Pro HTML5 Programming

Powerful APIs for Richer Internet Application Development

PETER LUBBERS
BRIAN ALBERS
FRANK SALIM

Apress®

Pro HTML5 Programming: Powerful APIs for Richer Internet Application Development

ISBN-13 (pbk): 978-1-4302-2790-8

ISBN-13 (electronic): 978-1-4302-2791-5

Printed and bound in the United States of America 9 8 7 6 5 4 3 2 1

President and Publisher: Paul Manning
Lead Editor: Clay Andres
Development Editor: Matthew Moodie
Technical Reviewer: Paul Haine
Editorial Board: Clay Andres, Steve Anglin, Mark Beckner, Ewan Buckingham, Gary Cornell, Jonathan Gennick, Jonathan Hassell, Michelle Lowman, Matthew Moodie, Duncan Parkes, Jeffrey Pepper, Frank Pohlmann, Douglas Pundick, Ben Renow-Clarke, Dominic Shakeshaft, Matt Wade, Tom Welsh
Coordinating Editor: Laurin Becker
Copy Editors: Heather Lang, Andy Rosenthal, Nancy Sixsmith
Compositor: Kimberly Burton
Indexer: Julie Grady
Artist: April Milne
Cover Designer: Anna Ishchenko

Distributed to the book trade worldwide by Springer Science+Business Media, LLC., 233 Spring Street, 6th Floor, New York, NY 10013. Phone 1-800-SPRINGER, fax (201) 348-4505, e-mail orders-ny@springer-sbm.com, or visit www.springeronline.com.

For information on translations, please e-mail rights@apress.com, or visit www.apress.com.

Apress and friends of ED books may be purchased in bulk for academic, corporate, or promotional use. eBook versions and licenses are also available for most titles. For more information, reference our Special Bulk Sales–eBook Licensing web page at www.apress.com/info/bulksales.

The source code for this book is available to readers at www.prohtml5.com and also at www.apress.com.

For my beautiful wife, Vittoria,
and for my sons—Sean and Rocky. I am so proud of you!
—Peter Lubbers

For John. You make it all worthwhile.
—Brian Albers

For people who still read books.
—Frank Salim

Contents at a Glance

Contents

Foreword

In June 2004, representatives from the semantic web community, major browser vendors, and the W3C met in San Jose, California to discuss the standards body's response to the rise of web applications. At the end of the second day, a vote was held to decide whether the W3C should augment HTML and the DOM to address the new requirements of web applications. Minutes from the event record the anonymous and curious result, "8 for, 14 against."

This schism lead to a divergence in effort: two days later, the WHATWG was formed from the major browser vendors to solve emerging issues. Meanwhile, the W3C pushed forward with the XHTML2 specification, only to drop it five years later to focus on an aligned HTML5 effort with the WHATWG.

Now, six years since, we stand to benefit greatly from the passionate minds that have designed HTML5. The features both codify de facto standards that have been in use for years and lay the groundwork for next-generation web applications. Putting them to use means a more engaging and responsive web experience for your users and, oftentimes, far less code for you.

In this book, you'll find a well-designed learning curve bringing you up to speed on the features within HTML5 and its associated specifications. You'll learn best practices of feature detection, appropriate use cases, and a lot of the whys that you won't find in the specifications. The code examples are not plain, trivial uses of each API but instead lead you through building actual web applications. I hope this book is able to serve you well, and I hope you'll be as excited about the next generation of the web as I am.

Paul Irish
Google and jQuery Dev Relations and Lead Developer for Modernizr

About the Authors

 ■ **Peter Lubbers** is the director of documentation and training at Kaazing. An HTML5 and WebSockets enthusiast, Peter is a frequent speaker at international events and teaches HTML5 training courses worldwide. Prior to joining Kaazing, Peter worked for almost ten years as an information architect at Oracle, where he wrote award-winning books and developed patent-pending software solutions. A native of the Netherlands, Peter served as a special forces commando in the Royal Dutch Green Berets. Peter lives on the edge of the Tahoe National Forest in California, and in his spare time, he runs ultramarathons. You can follow Peter on Twitter (@peterlubbers).

 ■ **Brian Albers** is the vice president of research and development at Kaazing. His career in web development spans a decade and a half, including his most recent position as a senior development manager at Oracle. Brian is a regular speaker at conferences, such as Web 2.0 Expo, AJAXWorld Expo, and JavaOne, where he focuses on Web and user interface technologies. A native Texan and current California resident, Brian spends as much time as possible escaping to Hawaii. When he cannot relax on the beach, Brian can be found frequenting a variety of virtual worlds in his spare time.

 ■ **Frank Salim** is one of the original engineers at Kaazing who helped craft the WebSockets gateway and client strategy. Frank is a San Diego native currently residing in Mountain View, California. He holds a degree in computer science from Pomona College. When he is not programming, Frank enjoys reading, painting, and inline skating.

About the Technical Reviewer

■ **Paul Haine** is a client-side developer currently working in London for the Guardian newspaper. He is the author of *HTML Mastery: Semantics, Standards, and Styling* (friends of ED, 2006) and runs a personal web site at www.joeblade.com.

Acknowledgments

I'd like to thank my wife Vittoria, for her love and patience, and my talented sons Sean and Rocky—reach for the stars, boys!

Thanks to my parents, Herman and Elisabeth, my sister Alice, and my brother David for always believing in me, and to my late grandmother Gebbechien whose courageous acts during the Nazi occupation of Holland were a great lesson to our family.

To my coauthors, the never-tiring Brian and the code-generating human Frank, it has been an honor to work with both of you.

Thanks also to Clay at Apress for all your support, and, finally, thanks to Jonas and John at Kaazing for pushing us to write a "real" book—an "unofficial e-book" would still be just a figment of our imagination, I am sure!

—Peter Lubbers

To my parents, Ken and Patty Albers, I offer my deepest love and appreciation for the sacrifices you made to bring me so many opportunities. Without your encouragement and the values you instilled in me, I would never have completed this or any other major life journey. You've been guiding me every step of the way.

To John, my deepest thanks for your patience every time that extra hour of work stretched to two, three, or more. You amaze and inspire me.

To Pitch, Bonnie, and Penelope, a scritch on the chin and a promise that dinner won't be so late any more. To the cats who came before, your purrs stay with me.

To my coworkers at Kaazing, much appreciation for the chance to work with the best and the brightest.

And a special thanks to the editorial staff at Apress for first believing that the time was right for an HTML5 book and then for having patience with us while we attempted to document a rapidly moving target.

—Brian Albers

I'd like to thank my parents, Mary and Sabri, who are responsible for my existence and without whom this book would literally not be possible.

—Frank Salim

Introduction

HTML5 is brand new. Indeed, it isn't even finished yet. And if you listen to some ornery pundits, they'll tell you that HTML5 won't be ready for ten years or more!

Why, then, would anyone think that now's the time for a book called *Pro HTML5 Programming*? That's easy. Because for anyone who's looking for an extra edge to make your web application stand above the rest, the time for HTML5 is right now. The authors of this book have been working with, developing, and teaching HTML5 technologies for more than two years now and can claim with certainty that adoption of the new standards is accelerating at dizzying speeds. Even over the course of writing this book, we've been forced to continually update our browser support matrix and reevaluate our assumptions about what is ready to use.

Most users don't really understand the power that's available in the browsers they are now using. Yes, they might notice some minor interface enhancement after their favorite browser has automatically updated. But they might have no idea that this new browser version just introduced a free-form drawing canvas or real-time network communication, or any number of other potential upgrades.

With this book, we aim to help you unlock the power HTML5.

Who This Book Is For

The content in this book is intended for the experienced web application developer who is familiar with JavaScript programming. In other words, we won't be covering the basics of web development in this text. There are many existing resources to get you up to speed in the fundamentals of web programming. That said, if you see yourself in any of the following bullets, this book will likely provide you with useful insight and information you are looking for:

- You sometimes find yourself thinking, "If only my browser could. . ."

- You find yourself using page source and developer tools to dissect a particularly impressive website.

- You enjoy reading the release notes of the latest browser updates to find out what's new.

- You are looking for ways to optimize or streamline your applications.

- You are willing to tailor your website to provide the best possible experience for users on relatively recent browsers.

If any of these apply to you, this book may be a good fit with your interests.

While we take care to point out the limitations of browser support where appropriate, our aim is not to give you elaborate workarounds to make your HTML5 application run seamlessly on a ten-year-old browser. Experience has shown that the workarounds and baseline browser support are evolving so rapidly that a book like this is not the best vehicle for such information. Instead, we will focus on the specification of HTML5 and how to use it. Detailed workarounds can be found on the Internet and will become less necessary over time.

An Overview of This Book

The eleven chapters of this book cover a selection of popular, useful, and powerful HTML5 APIs. In some cases, we have built on the capabilities introduced in earlier chapters to provide you with richer demonstrations.

Chapter 1, "Introduction to HTML5," starts off with the background of past and current versions of the HTML specification. The new high-level semantic tags are presented, along with basic changes and the rationale behind all the recent developments in HTML5. It's good to know this terrain.

Chapter 2, "Using the HTML5 Canvas API", and Chapter 3, "Working with HTML5 Audio and Video," describe the new visual and media elements. In these chapters, the focus is on finding simpler ways to spruce up your user interface without plugins or server-side interaction.

Chapter 4, "Using the HTML5 Geolocation API," introduces a truly new feature that was not easily emulated before now—the ability for an application to identify the user's current location and use that to customize the experience. Privacy is important here, so we cover some of the caveats, as well.

The next two chapters, "Using the Communication APIs" and "Using the HTML5 WebSocket API," present increasingly powerful ways that HTML5 lets you communicate with other websites and stream real-time data to an application with both simplicity and minimal overhead. The techniques in these chapters will enable you to simplify the many overly complex architectures deployed on the Web today.

Chapter 7, "Using the HTML5 Forms API," presents you with minimal tweaks you can make to your desktop or mobile web applications today to increase usability, as well as more fundamental changes you can make to detect page entry errors in very common usage scenarios.

Chapters 8, 9, and 10—"Using the HTML5 Web Workers API," "Using the HTML5 Storage API," and "Creating HTML5 Offline Web Applications"—deal with the internal plumbing of your applications. Here, you will find ways to optimize the existing functionality to obtain better performance and better data management.

Finally, Chapter 11, "The Future of HTML5," will give you a tasty preview of what's still to come.

Example Code and Companion Web Site

The code for the examples shown in this book is available online in the Source Code section of the Apress web site. Visit www.apress.com, click Source Code, and look for this book's title. You can download the source code from this book's home page. In addition, we are hosting a companion site for the book at www.prohtml5.com, from which you can also download the sample code and some practical extras.

Contacting the Authors

Thank you for buying this book. We hope you enjoy reading it and that you find it a valuable resource. Despite our best effort to avoid errors, we realize that things sometimes slip through the cracks, and we'd like to express, in advance, our regrets for any such slip-ups. We welcome your personal feedback, questions, and comments regarding this book's content and source code. You can contact us by sending us an e-mail at prohtml5@gmail.com.

CHAPTER 1

■ ■ ■

Overview of HTML5

This book is about HTML5 Programming. Before you can understand HTML5 programming, however, you need to take a step back and understand what HTML5 is, a bit of the history behind it, and the differences between HTML4 and HTML5.

In this chapter, we get right to the practical questions to which everyone wants answers. Why HTML5, and why all the excitement just now? What are the new design principles that make HTML5 truly revolutionary—but also highly accommodating? What are the implications of a plugin-free paradigm; what's in and what's out? What's new in HTML, and how does this kick off a whole new era for web developers? Let's get to it.

The Story So Far—The History of HTML5

HTML goes back a long way. It was first published as an Internet draft in 1993. The '90s saw an enormous amount of activity around HTML, with version 2.0, versions 3.2, and 4.0 (in the same year!), and finally, in 1999, version 4.01. In the course of its development, the World Wide Web Consortium (W3C) assumed control of the specification.

After the rapid delivery of these four versions though, HTML was widely considered a dead-end; the focus of web standards shifted to XML and XHTML, and HTML was put on the back burner. In the meantime, HTML refused to die, and the majority of content on the web continued to be served as HTML. To enable new web applications and address HTML's shortcomings, new features and specifications were needed for HTML.

Wanting to take the web platform to a new level, a small group of people started the Web Hypertext Application Working Group (WHATWG) in 2004. They created the HTML5 specification. They also began working on new features specifically geared to web applications—the area they felt was most lacking. It was around this time that the term Web 2.0 was coined. And it really *was* like a second new web, as static web sites gave way to more dynamic and social sites that required more features—a lot more features.

The W3C became involved with HTML again in 2006 and published the first working draft for HTML5 in 2008, and the XHTML 2 working group stopped in 2009. Another year passed, and that is where we stand today. Because HTML5 solves very practical problems (as you will see later), browser vendors are feverishly implementing its new features, even though the specification has not been completely locked down. Experimentation by the browsers feeds back into and improves the specification. HTML5 is rapidly evolving to address real and practical improvements to the web platform.

The Myth of 2022 and Why It Doesn't Matter

The HTML5 specification that we see today has been published as a working draft—it is not yet final. So when does it get cast in stone? Here are the key dates that you need to know. The first is 2012, which is the target date for the *candidate recommendation*. The second date is 2022, which is the *proposed recommendation*. Wait! Not so fast! Don't close this book to set it aside for ten years before you consider what these two dates actually mean.

The first and nearest date is arguably the most important one, because once we reach that stage, HTML5 will be complete. That's just two years away. The significance of the proposed recommendation (which we can all agree is a bit distant) is that there will then be two interoperable implementations. This means two browsers equipped with completely interoperable implementations of the entire specifications—a lofty goal that actually makes the 2022 deadline seem ambitious. After all, we haven't even achieved that in HTML4.

What *is* important, right now, is that browser vendors are actively adding support for many very cool new features. Depending on your audience, you can start using many of these features today. Sure, any number of minor changes will need to be made down the road, but that's a small price to pay for enjoying the benefits of living on the cutting edge. Of course, if your audience uses Internet Explorer 6.0, many of the new features won't work and will require emulation—but that's still not a good reason to dismiss HTML5. After all, those users, too, will eventually be jumping to a later version. Many of them will probably move to Internet Explorer 9.0 right away, and Microsoft promises to design that browser with increased HTML5 support. In practice, the combination of new browsers and improving emulation techniques means you can use many HTML5 features today or in the very near future.

Who Is Developing HTML5?

We all know that a certain degree of structure is needed, and somebody clearly needs to be in charge of the specification of HTML5. That challenge is the job of three important organizations:

- *Web Hypertext Application Technology Working Group (WHATWG)*: Founded in 2004 by individuals working for browser vendors Apple, Mozilla, Google, and Opera, WHATWG develops HTML and APIs for web application development and provides open collaboration of browser vendors and other interested parties.

- *World Wide Web Consortium (W3C)*: The W3C contains the HTML working group that is currently charged with delivering the HTML5 specification.

- *Internet Engineering Task Force (IETF)*: This task force contains the groups responsible for Internet protocols such as HTTP. HTML5 defines a new WebSocket API that relies on a new WebSocket protocol, which is under development in an IETF working group.

A New Vision

HTML5 is based on various design principles, spelled out in the WHATWG specification, that truly embody a new vision of possibility and practicality.

- Compatibility

- Utility

- Interoperability

- Universal access

Compatibility and Paving the Cow Paths

Don't worry; HTML5 is not an upsetting kind of revolution. In fact, one of its core principles is to keep everything working smoothly. If HTML5 features are not supported, the behavior must degrade gracefully. In addition, since there is about 20 years of HTML content out there, supporting all that existing content is important.

A lot of effort has been put into researching common behavior. For example, Google analyzed millions of pages to discover the common ID names for `DIV` tags and found a huge amount of repetition. For example, many people used `DIV id="header"` to mark up header content. HTML5 is all about solving real problems, right? So why not simply create a `<header>` element?

Although some features of the HTML5 standard are quite revolutionary, the name of the game is evolution not revolution. After all, why reinvent the wheel? (Or, if you must, then at least make a better one!)

Utility and the Priority of Constituencies

The HTML5 specification is written based upon a definite *Priority of Constituencies*. And as priorities go, "the user is king." This means, when in doubt, the specification values users over authors, over implementers (browsers), over specifiers (W3C/WHATWG), and over theoretical purity. As a result, HTML5 is overwhelmingly practical, though in some cases, less than perfect.

Consider this example. The following code snippets are all equally valid in HTML5:

```
id="prohtml5"
id=prohtml5
ID="prohtml5"
```

Sure, some will object to this relaxed syntax, but the bottom line is that the end user doesn't really care. We're not suggesting that you start writing sloppy code, but ultimately, it's the end user who suffers when any of the preceding examples generates errors and doesn't render the rest of the page.

HTML5 has also spawned the creation of XHTML5 to enable XML tool chains to generate valid HTML5 code. The serializations of the HTML or the XHTML version should produce the same DOM trees with minimal differences. Obviously, the XHTML syntax is a lot stricter, and the code in the last two examples would not be valid.

Secure by Design

A lot of emphasis has been given to making HTML5 secure right out of the starting gate. Each part of the specification has sections on security considerations, and security has been considered up front. HTML5 introduces a new origin-based security model that is not only easy to use but is also used consistently by different APIs. This security model allows us to do things in ways that used to be impossible. It allows us to communicate securely across domains without having to revert to all kinds of clever, creative, but ultimately insecure hacks. In that respect, we definitely will not be looking back to the good old days.

Separation of Presentation and Content

HTML5 takes a giant step toward the clean separation of presentation and content. HTML5 strives to create this separation wherever possible, and it does so using CSS. In fact, most of the presentational features of earlier versions of HTML are no longer supported (but will still work!), thanks to the compatibility design principle mentioned earlier. This idea is not entirely new, though; it was already in the works in HTML4 Transitional and XHTML1.1. Web designers have been using this as a best practice for a long time, but now, it is even more important to cleanly separate the two. The problems with presentational markup are:

- Poor accessibility

- Unnecessary complexity (it's harder to read your code with all the inline styling)

- Larger document size (due to repetition of style content), which translates into slower-loading pages

Interoperability Simplification

HTML5 is all about simplification and avoiding needless complexity. The HTML5 mantra? "Simple is better. Simplify wherever possible." Here are some examples of this:

- Native browser ability instead of complex JavaScript code

- A new, simplified `DOCTYPE`

- A new, simplified character set declaration

- Powerful yet simple HTML5 APIs

We'll say more about some of these later.

To achieve all this simplicity, the specification has become much bigger, because it needs to be much more precise—far more precise, in fact, than any previous version of the HTML specification. It specifies a legion of well-defined behaviors in an effort to achieve true browser interoperability by 2022. Vagueness simply will not make that happen.

The HTML5 specification is also more detailed than previous ones to prevent misinterpretation. It aims to define things thoroughly, especially web applications. Small wonder, then, that the specification is over 900 pages long!

HTML5 is also designed to handle errors well, with a variety of improved and ambitious error-handling plans. Quite practically, it prefers graceful error recovery to hard failure, again giving A-1 top priority to the interest of the end user. For example, errors in documents will not result in catastrophic failures in which pages do not display. Instead, error recovery is precisely defined so browsers can display "broken" markup in a standard way.

Universal Access

This principle is divided into three concepts:

- *Accessibility*: To support users with disabilities, HTML5 works closely with a related standard called Web Accessibility Initiative (WAI) Accessible Rich Internet Applications (ARIA). WAI-ARIA roles, which are supported by screen readers, can be already be added to your HTML elements.

- *Media Independence*: HTML5 functionality should work across all different devices and platforms if at all possible.

- *Support for all world languages*: For example, the new `<ruby>` element supports the Ruby annotations that are used in East Asian typography.

A Plugin–Free Paradigm

HTML5 provides native support for many features that used to be possible only with plugins or complex hacks (a native drawing API, native sockets, and so on). Plugins, of course, present problems:

- Plugins cannot always be installed.

- Plugins can be disabled or blocked (for example, the Apple iPad does not ship with a Flash plugin).

- Plugins are a separate attack vector.

- Plugins are difficult to integrate with the rest of an HTML document (because of plugin boundaries, clipping, and transparency issues).

Although some plugins have high install rates, they are often blocked in controlled corporate environments. In addition, some users choose to disable these plugins due to the unwelcome advertising displays that they empower. However, if users disable your plugin, they also disable the very program you're relying on to display your content.

Plugins also often have difficulty integrating their displays with the rest of the browser content, which causes clipping or transparency issues with certain site designs. Because plugins use a self-contained rendering model that is different from that of the base web page, developers face difficulties if pop-up menus or other visual elements need to cross the plugin boundaries on a page. This is where HTML5 comes on the scene, smiles, and waves its magic wand of *native* functionality. You can style elements with CSS and script with JavaScript. In fact, this is where HTML5 flexes its biggest muscle, showing us a power that just didn't exist in previous versions of HTML. It's not just that the new elements provide new functionality. It's also the added native interaction with scripting and styling that enables us to do much more than we could ever do before.

Take the new canvas element, for example. It enables us to do some pretty fundamental things that were not possible before (try drawing a diagonal line in a web page in HTML4). However, what's most interesting is the power that we can unlock with the APIs and the styling we can apply with just a few lines of CSS code. Like well-behaved children, the HTML5 elements also play nicely together. For example, you can grab a frame from a video element and display it on a canvas, and the user can just click the canvas to play back the video from the frame you just grabbed. This is just one example of what a native code has to offer over a plugin. In fact, virtually *everything* becomes easier when you're not working with a black box. What this all adds up to is a truly powerful new medium, which is why we decided to write a book about HTML5 *programming*, and not just about the new elements!

What's In and What's Out?

So, what really *is* part of HTML5? If you read the specification carefully, you might not find all of the features we describe in this book. For example, you will not find HTML5 Geolocation and Web Workers in there. So are we just making this stuff up? Is it all hype? No, not at all!

Many pieces of the HTML5 effort (for example, Web Storage and Canvas 2D) were originally part of the HTML5 specification and were then moved to separate standards documents to keep the specification focused. It was considered smarter to discuss and edit some of these features on a separate track before making them into official specifications. This way, one small contentious markup issue wouldn't hold up the show of the entire specification.

Experts in specific areas can come together on mailing lists to discuss a given feature without the crossfire of too much chatter. The industry still refers to the original set of features, including Geolocation, as HTML5. Think of HTML5, then, as an umbrella term that covers the core markup, as well as many cool new APIs. At the time of this writing, these features are part of HTML5:

- Canvas (2D and 3D)

- Channel messaging

- Cross-document messaging

- Geolocation

- MathML

- Microdata

- Server-Sent events

- Scalable Vector Graphics (SVG)

- WebSocket API and protocol

- Web origin concept

- Web storage

- Web SQL database

- Web Workers

- XMLHttpRequest Level 2

As you can see, a lot of the APIs we cover in this book are on this list. How did we choose which APIs to cover? We chose to cover features that were at least somewhat baked. Translation? They're available in some form in more than one browser. Other (less-baked) features may only work in one special beta version of a browser, while others are still just ideas at this point.

In this book, we will give you an up-to-date overview (at the time of this writing) of the browser support available for each of the HTML5 features we cover. However, whatever we tell you will soon be out of date, because this is very much a moving target. Don't worry though; there are some excellent online resources that you can use to check current (and future) browser support. The site `www.caniuse.com` provides an exhaustive list of features and browser support broken down by browser version and the site `www.html5test.com` checks the support for HTML5 features in the browser you use to access it.

Furthermore, this book does not focus on providing you with the emulation workarounds to make your HTML5 applications run seamlessly on antique browsers. Instead, we will focus primarily on the specification of HTML5 and how to use it. That said, for each of the APIs we do provide some example code that you can use to detect its availability. Rather than using *user agent* detection, which is often unreliable, we use *feature* detection. For that, you can also use *Modernizr*—a JavaScript library that provides very advanced HTML5 and CSS3 feature detection. We highly recommend you use Modernizr in your applications, because it is hands down the best tool for this.

MORE MOMENTS IN HTML

Frank says: "Hi, I'm Frank, and I sometimes paint.

One of the first HTML canvas demonstrations I saw was a basic painting application that mimicked the user interface of Microsoft Paint. Although it was decades behind the state of the art in digital painting and, at the time, ran in only a fraction of existing browsers, it got me thinking about the possibilities it represented.

When I paint digitally, I typically use locally installed desktop software. While some of these programs are excellent, they lack the characteristics that make web applications so great. In short, they are disconnected. Sharing digital paintings has, to date, involved exporting an image from a painting application and uploading it to the Web. Collaboration or critiques on a live canvas are out of the question. HTML5 applications can short-circuit the export cycle and make the creative process fit into the online world along with finished images.

The number of applications that cannot be implemented with HTML5 is dwindling. For text, the Web is already the ultimate two-way communication medium. Text-based applications are available in entirely web-based forms. Their graphical counterparts, like painting, video editing, and 3D modeling software, are just arriving now.

We can now build great software to create and enjoy images, music, movies, and more. Even better, the software we make will be on and off the Web: a platform that is ubiquitous, empowering, and online."

What's New in HTML5?

Before we start programming HTML5, let's take a quick look at what's new in HTML5.

New DOCTYPE and Character Set

First of all, true to design principle 3—simplification—the DOCTYPE for web pages has been greatly simplified. Compare, for example, the following HTML4 DOCTYPEs:

```
<!DOCTYPE HTML PUBLIC "-//W3C//DTD HTML 4.01 Transitional//EN"
 "http://www.w3.org/TR/html4/loose.dtd">
```

Who could ever remember any of these? We certainly couldn't. We would always just copy and paste some lengthy DOCTYPE into the page, always with a worry in the back of our minds, "Are you absolutely sure you pasted the right one?" HTML5 neatly solves this problem as follows:

```
<!DOCTYPE html>
```

Now *that's* a DOCTYPE you might just remember. Like the new DOCTYPE, the character set declaration has also been abbreviated. It used to be

```
<meta http-equiv="Content-Type" content="text/html; charset=utf-8">
```

Now, it is:

```
<meta charset="utf-8">
```

Using the new DOCTYPE triggers the browser to display pages in standards mode. For example, Figure 1-1 shows the information you will see if you open an HTML5 page in Firefox, and you click Tools ➤ Page Info. In this example, the page is rendered in standards mode.

Figure 1-1. A page rendered in standards-compliant mode

When you use the new HTML5 DOCTYPE, it triggers browsers to render the page in standards-compliant mode. As you may know, Web pages can have different rendering modes, such as Quirks, Almost Standards, and Standards (or no-quirks) mode. The DOCTYPE indicates to the browser which mode to use and what rules are used to validate your pages. In Quirks mode, browsers try to avoid breaking pages and render them even if they are not entirely valid. HTML5 introduces new elements and others (more on this in the next section) so that if you use deprecated elements, your page will not be valid.

New and Deprecated Elements

HTML5 introduces many new markup elements, which it groups into seven different content types. These are shown below in Table 1-1.

Table 1-1. HTML5 Content Types

Content Type	Description
Embedded	Content that imports other resources into the document, for example `audio`, `video`, `canvas`, and `iframe`
Flow	Elements used in the body of documents and applications, for example `form`, `h1`, and `small`
Heading	Section headers, for example `h1`, `h2`, and `hgroup`
Interactive	Content that users interact with, for example `audio` or `video` `controls`, `button`, and `textarea`
Metadata	Elements—commonly found in the `head` section— that set up the presentation or behavior of the rest of the document, for example `script`, `style`, and `title`
Phrasing	Text and text markup elements, for example `mark`, `kbd`, `sub`, and `sup`
Sectioning	Elements that define sections in the document, for example `article`, `aside`, and `title`

All of these elements can be styled with CSS. In addition, some of them, such as `canvas`, `audio`, and `video`, can be used by themselves, though they are accompanied by APIs that allow for fine-grained native programmatic control. These APIs will be discussed in much more detail later in this book.

It is beyond the scope of this book to discuss all these new elements, but the sectioning elements (discussed in the next section) are new. The `canvas`, `audio`, and `video` elements are also new in HTML5.

Likewise, we're not going to provide an exhaustive list of all the deprecated tags (there are many good online resources online for this), but many of the elements that performed inline styling have been removed in favor of using CSS, such as `big`, `center`, `font`, and `basefont`.

Semantic Markup

One content type that contains many new HTML5 elements is the *sectioning* content type. HTML5 defines a new *semantic* markup to describe an element's content. Using semantic markup doesn't provide any immediate benefits, but it does simplify the design of your HTML pages, and in the future, search engines will definitely be taking advantage of these elements as they crawl and index pages.

As we said before, HTML5 is all about paving the cow paths. Google analyzed millions of pages to discover the common ID names for `DIV` tags and found a huge amount of repetition. For example, since many people used `DIV id="footer"` to mark up footer content, HTML5 provides a set of new sectioning elements that you can use in modern browsers right now. Table 1-2 shows the different semantic markup elements.

Table 1-2. New sectioning HTML5 elements

Sectioning Element	Description
header	Header content (for a page or a section of the page)
footer	Footer content (for a page or a section of the page)
section	A section in a web page
article	Independent article content
aside	Related content or pull quotes
nav	Navigational aids

All of these elements can be styled with CSS. In fact, as we described in the utility design principle earlier, HTML5 pushes the separation of content and presentation, so you have to style your page using CSS styles in HTML5. Listing 1-1 shows what an HTML5 page might look like. It uses the new DOCTYPE, character set, and semantic markup elements—in short, the new sectioning content. The code file is also available in the code/intro folder.

Listing 1-1. An Example HTML5 Page

```
<!DOCTYPE html>
<html>

<head>
  <meta charset="utf-8" >
  <title>HTML5</title>
  <link rel="stylesheet" href="html5.css">

</head>

<body>

  <header>
    <h1>Header</h1>
    <h2>Subtitle</h2>
    <h4>HTML5 Rocks!</h4>
  </header>

  <div id="container">
```

```
    <nav>
        <h3>Nav</h3>
        <a href="http://www.example.com">Link 1</a>
        <a href="http://www.example.com">Link 2</a>
        <a href="http://www.example.com">Link 3</a>
    </nav>

        <section>
        <article>
          <header>
            <h1>Article Header</h1>
          </header>
          <p>Lorem ipsum dolor HTML5 nunc aut nunquam sit amet, consectetur adipiscing

            elit. Vivamus at est eros, vel fringilla urna.</p>
          <p>Per inceptos himenaeos. Quisque feugiat, justo at vehicula

            pellentesque, turpis lorem dictum nunc.</p>
          <footer>
            <h2>Article Footer</h2>
          </footer>
        </article>

        <article>
          <header>
            <h1>Article Header</h1>
          </header>
          <p>HTML5: "Lorem ipsum dolor nunc aut nunquam sit amet, consectetur adipiscing

            elit. Vivamus at est eros, vel fringilla urna. Pellentesque odio</p>

          <footer>
            <h2>Article Footer</h2>
          </footer>
        </article>

    </section>

        <aside>
        <h3>Aside</h3>
        <p>HTML5: "Lorem ipsum dolor nunc aut nunquam sit amet, consectetur adipiscing

          elit. Vivamus at est eros, vel fringilla urna. Pellentesque odio rhoncus</p>
    </aside>

        <footer>
        <h2>Footer</h2>
    </footer>
  </div>
</body>

</html>
```

Without styles, the page would be pretty dull to look at. Listing 1-2 shows some of the CSS code that can be used to style the content. Note that this style sheet uses some of the new CSS3 features, such as rounded corners (for example, `border-radius`) and rotate transformations (for example, `transform: rotate();`). Note that CSS3—just like HTML5 itself—is still under development and is modularized with subspecifications for easier browser uptake (for example, transformation, animation, and transition are all areas that are in separate subspecifications).

Experimental CSS3 features are prefixed with vendor strings to avoid namespace conflicts should the specifications change. To display rounded corners, gradients, shadows, and transformations, it is currently necessary to use prefixes such as `-moz-` (for Mozilla), `o-` (for Opera), and `-webkit-` (for WebKit-based browsers such as Safari and Chrome) in your declarations.

Listing 1-2. CSS File for the HTML5 Page

```
body {
        background-color:#CCCCCC;
        font-family:Geneva,Arial,Helvetica,sans-serif;
        margin: 0px auto;
        max-width:900px;
        border:solid;
        border-color:#FFFFFF;
}

header {
        background-color: #F47D31;
        display:block;
        color:#FFFFFF;
        text-align:center;
}

header h2 {
        margin: 0px;
}

h1 {
        font-size: 72px;
        margin: 0px;
}

h2 {
        font-size: 24px;
        margin: 0px;
        text-align:center;
        color: #F47D31;
}

h3 {
        font-size: 18px;
        margin: 0px;
        text-align:center;
        color: #F47D31;
}
```

```
h4 {
        color: #F47D31;
        background-color: #fff;
        -webkit-box-shadow: 2px 2px 20px #888;
        -webkit-transform: rotate(-45deg);
        -moz-box-shadow: 2px 2px 20px #888;
        -moz-transform: rotate(-45deg);
        position: absolute;
        padding: 0px 150px;
        top: 50px;
        left: -120px;
        text-align:center;

}

nav {
        display:block;
        width:25%;
        float:left;
}

nav a:link, nav a:visited {
        display: block;
        border-bottom: 3px solid #fff;
        padding: 10px;
        text-decoration: none;
        font-weight: bold;
        margin: 5px;
}

nav a:hover {
        color: white;
        background-color: #F47D31;
}

nav h3 {
        margin: 15px;
        color: white;
}

#container {
        background-color: #888;
}

section {
        display:block;
        width:50%;
        float:left;
}
```

```
article {
        background-color: #eee;
        display:block;
        margin: 10px;
        padding: 10px;
        -webkit-border-radius: 10px;
        -moz-border-radius: 10px;
        border-radius: 10px;
        -webkit-box-shadow: 2px 2px 20px #888;
        -webkit-transform: rotate(-10deg);
        -moz-box-shadow: 2px 2px 20px #888;
        -moz-transform: rotate(-10deg);
}

article header {
        -webkit-border-radius: 10px;
        -moz-border-radius: 10px;
        border-radius: 10px;
        padding: 5px;

}

article footer {
        -webkit-border-radius: 10px;
        -moz-border-radius: 10px;
        border-radius: 10px;
        padding: 5px;
}

article h1 {
        font-size: 18px;
}

aside {
        display:block;
        width:25%;
        float:left;
}

aside h3 {
        margin: 15px;
        color: white;
}

aside p {
        margin: 15px;
        color: white;
        font-weight: bold;
        font-style: italic;
}
```

```
footer {
        clear: both;
        display: block;
        background-color: #F47D31;
        color:#FFFFFF;
        text-align:center;
        padding: 15px;
}

footer h2 {
        font-size: 14px;
        color: white;
}


/* links */
a {
        color: #F47D31;
}

a:hover {
        text-decoration: underline;
}
```

Figure 1-2 shows an example of the page in Listing 1-1, styled with CSS (and some CSS3) styles. Keep in mind, however, that there is no such thing as a typical HTML5 page. Anything goes, really, and this example uses many of the new tags mainly for purposes of demonstration.

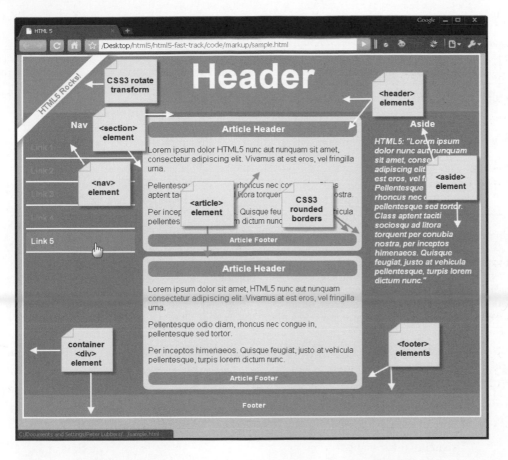

Figure 1-2. An HTML5 page with all the new semantic markup elements

One last thing to keep in mind is that browsers may seem to render things as if they actually understand these new elements. The truth is, however, that these elements could have been renamed `foo` and `bar` and then styled, and they would have been rendered the same way (but of course, they would not have any benefits in search engine optimization). The one exception to this is Internet Explorer, which requires that elements be part of the DOM. So, if you want to see these elements in IE, you must programmatically insert them into the DOM and display them as block elements.

Simplifying Selection Using the Selectors API

Along with the new semantic elements, HTML5 also introduces new simple ways to find elements in your page DOM. Table 1-3 shows the previous versions of the document object allowed developers to make a few calls to find specific elements in the page.

Table 1-3. Previous JavaScript Methods to Find Elements

Function	Description	Example
getElementById()	Returns the element with the specified id attribute value	`<div id="foo">` `getElementById("foo");`
getElementsByName()	Returns all elements whose name attribute has the specified value	`<input type="text" name="foo">` `getElementsByName("foo");`
getElementsByTagName()	Return all elements whose tag name matches the specified value	`<input type="text">` `getElementsByTagName("input");`

With the new Selectors API, there are now more precise ways to specify which elements you would like to retrieve without resorting to looping and iterating through a document using standard DOM. The Selectors API exposes the same selector rules present in CSS as a means to find one or more elements in the page. For example, CSS already has handy rules for selecting elements based on their nesting, sibling, and child patterns. The most recent versions of CSS add support for more pseudo-classes—for example, whether an object is enabled, disabled, or checked—and just about any combination of properties and hierarchy you could imagine. To select elements in your DOM using CSS rules, simply utilize one of the functions shown in Table 1-4.

Table 1-4. New QuerySelector methods

Function	Description	Example	Result
querySelector()	Return the first element in the page which matches the specified selector rules(s)	`querySelector("input.error");`	Return the first input field with a style class of "error"
querySelectorAll()	Returns all elements which match the specified rule or rules	`querySelectorAll("#results td");`	Return any table cells inside the element with id results

It is also possible to send more than one selector rule to the Selector API functions, for example:

```
// select the first element in the document with the
// style class highClass or the style class lowClass
var x = document.querySelector(".highClass", ".lowClass");
```

In the case of querySelector(), the first element that matches either rule is selected. In the case of querySelectorAll(), any element matching any of the listed rules is returned. Multiple rules are comma-separated.

The new Selector API makes it easy to select sections of the document that were painful to track before. Assume, for example, that you wanted the ability to find whichever cell of a table currently had the mouse hovering over it. Listing 1-3 shows how this is trivially easy with a selector. This file is also in the code/intro directory.

Listing 1-3. Using the Selector API

```
<!DOCTYPE html>
<html>

<head>
  <meta charset="utf-8" />
  <title>Query Selector Demo</title>

  <style type="text/css">
    td {
      border-style: solid;
      border-width: 1px;
      font-size: 300%;
    }

    td:hover {
      background-color: cyan;
    }

    #hoverResult {
      color: green;
      font-size: 200%;
    }
  </style>
</head>

<body>
  <section>
    <!-- create a table with a 3 by 3 cell display -->
    <table>
      <tr>
        <td>A1</td> <td>A2</td> <td>A3</td>
      </tr>
      <tr>
        <td>B1</td> <td>B2</td> <td>B3</td>
      </tr>
      <tr>
        <td>C1</td> <td>C2</td> <td>C3</td>
      </tr>
    </table>

    <div>Focus the button, hover over the table cells, and hit Enter to identify them
 using querySelector('td:hover').</div>
    <button type="button" id="findHover" autofocus>Find 'td:hover' target</button>
    <div id="hoverResult"></div>
```

19

```
<script type="text/javascript">
  document.getElementById("findHover").onclick = function() {
    // find the table cell currently hovered in the page
    var hovered = document.querySelector("td:hover");
    if (hovered)
        document.getElementById("hoverResult").innerHTML = hovered.innerHTML;
  }
</script>
</section>

</body>
</html>
```

As you can see from this example, finding the element a user is hovering over is a one-line exercise using:

```
var hovered = document.querySelector("td:hover");
```

■ **Note** Not only are the Selector APIs handy, but they are often faster than traversing the DOM using the legacy child retrieval APIs. Browsers are highly optimized for selector matching in order to implement fast style sheets.

It should not be too surprising to find that the formal specification of selectors is separated from the specification for CSS at the W3C. As you've seen here, selectors are generally useful outside of styling. The full details of the new selectors are outside the scope of this book, but if you are a developer seeking the optimal ways to manipulate your DOM, you are encouraged to use the new Selectors API to rapidly navigate your application structure.

JavaScript Logging and Debugging

Though they're not technically a feature of HTML5, JavaScript logging and in-browser debugging tools have been improved greatly over the past few years. The first great tool for analyzing web pages and the code running in them was the Firefox add-on, Firebug.

Similar functionality can now be found in all the other browsers' built-in development tools: Safari's Web Inspector, Google's Chrome Developer Tools, Internet Explorer's Developer Tools, and Opera's Dragonfly. Figure 1-3 shows the Google Chrome Developer Tools (use the shortcut key CTRL + Shift + J to access this) that provide a wealth of information about your web pages; these include a debugging console, a resource view, and a storage view, to name just a few.

Figure 1-3. Developer Tools view in Chrome

Many of the debugging tools offer a way to set breakpoints to halt code execution and analyze the state of the program and the current state of the variables. The `console.log` API has become the de facto logging standard for JavaScript developers. Many browsers offer a split-pane view that allows you to see messages logged to the console. Using `console.log` is much better than making a call to `alert()`, since it does not halt program execution.

window.JSON

JSON is a relatively new and increasingly popular way to represent data. It is a subset of JavaScript syntax that represents data as object literals. Due to its simplicity and natural fit in JavaScript programming, JSON has become the de facto standard for data interchange in HTML5 applications. The canonical API for JSON has two functions, `parse()` and `stringify()` (meaning serialize or convert to string).

To use JSON in older browsers, you need a JavaScript library (several can be found at `http://json.org`). Parsing and serializing in JavaScript are not always as fast as you would like, so to speed up things, newer browsers now have a native implementation of JSON that can be called from JavaScript. The native JSON object is specified as part of the ECMAScript 5 standard covering the next generation of the JavaScript language. It is one of the first parts of ECMAScript 5 to be widely implemented. Every modern browser has `window.JSON`, and you can expect to see quite a lot of JSON used in HTML5 applications.

21

DOM Level 3

One of the most maligned parts of web application development has been event handling. While most browsers support standard APIs for events and elements, Internet Explorer differs. Early on, Internet Explorer implemented an event model that differed from the eventual standard. Internet Explorer 9 (IE9) will support DOM Level 2 and 3 features, so you can finally use the same code for DOM manipulation and event handling in all HTML5 browsers. This includes the ever-important `addEventListener()` and `dispatchEvent()` methods.

Monkeys, Squirrelfish, and Other Speedy Oddities

The latest round of browser innovations isn't just about new tags and new APIs. One of the most significant recent changes is the rapid evolution of JavaScript/ECMAScript engines in the leading browsers. Just as new APIs open up capabilities that were impossible in last-generation browsers, speedups in the execution of the overall scripting engine benefit both existing web applications and those using the latest HTML5 features. Think your browser can't handle complex image or data processing, or the editing of lengthy manuscripts? Think again.

For the last few years, browser vendors have been in a virtual arms race to see who could develop the fastest JavaScript engine. While the earliest iterations of JavaScript were purely interpreted, the newest engines compile script code directly to native machine code, offering speedups of orders of magnitude compared to the browsers of the mid-2000s.

The action pretty much began when Adobe donated its just-in-time (JIT) compilation engine and virtual machine for ECMAScript—code named Tamarin—to the Mozilla project in 2006. Although only pieces of the Tamarin technology remain in the latest versions of Mozilla, the donation of Tamarin helped spawn new scripting engines in each of the browsers, with names that are just as intriguing as the performance they claim.

Table 1-5. Web Browser JavaScript Engines

Browser	Engine Name	Notes
Apple Safari 5	Nitro (otherwise know as SquirrelFish Extreme)	Released in Safari 4 and refined in version 5, it introduces byte code optimizations and a context-threaded native compiler.
Google Chrome 5	V8	Since Chrome 2, it uses generational garbage collection for high memory scalability without interruptions.
Microsoft Internet Explorer 9	Chakra	This focuses on background compilation and an efficient type system and demonstrates a tenfold improvement over IE8.
Mozilla Firefox 4	JägerMonkey	Refined from version 3.5, this combines fast interpretation with native compilation from trace trees.
Opera 10.60	Carakan	This one uses register-based byte code and selective native compilation and claims improvements of 75% on version 10.50.

All in all, this healthy competition among browser vendors is bringing the performance of JavaScript ever closer to that of native desktop application code.

STILL MORE MOMENTS IN HTML

Peter says: "Speaking of competition, and speedy oddities, my name is Peter and running is my thing—a lot of running.

Ultra running is a great sport where you meet great people. While running the last miles of a 100-mile race or a 165-mile trail run, you really get to know some very interesting people in a very new way. At that point, you're really stripped down to your essence, the place where great friendships can happen. There's still the element of competition, to be sure, but most of all there's a deep sense of camaraderie. But I digress here.

To keep track of how my friends are doing in races that I can't attend (for example, when I am writing an HTML5 book), I usually follow along on the race websites. Not surprisingly, the 'live tracking' options are often quite unreliable.

A few years ago, I stumbled upon a site for a European race that had all the right ideas. They gave GPS trackers to the front runners and then displayed these racers on a map (we'll build some similar demonstrations in this book using Geolocation and WebSocket). Despite the fact that it was quite a primitive implementation (users had to actually click "refresh the page" to see updates!), I could instantly see the incredible potential.

Now, just a few years later, HTML5 provides us with tools to build these sorts of live race tracking websites with APIs such as Geolocation for location-aware applications and WebSockets for real-time updates. There's no doubt in my mind—HTML5 has crossed the finish line a winner!"

Summary

In this chapter, we have given you a general overview of the big essentials of HTML5.

We charted the history of its development and some of the important dates coming up. We also outlined the four new design principles behind the HTML5 era that is now dawning: compatibility, utility, interoperability, and universal access. Each one of these principles opens the door to a world of possibilities and closes the door on a host of practices and conventions that are now rendered obsolete. We then introduced HTML5's startling new plugin-free paradigm and answered the question on the tip of everyone's tongue—what's in and what's out? We reviewed what's new in HTML5, such as a new `DOCTYPE` and character set, lots of new markup elements, and we discussed the race for JavaScript supremacy.

In the next chapter, we'll begin by exploring the programming side of HTML5, starting with the Canvas API.

CHAPTER 2

■ ■ ■

Using the HTML5 Canvas API

In this chapter, we'll explore what you can do with the HTML5 Canvas API—a cool API that enables you to dynamically generate and render graphics, charts, images, and animation. We'll walk you through using the basics of the rendering API to create a drawing that can scale and adjust to the browser environment. We'll show you how to create dynamic pictures based on user input in a heatmap display. Of course, we'll also alert you to the pitfalls of using HTML5 Canvas and share tricks to overcome them.

This chapter presumes only a minimal amount of graphics expertise, so don't be afraid to jump in and try out one of the most powerful features of HTML.

Overview of HTML5 Canvas

An entire book could be written about the use of the HTML5 Canvas API (and it wouldn't be a small book). Because we have only a chapter, we're going to cover (what we think is) the most commonly used functionality in this very extensive API.

History

The canvas concept was originally introduced by Apple to be used in Mac OS X WebKit to create *dashboard widgets*. Before the arrival of canvas, you could only use drawing APIs in a browser through plugins such as Adobe plugins for Flash and Scalable Vector Graphics (SVG), Vector Markup Language (VML) only in Internet Explorer, or other clever JavaScript hacks.

Try, for example, to draw a simple diagonal line without a **canvas** element—it sounds simple, but it is a fairly complex task if you do not have a simple two-dimensional drawing API at your disposal. HTML5 Canvas provides just that and because it is an extremely useful thing to have in the browser, it was added to the HTML5 specification.

Early on, Apple hinted at possibly reserving the intellectual property rights in the WHATWG draft of the canvas specification, which caused concern at the time among some followers of web standardization. In the end, however, Apple disclosed the patents under the W3C's royalty-free patent licensing terms.

SVG VERSUS CANVAS

Peter says: "Canvas is essentially a *bitmap* canvas, and as such images that are drawn on a canvas are final and cannot be resized in the way that Scalable Vector Graphic (SVG) images can. Furthermore, objects drawn on a canvas are not part of the page's DOM or part of any namespace—something that is considered a weakness. SVG images, on the other hand can be scaled seamlessly at different resolutions and allow for hit detection (knowing precisely where an image is clicked).

Why then, would the WHATWG HTML5 specification not use SVG exclusively? Despite its obvious shortcomings, the HTML5 Canvas API has two things going for it: it performs well because it does not have to store objects for every primitive it draws, and it is relatively easy to implement the Canvas API based on many of the popular two-dimensional drawing APIs found in other programming languages. Ultimately, it is better to have one bird in the hand than two in the bush."

What Is a Canvas?

When you use a `canvas` element in your web page, it creates a rectangular area on the page. By default, this rectangular area is 300 pixels wide and 150 pixels high, but you can specify the exact size and set other attributes for your `canvas` element. Listing 2-1 shows the most basic `canvas` element that can be added to an HTML page.

Listing 2-1. A basic canvas element

```
<canvas></canvas>
```

Once you have added a `canvas` element to your page, you can use JavaScript to manipulate it any way you want. You can add graphics, lines, and text to it; you can draw on it; and you can even add advanced animations to it.

The HTML5 Canvas API supports the same two-dimensional drawing operations that most modern operating systems and frameworks support. If you have ever programmed two-dimensional graphics in recent years, you will probably feel right at home with the HTML5 Canvas API because it is designed to be similar to existing systems. If you haven't, you're about to discover how much more powerful a rendering system can be than the previous images and CSS tricks developers have used for years to create web graphics.

To programmatically use a canvas, you have to first get its *context*. You can then perform actions on the context and finally apply those actions to the context. You can think of making canvas modifications as similar to database transactions: you start a transaction, perform certain actions, and then commit the transaction.

Canvas Coordinates

As shown in Figure 2-1, coordinates in a canvas start at `x=0,y=0` in the upper-left corner—which we will refer to as the *origin*—and increase (in pixels) horizontally over the x-axis and vertically over the y-axis.

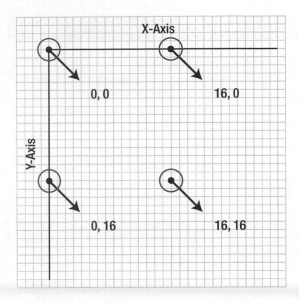

Figure 2-1. x and y coordinates on a canvas

When Not to Use Canvas

Although the **canvas** element is great and very useful, you should *not* use the **canvas** element when another element will suffice. For example, it would not be a good idea to dynamically draw all the different headings for an HTML document on a canvas instead of simply using heading styles (H1, H2, and so on) that are meant for that purpose.

Fallback Content

In case your web page is accessed by a browser that does not support the **canvas** element or a subset of the HTML5 Canvas API features, it is a good idea to provide an alternate source (see Table 2-1 in the "Browser Support for HTML5 Canvas" section for more on browser support). For example, you can provide an alternate image or just some text that explains what the user could be enjoying if they actually used a modern browser. Listing 2-2 shows how alternate text can be specified inside a **canvas** element. Browsers that do not support the **canvas** element will simply render this fallback content.

Listing 2-2. Use of fallback text inside a canvas element

```
<canvas>
  Update your browser to enjoy canvas!
</canvas>
```

Instead of the previous text shown, you can also point to an image that can be displayed in case the browser does not support the **canvas** element.

WHAT ABOUT CANVAS ACCESSIBILITY?

Peter says: "Providing alternate images or alternate text raises the subject of *accessibility*—an area in which the HTML5 Canvas specification is, unfortunately, still lacking significantly. For example, there is no native method for inserting text alternatives for images that are being inserted into a canvas, and there is no native method to provide alternate text to match text generated with the canvas text API. At the time of this writing, there are no accessibility hooks that can be used with the dynamically generated content in a canvas, but a task force is working on designing them. Let's hope this improves with time."

CSS and Canvas

As with most HTML elements, CSS can be applied to the **canvas** element itself to add borders, padding, margins, etc. Additionally, some CSS values are inherited by the contents of the **canvas**; fonts are a good example, as fonts drawn into a **canvas** default to the settings of the **canvas** element itself.

Furthermore, properties set on the **context** used in **canvas** operations follow the syntax you may already be familiar with from CSS. Colors and fonts, for example, use the same notation on the **context** that they use throughout any HTML or CSS document.

Browser Support for HTML5 Canvas

With the exception of Internet Explorer, all browsers now provide support for HTML5 Canvas. However, there are some parts of the specification that were added later that are not supported as widely. An example of this is the Canvas Text API. As a whole, however, the specification is at a very advanced stage and is unlikely to change a whole lot. As shown in Table 2-1, HTML5 Canvas is already supported in many browsers at the time of this writing.

Table 2-1. Browser support for HTML5 Canvas

Browser	Details
Chrome	Supported in version 1.0 and greater
Firefox	Supported in version 1.5 and greater
Internet Explorer	Not supported
Opera	Supported in version 9.0 and greater
Safari	Supported in version 1.3 and greater

As you can see, HTML5 Canvas is supported in all the browsers except Internet Explorer. If you want to use canvas in Internet Explorer, you can use the open-source project *explorercanvas* (http://code.google.com/p/explorercanvas). To use explorercanvas, you just need to check if Internet

Explorer is the current browser and include a `script` tag in your web pages to launch explorercanvas, such as the following:

```
<head>
<!--[if IE]><script src="excanvas.js"></script><![endif]-->
</head>
```

Universal support for the Canvas is highly desired by developers, and new projects are launched all the time to try to bring support for Canvas to older or nonstandard browser environments. Microsoft has announced support for canvas in Internet Explorer 9, so native support in all major web browsers is on the horizon.

Due to the varying levels of support, it is a good idea to first test whether HTML5 Canvas is supported before you use the APIs. The section "Checking for Browser Support" later in this chapter will show you how you can programmatically check for browser support.

Using the HTML5 Canvas APIs

In this section, we'll explore the use of the HTML5 Canvas APIs in more detail. For the sake of illustration—no pun intended—we will use the various HTML5 Canvas APIs to build a logo-like display of a forest scene with trees and a beautiful trail-running path suitable for a long-distance race event. Although our example will not win any awards for graphical design, it should serve to illustrate the various capabilities of HTML5 Canvas in a reasonable order.

Checking for Browser Support

Before you use the HTML5 `canvas` element, you will want to make sure there is support in the browser. This way, you can provide some alternate text in case there is no support in their antique browser. Listing 2-3 shows one way you can use to test for browser support.

Listing 2-3. Checking for browser support

```
try {
  document.createElement("canvas").getContext("2d");
  document.getElementById("support").innerHTML =
    "HTML5 Canvas is supported in your browser.";
} catch (e) {
  document.getElementById("support").innerHTML = "HTML5 Canvas is not supported ↵
                                              in your browser.";
}
```

In this example, you try to create a canvas object and access its context. If there is an error, you will catch it and know that Canvas is not supported. A previously defined `support` element on the page is updated with a suitable message to reflect whether there is browser support or not.

This test will indicate whether the `canvas` element itself is supported by the browser. It will not indicate which capabilities of the Canvas are supported. At the time of this writing, the API is stable and well-supported, so this should generally not be an issue to worry about.

Additionally, it is a good idea to supply fallback content to your `canvas` element, as shown in Listing 2-3.

Adding a Canvas to a Page

Adding a **canvas** element in an HTML page is pretty straight-forward. Listing 2-4 shows the **canvas** element that can be added to an HTML page.

Listing 2-4. The canvas element

```
<canvas height="200" width="200"></canvas>
```

The resulting canvas will show up as an "invisible" 200 × 200 pixel rectangle on your page. If you want to add a border around it, you could use the HTML code shown in Listing 2-5 to style the canvas with normal CSS borders.

Listing 2-5. Canvas element with a solid border

```
<canvas id="diagonal" style="border: 1px solid;" width="200" height="200">
</canvas>
```

Note the addition of the ID **diagonal** to make it easy to locate this **canvas** element programmatically. An ID attribute is crucial to any canvas because all the useful operations on this element must be done through scripting. Without an ID, you will have difficulty locating the element to interoperate with it.

Figure 2-2 shows what the canvas in Listing 2-5 would look like in a browser.

Figure 2-2. A simple HTML5 canvas element on an HTML page

Not very exciting, but as any artist would tell you, it is full of potential. Now, let's do something with this pristine canvas. As mentioned before, it is not easy to draw a diagonal line on a web page without HTML5 Canvas. Let's see how easy it is now that we *can* use Canvas. Listing 2-6 shows how, with just a few lines of code, you can draw a diagonal line on the canvas we added to the page earlier.

Listing 2-6. Creating a diagonal line on a canvas

```
<script>
  function drawDiagonal() {
    // Get the canvas element and its drawing context
    var canvas = document.getElementById('diagonal');
    var context = canvas.getContext('2d');

    // Create a path in absolute coordinates
    context.beginPath();
    context.moveTo(70, 140);
    context.lineTo(140, 70);

    // Stroke the line onto the canvas
    context.stroke();
  }

  window.addEventListener("load", drawDiagonal, true);
</script>
```

Let's examine the JavaScript code used to create the diagonal line. It is a simple example, but it captures the essential flow of working with the HTML5 Canvas API:

You first gain access to the canvas object by referencing a particular canvas's ID value. In this example, the ID is diagonal. Next, you create a context variable and you call the canvas object's getContext method, passing in the type of canvas you are looking for. You pass in the string "2d" to get a two-dimensional context—the only available context type at this time.

■ **Note** A three-dimensional context might be supported in a future version of the specification.

You then use the context to perform drawing operations. In this case, you can create the diagonal line by calling three methods—beginPath, moveTo, and lineTo—passing in the line's start and end coordinates.

The drawing methods moveTo and lineTo do not actually create the line; you finalize a canvas operation and draw the line by calling the context.stroke(); method. Figure 2-3 shows the diagonal line created with the example code.

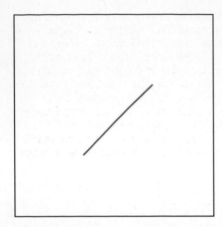

Figure 2-3. Diagonal line on a canvas

Triumph! Although this simple line may not appear to be the start of a revolution, keep in mind that drawing a diagonal line between two arbitrary points using classic HTML techniques was a very difficult maneuver involving stretched images, strange CSS and DOM objects, or other forms of black magic. Let us never speak of them again.

As you can see from this example's code, all operations on the canvas are performed via the context object. This will hold true for the rest of your interaction with the canvas because all the important functions with visual output are accessible only from the context, not the canvas object itself. This flexibility allows the canvas to support different types of drawing models in the future, based on the type of context that is retrieved from the canvas. Although we will frequently refer in this chapter to actions we will take on the canvas, keep in mind that this actually means that we will be working with the context object that the canvas supplies.

As demonstrated in the previous example, many operations on the context do not immediately update the drawing surface. Functions such as `beginPath`, `moveTo`, and `lineTo` do not modify the canvas appearance immediately. The same is true of many functions that set the styling and preferences of the canvas. Only when a path is *stroked* or *filled* does it appear on the display. Otherwise, the canvas will only be immediately updated when images are displayed, text is shown, or rectangles are drawn, filled, or cleared.

Applying Transformations to Drawings

Now let's look at another way to draw on the canvas using *transformation*. In the following example, the result is identical to the previous example, but the code used to draw the diagonal line is different. For this simple example, you could argue that the use of transformation adds unnecessary complexity. However, you can think of using transformation as a best practice for more complex canvas operations and you'll see that we'll use it a lot throughout the remaining examples, and it is critical to understanding the HTML5 Canvas API's complex capabilities.

Perhaps the easiest way to think of the transformation system—at least, the easiest way that does not involve a great amount of mathematical formulae and hand-waving—is as a modification layer that sits between the commands you issue and the output on the canvas display. This modification layer is always present, even if you choose not to interact with it.

Modifications, or *transformations* in the parlance of drawing systems, can be applied sequentially, combined, and modified at will. Every drawing operation is passed through the modification layer to be modified before it appears on the canvas. Although this adds an extra layer of complexity, it also adds tremendous power to the drawing system. It grants access to the powerful modifications that modern image-editing tools support in real time, yet in an API that is only as complex as it absolutely needs to be.

Don't be fooled into thinking that you are optimizing performance if you don't use transformation calls in your code. The canvas implementation uses and applies transformations implicitly in its rendering engine, whether or not you call them directly. It is wiser to understand the system up front because it will be crucial to know if you step outside the most basic drawing operations.

A key recommendation for reusable code is that you usually want to *draw at the origin* (coordinate 0,0) and apply transformations—scale, translate, rotate, and so forth—to modify your drawing code into its final appearance, as shown in Figure 2-4.

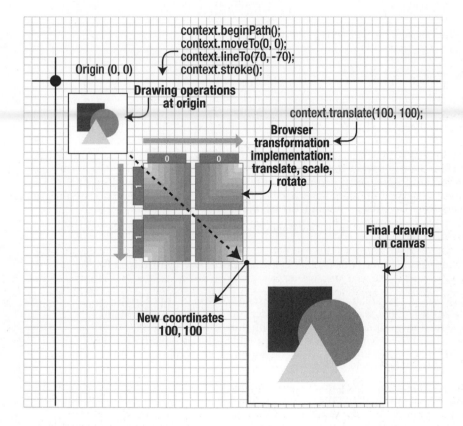

Figure 2-4. Overview of transformation and drawing at the origin

Listing 2-7 shows this best practice in action using the simplest transform: `translate`.

Listing 2-7. Using translation to create a diagonal line on a canvas

```
<script>
  function drawDiagonal() {
    var canvas = document.getElementById('diagonal');
    var context = canvas.getContext('2d');

    // Save a copy of the current drawing state
    context.save();

    // Move the drawing context to the right, and down
    context.translate(70, 140);

    // Draw the same line as before, but using the origin as a start
    context.beginPath();
    context.moveTo(0, 0);
    context.lineTo(70, -70);
    context.stroke();

    // Restore the old drawing state
    context.restore();
  }

  window.addEventListener("load", drawDiagonal, true);
</script>
```

Let's examine the JavaScript code used to create this second, translated diagonal line.

1. First, you access the canvas object by referencing its ID value (in this case, diagonal).

2. You then retrieve a context variable by calling the canvas object's getContext function.

3. Next, you want to save the still unmodified context so you can get back to its original state at the end of the drawing and transformation operation. If you do not save the state, the modifications you're making during the operation (translate, scale, and so on) will continue to be applied to the context in future operations, and that might not be desirable. Saving the context state before transforming it will allow us to restore it later.

4. The next step is to apply the translate method to the context. With this operation, the translation coordinates you supply will be added to the eventual drawing coordinates (the diagonal line) at the time any drawing is rendered, thus moving the line to its final location, but only after the drawing operation is complete.

5. After the translation has been applied, you can perform the normal drawing operations to create the diagonal line. In this case, you can create the diagonal line by calling three methods—beginPath, moveTo, and lineTo—this time drawing at the origin (0,0) instead of coordinates 70,140.

6. After the line has been sketched, you can render it to the canvas (for example, draw the line) by calling the context.stroke method.

7. Finally, you restore the context to its clean original state, so that future canvas operations are performed without the translation that was applied in this operation. Figure 2-5 shows the diagonal line created with the example code.

Figure 2-5. Translated diagonal line on a canvas

Even though your new line looks remarkably like the old one, you created it using the power of transformations, something that will become more apparent as we progress through the rest of this chapter.

Working with Paths

Although we could offer many more exciting examples for drawing lines, we are ready now to progress to something a bit more complex: *paths*. Paths in the HTML5 Canvas API represent any shape you care to render. Our original line example was a path, as you might have gathered from the conspicuous `beginPath` call used to start it off. But paths can be as complicated as you desire, with multiple line and curve segments and even subpaths. If you are looking to draw almost any shape on a canvas, the path API will be your focus point.

When embarking on any routine to draw a shape or path, the first call you make is `beginPath`. This simple function takes no arguments, but it signals to the canvas that you wish to start a new shape description. This function is mostly useful to the canvas so that it can calculate the interior and exterior of the shape you are creating for later fills and strokes.

A path always tracks the concept of a current location, which defaults to the origin. The canvas internally tracks the current location, but you will modify it with your drawing routines.

Once the shape is begun, you can use a variety of functions on the context to plot the layout of your shape. You've already seen the simplest context pathing functions in action:

- moveTo(x, y): moves the current location to a new destination of (x, y) without drawing.

- lineTo(x, y): moves the current location to a new destination of (x, y) drawing a straight line from the current position to the new one.

Essentially, the difference between these two calls is that the first is akin to lifting a drawing pen and moving to a new location, whereas the second tells the canvas to leave the pen on the paper and move it in a straight line to the new destination. However, it is worth pointing out again that *no actual drawing occurs until you stroke or fill the path*. At present, we are merely defining the positions in our path so that it can be drawn later.

The next special pathing function is a call to closePath. This command is very similar in behavior to the lineTo function, with the difference being that the destination is automatically assumed to be the origination of the path. However, the closePath also informs the canvas that the current shape has closed or formed a completely contained area. This will be useful for future fills and strokes.

At this point, you are free to continue with more segments in your path to create additional subpaths. Or you can beginPath at any time to start over and clear the path list entirely.

As with most complex systems, it is often better to see them in action. Let's depart from our line examples and use the HTML5 Canvas API to start to create a new scene that illustrates a forest with a trail-running path. This scene will serve as a logo of sorts for our race event. And as with any picture, we will start with a basic element, which in this case is the canopy of a simple pine tree. Listing 2-8 shows how to draw the pine tree's canopy.

Listing 2-8. Function that creates a path for a tree canopy

```
function createCanopyPath(context) {
  // Draw the tree canopy
  context.beginPath();

  context.moveTo(-25, -50);
  context.lineTo(-10, -80);
  context.lineTo(-20, -80);
  context.lineTo(-5, -110);
  context.lineTo(-15, -110);

  // Top of the tree
  context.lineTo(0, -140);

  context.lineTo(15, -110);
  context.lineTo(5, -110);
  context.lineTo(20, -80);
  context.lineTo(10, -80);
  context.lineTo(25, -50);

  // Close the path back to its start point
  context.closePath();
}
```

As you can see from the code, we used the same move and line commands from before, but more of them. These lines form the branches of a simple tree shape, and we close the path back at the end. Our tree will leave a notable gap at the bottom, and we will use this in future sections to draw the trunk. Listing 2-9 shows how to use that canopy drawing function to actually render our simple tree shape onto a canvas.

Listing 2-9. *Function that draws a tree on the canvas*

```
function drawTrails() {
  var canvas = document.getElementById('trails');
  var context = canvas.getContext('2d');

  context.save();
  context.translate(130, 250);

  // Create the shape for our canopy path
  createCanopyPath(context);

  // Stroke the current path
  context.stroke();
  context.restore();
}
```

All the calls in this routine should be familiar to you already. We fetch the canvas context, save it for future reference, translate our position to a new location, draw the canopy, stroke it onto the canvas, and then restore our state. Figure 2-6 shows the results of our handiwork, a simply line representation of a tree canopy. We'll expand on this as we go forward, but it's a good first step.

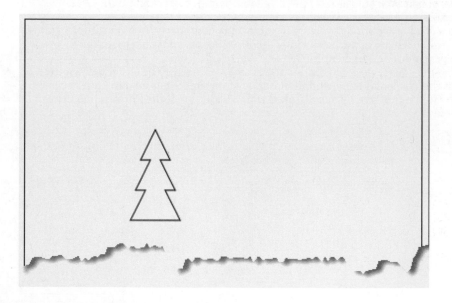

Figure 2-6. *A simple path of a tree canopy*

Working with Stroke Styles

The HTML5 Canvas API wouldn't be powerful or popular if developers were stuck using simple stick drawings and black lines. Let's use the stroke styling capabilities to make our canopy a little more tree-like. Listing 2-10 shows some basic commands that can modify the properties of the context in order to make the stroked shape look more appealing.

Listing 2-10. Using a stroke style

```
// Increase the line width
context.lineWidth = 4;

// Round the corners at path joints
context.lineJoin = 'round';

// Change the color to brown
context.strokeStyle = '#663300';

// Finally, stroke the canopy
context.stroke();
```

By adding the above properties before stroking, we change the appearance of any future stroked shapes—at least until we restore the context back to a previous state.

First, we increase the width of the stroked lines to four pixels.

Next, we set the `lineJoin` property to `round`, which causes the joints of our shape's segments to take on a more rounded corner shape. We could also set the `lineJoin` to `bevel` or `miter` (and the corresponding `context.miterLimit` value to tweak it) to choose other corner options.

Finally, we change the color of the stroke by using the `strokeStyle` property. In our example, we are setting the color to a CSS value, but as you will see in later sections, it is also possible to set the `strokeStyle` to be an image pattern or a gradient for fancier displays.

Although we are not using it here, we could also set the `lineCap` property to be either `butt`, `square`, or `round` to specify how lines should display at the endpoints. Alas, our example has no dangling line ends. Figure 2-7 shows our spruced-up tree canopy, now stroked with a wider, smoother, brown line instead of the flat black line from before.

Figure 2-7. Stylish stroked tree canopy

Working with Fill Styles

As you might expect, stroking is not the only way to affect the appearance of canvas shapes. The next common way to modify a shape is to specify how its paths and subpaths are filled. Listing 2-11 shows how simple it is to fill our canopy with a pleasant, green color.

Listing 2-11. Using a fill style

```
// Set the fill color to green and fill the canopy
context.fillStyle = '#339900';
context.fill();
```

First, we set the `fillStyle` to the appropriate color. As we will see later, it is also possible to set the fill to be a gradient or an image pattern. Then, we simply call the context's `fill` function to let the canvas fill all the pixels inside all the closed paths of our current shape, as shown in Figure 2-8.

Figure 2-8. Filled tree canopy

Because we stroked our canopy before filling it, the fill covers part of the stroked path. This is due to the fact that the wide stroke—in our case, four pixels wide—is centered along the line of the path shape. The fill applies to all pixels on the interior of the shape, and as such it will cover half of the stroked line pixels. Should you prefer the full stroke to appear, you can simply fill *before* stroking the path.

Filling Rectangular Content

Every tree deserves a strong foundation. Thankfully, we left space for our tree trunk in the original shape path. Listing 2-12 shows how we can add the simplest rendering of a tree trunk by using the `fillRect` convenience function.

Listing 2-12. Using the fillRect convenience fucntion

```
// Change fill color to brown
context.fillStyle = '#663300';

// Fill a rectangle for the tree trunk
context.fillRect(-5, -50, 10, 50);
```

Here, we once again set a brown fill style. But instead of explicitly drawing the corners of our trunk rectangle using the `lineTo` ability, we will draw the entire trunk in one step by using `fillRect`. The `fillRect` call takes the x and y location, as well as the width and height, and then immediately fills it with the current fill style.

Although we are not using them here, corresponding functions exist to `strokeRect` and `clearRect`. The former will draw the outline of the rectangle based on a given position and dimension, while the latter will remove any content from the rectangular area and reset it to its original, transparent color.

CANVAS ANIMATIONS

Brian says: "The ability to clear rectangles in the canvas is core to creating animations and games using the HTML5 Canvas API. By repeatedly drawing and clearing sections of the canvas, it is possible to present the illusion of animation, and many examples of this already exist on the Web. However, to create animations that perform smoothly, you will need to utilize *clipping* features and perhaps even a secondary buffered canvas to minimize the flickering caused by frequent canvas clears. Although animations are beyond the scope of this book, feel free to explore!"

Figure 2-9 shows our simple, flatly filled tree trunk attached to our previous canopy path.

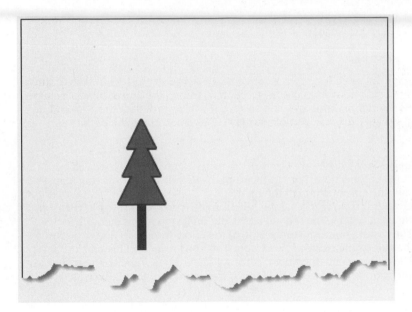

Figure 2-9. Tree with filled rectangular trunk

Drawing Curves

The world, particularly the natural world, is not filled with straight lines and rectangles. Fortunately, the canvas provides a variety of functions for creating curves in our paths. We will demonstrate the simplest option—a *quadratic* curve—to form a path through our virtual forest. Listing 2-13 demonstrates the addition of two quadratic curves.

Listing 2-13. Drawing a curve

```
// Save the canvas state and draw the path
context.save();

context.translate(-10, 350);
context.beginPath();

// The first curve bends up and right
context.moveTo(0, 0);
context.quadraticCurveTo(170, -50, 260, -190);

// The second curve continues down and right
context.quadraticCurveTo(310, -250, 410,-250);

// Draw the path in a wide brown stroke
context.strokeStyle = '#663300';
context.lineWidth = 20;
context.stroke();

// Restore the previous canvas state
context.restore();
```

As before, one of the first things we will do is save our canvas context state, because we will be modifying the translation and stroke options here. For our forest path, we will start by moving back to the origin and drawing a first quadratic curve up and to the right.

As shown in Figure 2-10, the `quadraticCurveTo` function begins at the current drawing location and takes two x, y point locations as its parameters. The second one is the final stop in our curve. The first one represents a *control point*. The control point sits to the side of the curve (not on it) and acts almost as a gravitational pull for the points along the curve path. By adjusting the location of the control point, you can adjust the curvature of the path you are drawing. We draw a second quadratic curve up and to the right to complete our path; then stroke it just as we did for our tree canopy before (only wider).

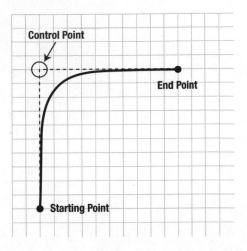

Figure 2-10. Quadratic curve start, end, and control points

Other options for curves in the HTML5 Canvas API include the bezierCurveTo, arcTo, and arc functions. These curves take additional control points, a radius, or angles to determine the characteristics of the curve. Figure 2-11 shows the two quadratic curves stroked on our canvas to create a path through the trees.

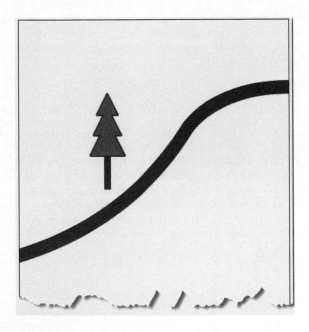

Figure 2-11. Quadratic curves for a path

Inserting Images into a Canvas

Images can be extremely handy to display inside a canvas. They can be stamped, stretched, modified with transformations, and often be the focus of the entire canvas. Thankfully, the HTML5 Canvas API includes a few simple commands for adding image content to the canvas.

But images also add a complication to the canvas operations: you must wait for them to load. Browsers will usually be loading images asynchronously as your page script is rendering. However, if you attempt to render an image onto a canvas before it has completely loaded, the canvas will fail to render any image at all. As such, you should be careful to make sure the image is loaded completely before you attempt to render it.

To solve this problem in our simple forest trail example, we will load an image of a bark texture to use directly in the canvas. In order to make sure that the image has completed loading before we render, we will switch the loading code to only execute as a callback from image loading completion, as shown in Listing 2-14.

Listing 2-14. Loading the image

```
// Load the bark image
var bark = new Image();
bark.src = "bark.jpg";

// Once the image is loaded, draw on the canvas
bark.onload = function () {
  drawTrails();
}
```

As you can see, we've added an `onload` handler to the `bark.jpg` image to call the main `drawTrails` function only when the image loading has completed. This guarantees that the image will be available to the next calls we add to the canvas rendering, as shown in Listing 2-15.

Listing 2-15. Drawing an image on a canvas

```
// Draw the bark pattern image where
//  the filled rectangle was before
context.drawImage(bark, -5, -50, 10, 50);
```

Here, we have replaced the previous call to `fillRect` with a simple routine to display our bark image as the new trunk for our tree. Although the image is a subtle replacement, it provides more texture to our display. Note that in this call, we are specifying an x, y, width, and height argument in addition to the image itself. This option will scale the image to fit into the 10×50 pixel space that we have allocated for our trunk. We could also have passed in source dimensions to have more control over the clipping area of the incoming image to be displayed.

As you can see in Figure 2-12, the change to the appearance of our trunk is only slightly different from the filled rectangle we used before.

Figure 2-12. *Tree with an image used for trunk*

Using Gradients

Not satisfied with the tree trunk? Well, neither are we. Let's take another approach to drawing our tree trunk that uses a little more finesse: gradients. Gradients allow you to apply a gradual algorithmic sampling of colors as either a stroke or fill style, just like the patterns were applied in the last section. Creating gradients requires a three-step process:

1. Create the gradient object itself.

2. Apply color stops to the gradient object, signaling changes in color along the transition.

3. Set the gradient as either a fillStyle or a strokeStyle on the context.

It is perhaps easiest to think of gradients as a smooth change of color that moves along a line. For example, if you supply points A and B as the arguments to the creation of a gradient, the color will be transitioned for any stroke or fill that moves in the direction of point A to point B.

To determine what colors are displayed, simply use the `addColorStop` function on the gradient object itself. This function allows you to specify an offset and a color. The color argument is the color you want to be applied in the stroke or fill at the offset position. The offset position is a value between 0.0 and 1.0, representing how far along the gradient line the color should be reached.

If you create a gradient from point (0,0) to point (0,100) and specify a white color stop at offset 0.0 and a black offset at offset 1.0, then when the stroke or fill occurs, you will see the color gradually shift from white (the beginning color stop) to black (the end color stop) as the rendering moves from point (0,0) to point (0,100).

As with other color values, it is possible to supply an alpha (for example, transparency) value as part of the color and make that alpha value transition as well. To do so, you will need to use another textual representation of the color value, such as the CSS `rgba` function that includes an alpha component.

Let's see this in more detail with a code sample that applies two gradients to a `fillRect` representing our final tree trunk, as shown in Listing 2-16.

Listing 2-16. Using a gradient

```
// Create a 3 stop gradient horizontally across the trunk
var trunkGradient = context.createLinearGradient(-5, -50, 5, -50);

// The beginning of the trunk is medium brown
trunkGradient.addColorStop(0, '#663300');

// The middle-left of the trunk is lighter in color
trunkGradient.addColorStop(0.4, '#996600');

// The right edge of the trunk is darkest
trunkGradient.addColorStop(1, '#552200');

// Apply the gradient as the fill style, and draw the trunk
context.fillStyle = trunkGradient;
context.fillRect(-5, -50, 10, 50);

// A second, vertical gradient creates a shadow from the
//   canopy on the trunk
var canopyShadow = context.createLinearGradient(0, -50, 0, 0);

// The beginning of the shadow gradient is black, but with
//   a 50% alpha value
canopyShadow.addColorStop(0, 'rgba(0, 0, 0, 0.5)');

// Slightly further down, the gradient completely fades to
//   fully transparent. The rest of the trunk gets no shadow.
canopyShadow.addColorStop(0.2, 'rgba(0, 0, 0, 0.0)');

// Draw the shadow gradient on top of the trunk gradient
context.fillStyle = canopyShadow;
context.fillRect(-5, -50, 10, 50);
```

Applying these two gradients creates a nice, smooth light source on our rendered tree as shown in Figure 2-13, making it appear curved and covered by a slight shadow from the canopy above. Let's keep it.

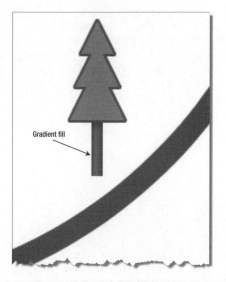

Figure 2-13. Tree with gradient trunk

Besides the linear gradient used in our example, the HTML5 Canvas API also supports a radial gradient option that allows you to specify two circular representations in which the color stops are applied to the cone between the two circles. The radial gradient uses the same color stops as the linear gradient, but takes its arguments in the form shown in Listing 2-17.

Listing 2-17. Example of applying a radial gradient

```
createRadialGradient(x0, y0, r0, x1, y1, r1)
```

In this example, the first three arguments represent a circle centered at (x0, y0) with radius r0, and the last three arguments represent a second circle centered at (x1, y1) with radius r1. The gradient is drawn across the area between the two circles.

Using Background Patterns

Direct rendering of images has many uses, but in some cases it is beneficial to use an image as a background tile, similar to the capability available in CSS. We've already seen how it is possible to set a stroke or fill style to be a solid color. The HTML5 Canvas API also includes an option to set an image as a repeatable pattern for either a path stroke or fill.

To make our forest trail appear a bit more rugged, we will demonstrate the capability by replacing the previous stroked trail curve with one that uses a background image fill. In doing so, we'll swap out our now-unused bark image for a gravel image that we will put to use here. Listing 2-18 shows we replace the call to `drawImage` with a call to `createPattern`.

Listing 2-18. Using a background pattern

```
// Replace the bark image with
// a trail gravel image
var gravel = new Image();
gravel.src = "gravel.jpg";
gravel.onload = function () {
    drawTrails();
}

// Replace the solid stroke with a repeated
// background pattern
context.strokeStyle = context.createPattern(gravel, 'repeat');
context.lineWidth = 20;
context.stroke();
```

As you can see, we are still calling `stroke()` for our path. However, this time we have set a `strokeStyle` property on the context first, passing in the result of a call to `context.createPattern`. Oh, and once again the image needs to be previously loaded in order for the canvas to perform the operation. The second argument is a repetition pattern that can be one of the choices shown in Table 2-2.

Table 2-2. Repetition Patterns

Repeat	Value
repeat	(Default) The image is repeated in both directions
repeat-x	The image is repeated only in the X dimension
repeat-y	The image is repeated only in the Y dimension
no-repeat	The image is displayed once and not repeated

Figure 2-14 shows the result of the use of a background image rather than an explicitly drawn image to represent our trail.

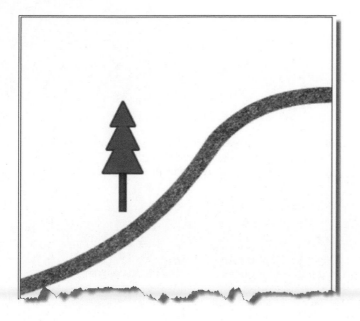

Figure 2-14. A trail with a repeating background pattern

Scaling Canvas Objects

What kind of forest has only one tree? Let's fix that right away. To make this a little easier, we will adjust our code sample to isolate the tree drawing operations to a single routine, called **drawTree**, as shown in Listing 2-19.

Listing 2-19. Function to draw the tree object

```
// Move tree drawing into its own function for reuse
function drawTree(context) {
  var trunkGradient = context.createLinearGradient(-5, -50, 5, -50);
  trunkGradient.addColorStop(0, '#663300');
  trunkGradient.addColorStop(0.4, '#996600');
  trunkGradient.addColorStop(1, '#552200');
  context.fillStyle = trunkGradient;
  context.fillRect(-5, -50, 10, 50);

  var canopyShadow = context.createLinearGradient(0, -50, 0, 0);
  canopyShadow.addColorStop(0, 'rgba(0, 0, 0, 0.5)');
  canopyShadow.addColorStop(0.2, 'rgba(0, 0, 0, 0.0)');
  context.fillStyle = canopyShadow;
  context.fillRect(-5, -50, 10, 50);

  createCanopyPath(context);
```

```
    context.lineWidth = 4;
    context.lineJoin = 'round';
    context.strokeStyle = '#663300';
    context.stroke();

    context.fillStyle = '#339900';
    context.fill();
}
```

As you can see, the `drawTree` function contains all the code we previously created to draw the canopy, trunk, and trunk gradient. Now we will use one of the transformation routines—`context.scale`—to draw a second tree at a new location and with a larger size, as shown in Listing 2-20.

Listing 2-20. Drawing the tree objects

```
// Draw the first tree at X=130, Y=250
context.save();
context.translate(130, 250);
drawTree(context);
context.restore();

// Draw the second tree at X=260, Y=500
context.save();
context.translate(260, 500);

// Scale this tree twice normal in both dimensions
context.scale(2, 2);
drawTree(context);
context.restore();
```

The `scale` function takes two factors for the x and y dimensions as its arguments. Each factor tells the canvas implementation how much larger (or smaller) to make the size in that dimension; an X factor of 2 would make all subsequent draw routines twice as wide, while a Y factor of 0.5 would make all subsequent operations half as tall as before. Using these routines, we now have an easy way to create a second tree in our trails canvas, as shown in Figure 2-15.

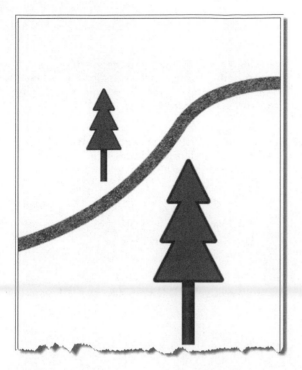

Figure 2-15. *Tree with a larger scale*

ALWAYS PERFORM SHAPE AND PATH ROUTINES AT THE ORIGIN

Brian says (and really means it, this time): "This example illustrates one of the reasons why it is a good idea to perform shape and path routines at the origin; then translate them when complete, as we do here in our code. The reason is that transforms such as `scale` and `rotate` operate from the origin.

If you perform a `rotate` transform to a shape drawn off origin, a `rotate` transform will rotate the shape around the origin rather than rotating in place. Similarly, if you performed a scale operation to shapes before translating them to their proper position, all locations for path coordinates would also be multiplied by the scaling factor. Depending on the scale factor applied, this new location could even be off the canvas altogether, leaving you wondering why your scale operation just 'deleted' the image."

Using Canvas Transforms

Transform operations are not limited to scales and translates. It is also possible to rotate the drawing context using the `context.rotate(angle)` function or even to modify the underlying transform directly for more advanced operations such as shearing of the rendered paths. If you wanted to rotate the display of an image, you would merely need to call the series of operations shown in Listing 2-21.

Listing 2-21. A rotated image

```
context.save();

// rotation angle is specified in radians
context.rotate(1.57);
context.drawImage(myImage, 0, 0, 100, 100);

context.restore();
```

In Listing 2-22, however, we will show how you can apply an arbitrary transform to the path coordinates to radically alter the display of our existing tree path in order to create a shadow effect.

Listing 2-22. Using a transform

```
// Create a 3 stop gradient horizontally across the trunk
// Save the current canvas state for later
context.save();

// Create a slanted tree as the shadow by applying
//   a shear transform, changing X values to increase
//   as Y values increase
context.transform(1, 0,-0.5, 1, 0, 0);

// Shrink the shadow down to 60% height in the Y dimension
context.scale(1, 0.6);

// Set the tree fill to be black, but at only 20% alpha
context.fillStyle = 'rgba(0, 0, 0, 0.2)';
context.fillRect(-5, -50, 10, 50);

// Redraw the tree with the shadow effects applied
createCanopyPath(context);
context.fill();

// Restore the canvas state
context.restore();
```

Modifying the context transform directly as we've done here is something you should attempt only if you are familiar with the matrix mathematics underpinning two-dimensional drawing systems. If you check the math behind this transform, you will see that we are shifting the X values of our drawing by a factor of the corresponding Y values in order to shear the gray tree being used as a shadow. Then, by applying a scale factor of 60%, the sheared tree is decreased in size.

Note that the sheared "shadow" tree is rendered first, so that the actual tree appears above it in *Z-order* (the order in which the canvas objects overlap). Also, the shadow tree is drawn using the CSS notation for RGBA, which allows us to set the alpha value to only 20% of normal. This creates the light, semitransparent look for the shadow tree. Once applied to our scaled trees, the output renders as shown in Figure 2-16.

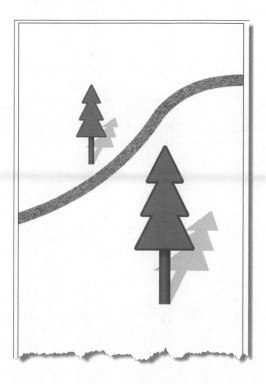

Figure 2-16. Trees with transformed shadows

Using Canvas Text

As we approach the end of our trail creation, let's demonstrate the power of the HTML5 Canvas API text functions by adding a fancy title to the top of our display. It is important to note that text rendering on a canvas is treated the same way as any other path object: text can be stroked or filled, and all rendering transformations and styles can apply to text just as they do to any other shape.

As you might expect, the text drawing routines consist of two functions on the context object:

- `fillText (text, x, y, maxwidth)`

- `strokeText (text, x, y, maxwidth)`

Both functions take the text as well as the location at which it should be drawn. Optionally, a `maxwidth` argument can be provided to constrain the size of the text by automatically shrinking the font to fit the given size. In addition, a `measureText` function is available to return a metrics object containing the width of the given text should it be rendered using the current context settings.

As is the case with all browser text display, the actual appearance of the text is highly configurable using context properties that are similar to their CSS counterparts, as shown in Table 2-3.

Table 2-3. Possible settings for background pattern repetition

Property	Values	Note
font	CSS font string	Example: italic Arial, sans-serif
textAlign	start, end, left, right, center	Defaults to start
textBaseline	top, hanging, middle, alphabetic, ideographic, bottom	Defaults to alphabetic

All these context properties can be set to alter the context or accessed to query the current values. In Listing 2-23, we will create a large text message with the font face **Impact** and fill it with the background pattern of our existing bark image. In order to center the text across the top of our canvas, we will declare a maximum width and a `center` alignment.

Listing 2-23. Using canvas text

```
// Draw title text on our canvas
context.save();

// The font will be 60 pixel, Impact face
context.font = "60px impact";

// Use a brown fill for our text
context.fillStyle = '#996600';
// Text can be aligned when displayed
context.textAlign = 'center';

// Draw the text in the middle of the canvas with a max
//  width set to center properly
context.fillText('Happy Trails!', 200, 60, 400);
context.restore();
```

As you can see from the result in Figure 2-17, the trail drawing just got a whole lot—you guessed it—happier.

Figure 2-17. Background pattern-filled text

Applying Shadows

Finally, we will use the built-in canvas shadow API to add a blurred shadow effect to our new text display. Like many graphical effects, shadows are best applied in moderation, even though the HTML5 Canvas API allows you to apply shadows to any operation we have already covered.

Once again, shadows are controlled by a few global **context** properties, as shown in Table 2-4.

Table 2-4. Shadow properties

Property	Values	Note
shadowColor	Any CSS color	Can include an alpha component
shadowOffsetX	Pixel count	Positive values move shadow to the right, negative left
shadowOffsetY	Pixel count	Positive values move shadow down, negative up
shadowBlur	Gaussian blur	Higher values cause blurrier shadow edges

The shadow effect is triggered on any path, text, or image render if the `shadowColor` and at least one of the other properties is set to a nondefault value. Listing 2-24 shows how we can apply a shadow to our new trails title text.

Listing 2-24. Applying a shadow

```
// Set some shadow on our text, black with 20% alpha
context.shadowColor = 'rgba(0, 0, 0, 0.2)';

// Move the shadow to the right 15 pixels, up 10
context.shadowOffsetX = 15;
context.shadowOffsetY = -10;

// Blur the shadow slightly
context.shadowBlur = 2;
```

With these simple additions, the canvas renderer will automatically apply shadows until the canvas state is restored or the shadow properties are reset. Figure 2-18 shows the newly applied shadows.

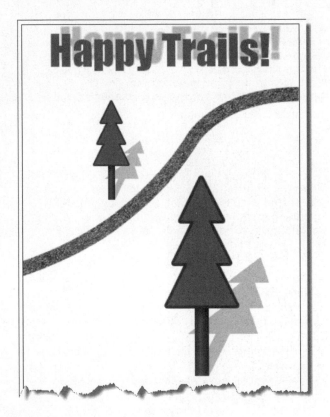

Figure 2-18. Title with shadowed text

As you can see, the shadow generated by CSS is positional only and not in sync with the transformational shadow we created for our tree. For the sake of consistency, you should probably only use one approach to drawing shadows in a given canvas scene.

Working with Pixel Data

One of the most useful—albeit nonobvious—aspects of the Canvas API is the ability for developers to easily get access to the underlying pixels in the canvas. This access works in both directions: it is trivial to get access to the pixel values as a numerical array, and it is equally easy to modify those values and apply them back to the canvas. In fact, it is entirely possible to manipulate the canvas entirely through the pixel value calls and forgo the rendering calls we've discussed in this chapter. This is made possible by the existence of three functions on the context API.

First up is context.getImageData(sx, sy, sw, sh). This function returns a representation of the current state of the canvas display as a collection of integers. Specifically, it returns an object containing three properties:

- width: The number of pixels in each row of the pixel data

- height: The number of pixels in each column of the pixel data

- data: A one-dimensional array containing the actual RGBA values for each pixel retrieved from the canvas. This array contains four values for each pixel—a red, green, blue, and alpha component—each with a value from 0 to 255. Therefore, each pixel retrieved from the canvas becomes four integer values in the data array. The data array is populated by pixels from left to right and top to bottom (for example, across the first row, then across the second row, and so on), as shown in Figure 2-19.

Figure 2-19. Pixel data and the internal data structure that represents it

The data returned by the call to getImageData is limited to the region defined by the four parameters. Only canvas pixels contained in the rectangular region surrounded by the source x, y, width, and height parameters will be retrieved. Therefore, to access all pixel values as data, you should pass in getImageData(0, 0, canvas.width, canvas.height).

Because there are four image data values representing each pixel, it can be a little tricky to calculate exactly which index represents the values for a given pixel. The formula is as follows.

For any pixel at coordinate (x,y) in a canvas with a given width and height, you can locate the component values:

- **Red component:** ((width * y) + x) * 4

- **Green component:** ((width * y) + x) * 4 + 1

- **Blue component:** ((width * y) + x) * 4 + 2

- **Alpha component:** ((width * y) + x) * 4 + 3

Once you have access to the object with image data, it is quite easy to modify the pixel values in the data array mathematically, because they are each simply integers from 0 to 255. Changing the red, green, blue, or alpha values for one or more pixels makes it easy to update the canvas display by using the second function: context.putImageData(imagedata, dx, dy).

putImageData allows you to pass in a set of image data in the same format as it was originally retrieved; that's quite handy because you can modify the values the canvas originally gave you and put them back. Once this function is called, the canvas will immediately update to reflect the new values of the pixels you passed in as the image data. The dx and dy parameters allow you to specify an offset for where to start applying your data array into the existing canvas, should you choose to use one.

Finally, if you want to start from scratch with a set of blank canvas data, you can call context.createImageData(sw, sh) to create a new set of image data tied to the canvas object. This set of data can be programmatically changed as before, even though it does not represent the current state of the canvas when retrieved.

Implementing Canvas Security

There is an important caveat to using pixel manipulation, as described in the previous section. Although most developers would use pixel manipulation for legitimate means, it is quite possible that the ability to fetch and update data from a canvas could be used for nefarious purposes. For this reason, the concept of an *origin-clean* canvas was specified, so that canvases that are *tainted* with images from origins other than the source of the containing page cannot have their data retrieved.

As shown in Figure 2-20, if a page served up from http://www.example.com contains a canvas element, it is entirely possible that the code in the page could try to render an image from http://www.remote.com inside the canvas. After all, it is perfectly acceptable to render images from remote sites inside any given web page.

Figure 2-20. Local and remote image sources

However, before the arrival of the Canvas API, it was not possible to programmatically retrieve the pixel values of a downloaded image. Private images from other sites could be displayed in a page but not read or copied. Allowing scripts to read image data from other origins would effectively share users' photographs and other sensitive online image file with the entire web.

In order to prevent this, any canvas that contains images rendered from remote origins will throw a security exception if the `getImageData` function is called. It is perfectly acceptable to render remote images into a canvas from another origin as long as you (or any other scriptwriter) do not attempt to fetch the data from that canvas after it has been tainted. Be aware of this limitation and practice safe rendering.

Building an Application with HTML5 Canvas

There are many different application possibilities for using the Canvas API: graphs, charts, image editing, and so on. However, one of the most intriguing uses for the canvas is to modify or overlay existing content. One popular type of overlay is known as a heatmap. Although the name implies a temperature measurement, the heat in this case can refer to any level of measurable activity. Areas on the map with high levels of activity are colored as hot (for example, red, yellow, or white). Areas with less activity show no color change at all, or minimal blacks and grays.

For example, a heatmap can be used to indicate traffic on a city map, or storm activity on a global map. And situations such as these are easy to implement in HTML5 by combining a canvas display with an underlying map source. Essentially, the canvas can be used to overlay the map and draw the heat levels based on the appropriate activity data.

Let's build a simple heatmap using the capabilities we learned about in the Canvas API. In this case, our heat data source will be not external data, but the movement of our mouse across the map. Moving the mouse over a portion of the map will cause the heat to increase, and holding the mouse at a given position will rapidly increase the temperature to maximum levels. We can overlay such a heatmap display(shown in Figure 2-21) on a nondescript terrain map, just to provide a sample case.

Heatmap

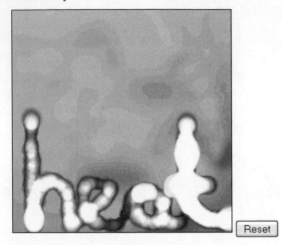

Figure 2-21. The heatmap application

Now that you've seen the end result of our heatmap application, let's step through the code sample. As usual, the working examples are available online for your download and perusal.

Let's start with the HTML elements declared in this example. For this display, the HTML consists of only a title, a canvas, and a button we can use to reset the heatmap. The background display for the canvas consists of a simple `mapbg.jpg` applied to the canvas via CSS as shown in Listing 2-25.

Listing 2-25. The heatmap canvas element

```
<style type="text/css">
  #heatmap {
      background-image: url("mapbg.jpg");
  }
</style>

<h2>Heatmap </h2>
<canvas id="heatmap" class="clear" style="border: 1px solid ; " height="300"↩
 width="300"> </canvas>
<button id="resetButton">Reset</button>
```

We also declare some initial variables to be used later in the example.

```
var points = {};
var SCALE = 3;
var x = -1;
var y = -1;
```

Next, we will set the canvas to have a high transparency value for its global drawing operations, and set the composite mode to cause new draws to lighten the underlying pixels rather than replace them.

Then, as shown in Listing 2-26, we will set a handler to change the display—addToPoint—every time the mouse moves or one-tenth of a second passes.

Listing 2-26. The loadDemo function

```
function loadDemo() {
  document.getElementById("resetButton").onclick = reset;

  canvas = document.getElementById("heatmap");
  context = canvas.getContext('2d');
  context.globalAlpha = 0.2;
  context.globalCompositeOperation = "lighter"

function sample() {
  if (x != -1) {
    addToPoint(x,y)
  }
  setTimeout(sample, 100);
}

canvas.onmousemove = function(e) {
  x = e.clientX - e.target.offsetLeft;
  y = e.clientY - e.target.offsetTop;
  addToPoint(x,y)
}

  sample();
}
```

If the user clicks **Reset**, the entire canvas area is cleared and reset to its original state by using the canvas' clearRect function, as shown in Listing 2-27.

Listing 2-27. The reset function

```
function reset() {
  points = {};
  context.clearRect(0,0,300,300);
  x = -1;
  y = -1;
}
```

Next we create a lookup table of colors to use when drawing heat on the canvas. Listing 2-28 shows how the colors range in brightness from least to greatest, and they will be used to represent varying levels of heat on the display. The greater the value of the intensity, the brighter the returned color.

Listing 2-28. The getColor function

```
function getColor(intensity) {
  var colors = ["#072933", "#2E4045", "#8C593B", "#B2814E", "#FAC268", "#FAD237"];
  return colors[Math.floor(intensity/2)];
}
```

Whenever the mouse moves or hovers over an area of the canvas, a point is drawn. The point grows in size (and brightness) the longer the mouse stays in the immediate area. As shown in Listing 2-29, we use the `context.arc` function to draw a circle of a given radius, and we draw a brighter, hotter color for larger radius values by passing the radius to our `getColor` function.

Listing 2-29. The drawPoint function

```
function drawPoint(x, y, radius) {
  context.fillStyle = getColor(radius);
  radius = Math.sqrt(radius)*6;

  context.beginPath();
  context.arc(x, y, radius, 0, Math.PI*2, true)

  context.closePath();
  context.fill();
}
```

In the `addToPoint` function—which you will recall is accessed every time the mouse moves or hovers over a point—a heat value is increased and stored for that particular point on the canvas. Listing 2-30 shows that the maximum point value is 10. Once the current value of heat for a given pixel is found, the appropriate pixel is passed to `drawPoint` with its corresponding heat/radius value.

Listing 2-30. The addToPoint function

```
function addToPoint(x, y) {
  x = Math.floor(x/SCALE);
  y = Math.floor(y/SCALE);

  if (!points[[x,y]]) {
    points[[x,y]] = 1;
  } else if (points[[x,y]]==10) {
    return
  } else {
    points[[x,y]]++;
  }
  drawPoint(x*SCALE,y*SCALE, points[[x,y]]);
}
```

Finally, the initial `loadDemo` function is registered to be called whenever the window completes loading.

```
window.addEventListener("load", loadDemo, true);
```

Together, these one hundred or so lines of code illustrate how much you can do with the HTML5 Canvas API in a short amount of time, without using any plugins or external rendering technology. With an infinite number of data sources available it is easy to see how they can be visualized simply and effectively.

Practical Extra: Full Page Glass Pane

In the example application, you saw how you can apply a canvas on top of a graphic. You can also apply a canvas on top of the entire browser window or portions of the same—a technique commonly referred to as glass pane. Once you have positioned the glass pane canvas on top of a web page, you can do all kinds of cool and handy things with it.

For example, you can use a routine to retrieve the absolute position of all the DOM elements on a page and create a step-by-step help function that can guide users of a web application through the steps they must perform to start and use the application.

Or, you can use the glass pane canvas to scribble feedback on someone's web page using the mouse events for drawing input. Some things to keep in mind if you try to use a canvas in this capacity:

- You will need to set the canvas positioning to absolute and give it a specific position, width, and height. Without an explicit width and height setting, the canvas will remain at a zero pixel size.

- Don't forget to set a high Z-index on the canvas so that it floats above all the visible content. A canvas rendered under all the existing content doesn't get much chance to shine.

- Your glass pane canvas can block access to events in the content below, so be sparing in how you use it and remove it when it is unnecessary.

Summary

As you can see, the HTML5 Canvas API provides a very powerful way to modify the appearance of your web application without resorting to odd document hacks. Images, gradients, and complex paths can be combined to create nearly any type of display you may be looking to present. Keep in mind that you generally need to draw at the origin, load any images you want to display before attempting to draw them, and be mindful of tainting your canvas with foreign image sources. However, if you learn to harness the power of the canvas, you can create applications that were never possible in a web page before.

CHAPTER 3

■■■

Working with HTML5 Audio and Video

In this chapter, we'll explore what you can do with two important HTML5 elements—*audio* and *video*—and we'll show you how they can be used to create compelling applications. The audio and video elements add new media options to HTML5 applications that allow you to use audio and video without plugins while providing a common, integrated, and scriptable API.

First, we'll discuss audio and video container files and codecs, and why we ended up with the codecs supported today. We'll go on to describe lack of common codec support—the most important drawback for using the media elements—and we'll discuss how we hope that this won't be such a big issue in the future. We'll also show you a mechanism for switching to the most appropriate type of content for the browser to display.

Next, we'll show you how you can use control audio and video programmatically using the APIs and finally we'll explore the use of the HTML5 Audio and Video in your applications.

Overview of HTML5 Audio and Video

In the following sections, we'll discuss some of the key concepts related to HTML5 audio and video: containers and codecs.

Video Containers

An audio or video file is really just a *container* file, similar to a ZIP archive file that contains a number of files. Figure 3-1 shows how a video file (a video container) contains audio tracks, video tracks, and additional metadata. The audio and video tracks are combined at runtime to play the video. The metadata contains information about the video such as cover art, title and subtitle, captioning information, and so on.

Figure 3-1. Overview of the video container

Some of the popular video container formats include the following:

- Audio Video Interleave (.avi)
- Flash Video (.flv)
- MPEG 4 (.mp4)
- Matroska (.mkv)
- Ogg (.ogv)

Audio and Video Codecs

Audio and video *coders/decoders* (*codecs*) are algorithms used to encode and decode a particular audio or video stream so that they can be played back. Raw media files are enormous, so without encoding, a video or audio clip would consist of tremendous amounts of data that could be too large to transmit across the Internet in a reasonable amount of time. Without a decoder, the recipient would not be able to reconstitute the original media source from the encoded form. A codec is able to understand a specific container format and decodes the audio and video tracks that it contains.

Some example audio codecs are the following:

- AAC

- MPEG-3

- Ogg Vorbis

Example video codecs are the following:

- H.264

- VP8

- Ogg Theora

The Codec Wars and the Tentative Truce

Some of the codecs are patent-encumbered, while others are freely available. For example, the Vorbis audio codec and the Theora video codec are freely available, while the use of the MPEG-4 and H.264 codecs are subject to license fees.

Originally, the HTML5 specification was going to require that certain codecs were supported. However, some vendors did not wish to include Ogg Theora as it was not part of their existing hardware and software stacks. Apple's iPhone, for example, includes hardware accelerated decoding for h264 video but not Theora. Free systems, on the other hand, cannot include proprietary for-pay codecs without hurting downstream distribution. On top of that, the performance that certain proprietary codecs provide is a factor in the browser uptake of free codecs. This situation has led to a stalemate; there does not appear to be a single codec that all browser vendors are willing to implement.

For now, the codec requirement has been dropped from the specification. However, this decision may be revisited in the future. For now, understand the current browser support and understand that you may need to re-encode your media for different environments. (You should probably be doing this already.)

We do expect that support for different codecs will increase and converge over time, making the choice of common media types easy and ubiquitous. It is also possible that one codec will grow to be the de facto standard codec for the Web. Additionally, the media tags have a built in mechanism for switching to the most appropriate type of content for the browser to display to make supporting different environments easy.

HERE COMES WEBM

Frank says: "Google introduced the WebM video format in May 2010. WebM is a new format for audio and video intended to clear up the murky media format situation on the Web. WebM files have the .webm extension and consist of VP8 video and Ogg Vorbis audio in a container based on Matroska. Google released the WebM specification and software under permissive licenses covering source code and patent rights. As a high quality format that is free for both implementers and publishers, WebM represents a significant development in the codec landscape.

As far as browsers go, at least Firefox, Opera, and Chrome will support WebM natively. Opera 10.60 is already shipping with WebM support. Mozilla and Google have committed to shipping WebM in the next versions of their browsers."

Audio and Video Restrictions

There are a few things that are not supported in the HTML5 audio and video specification:

- *Streaming* audio and video. That is, there is currently no standard for bitrate switching in HTML5 video; only full media files are supported by current implementations. However, there are aspects of the spec that are designed to support streaming media in the future once the formats are supported.

- Media is restricted by HTTP cross-origin resource sharing. See Chapter 5 for more information about cross-origin resource sharing.

- Full-screen video is not scriptable because it could be considered a security violation to let a scriptable element take over the full screen. However, browsers have the option of letting users choose to view videos in full screen through additional controls.

- Accessibility for audio and video elements is not fully specified yet. Work is underway on a specification called WebSRT for subtitle support based on the popular SRT format.

Browser Support for HTML5 Audio and Video

As shown in Table 3-1, HTML5 `audio` and `video` elements are already supported in many browsers at the time of this writing. The table also shows the supported codecs.

Table 3-1. *Browser support for HTML5 Video*

Browser	Details	Codec, Container Support
Chrome	Version 3.0 and greater	Theora and Vorbis, Ogg Container H.264 and AAC, MPEG 4
Firefox	Version 3.5 and greater	Theora and Vorbis, Ogg Container
Internet Explorer	Not supported	N/A
Opera	Version 10.5 and greater	Theora and Vorbis, Ogg Container (10.5 and greater) VP8 and Vorbis, WebM Format (10.6 and greater)
Safari	Version 3.2 and greater	H.264 and AAC, MPEG 4 Container

It is always good idea to first test whether HTML5 Audio and Video are supported. The section *"Checking for Browser Support"* later in this chapter will show you how you can programmatically check for browser support.

Using the HTML5 Audio and Video APIs

In this section, we'll explore the use of the HTML5 Audio and Video in your applications. There are two main benefits to using these HTML5 media tags over previous video-embedding techniques—usually videos embedded using the Flash, QuickTime, or Windows Media plugins—that aim to make life easier for users and developers:

- *The new audio and video tags remove deployment hurdles by being part of the native browser environment.* Although some plugins have high install rates, they are often blocked in controlled corporate environments. Some users choose to disable these plugins due to the... ostentatious... advertising displays those plugins are also capable of, which also removes their capability to be used for media playback. Plugins are also separate vectors of attack for security issues. And plugins often have difficulty integrating their displays with the rest of browser content, causing clipping or transparency issues with certain site designs. Because plugins use a self-contained rendering model that is different from that of the base web page, developers face difficulties if elements such as popup menus or other visual elements need to cross plugin boundaries in a page.

- *The media elements expose a common, integrated, and scriptable API to the document.* As a developer, your use of the new media elements allows very simple ways to script the control and playback of content. We will see multiple examples of this later in the chapter.

Of course, there is one primary drawback to using the media tags: lack of common codec support, as discussed in the earlier sections of this chapter. However, we expect that support for codecs will increase and converge over time, making the choice of common media types easy and ubiquitous. Plus, the media tags have a built-in mechanism for switching to the most appropriate type of content for the browser to display, as you will soon see.

Checking for Browser Support

The easiest way to check for support of the `video` and `audio` tags is to dynamically create one or both with scripting and check for the existence of a function:

```
var hasVideo = !!(document.createElement('video').canPlayType);
```

This simple code line will dynamically create a `video` element and check for the existence of the `canPlayType()` function. By using the `!!` operator, the result is converted to a Boolean value, which indicates whether or not a video object could be created.

However, if video or audio support is not present, you may choose to use an enabling script that introduces media script tags into older browsers, allowing the same scriptability but using technologies such as Flash for playback.

Alternatively, you can choose to include alternate content between your `audio` or `video` tags, and the alternate content will display in place of the unsupported tag. This alternate content can be used for a Flash plugin to display the same video if the browser doesn't support the HTML5 tags. If you merely wish to display a text message for nonsupporting browsers, it is quite easy to add content inside the `video` or `audio` elements such as the following:

```
<video src="video.ogg" controls>
  Your browser does not support HTML5 video.
</video>
```

However, if you choose to use an alternative method to render video for browsers without HTML5 media support, you can use the same element content section to provide a reference to an external plugin displaying the same media:

```
<video src="video.ogg">
  <object data="videoplayer.swf" type="application/x-shockwave-flash">
    <param name="movie" value="video.swf"/>
  </object>
</video>
```

By embedding an `object` element that displays a Flash video inside the `video` element, the HTML5 video will be preferred if it is available, and the Flash video will be used as a fallback. Unfortunately, this requires multiple versions of the video to be served up until HTML5 support is ubiquitous.

MEDIA FOR EVERYONE

Brian says: "Making your web applications accessible to everyone isn't just the right thing to do; it's good business and, in some cases, it's the law! Users with limited vision or hearing should be presented with alternative content that meets their needs.

The standards bodies designing HTML5 are keenly aware of the lack of built-in support for accessible video and audio, such as closed captioning, and are in the process of planning it now. In the meantime, developers should provide links to transcripts at a minimum, and should consider using the power of the scripting APIs in video to add synchronized text displays on or nearby the video itself.

Keep in mind that the alternative content located between the `video` and `audio` elements is only displayed if the browser does not support those elements at all, and therefore is not suitable for accessible displays where the browser may support HTML5 media, but the user may not."

Understanding Media Elements

Due to a wise design decision, there is much commonality between the `audio` and `video` elements in HTML5. Both audio and video support many of the same operations—play, pause, mute/unmute, load, and so on—and therefore, the common behavior was separated out into the *media* element section of the specification. Let's start examining the media elements by observing what they have in common.

The Basics: Declaring Your Media Element

For the sake of example, we will use an `audio` tag to try out the common behaviors of HTML5 media. The examples in this section will be very media-heavy (surprise!), but they are included in the example support files that come with this book.

For the very simplest example (the example file `audio.html`), let's create a page that shows an audio player for a soothing, satisfying, and very public domain audio clip: Johann Sebastian Bach's "Air":

```
<!DOCTYPE html>
<html>
  <title>HTML5 Audio </title>
  <audio controls src="johann_sebastian_bach_air.ogg">
          An audio clip from Johann Sebastian Bach.
  </audio>
</html>
```

This clip assumes that the HTML document and the audio file—in this case, `johann_sebastian_bach_air.ogg`—are served from the same directory. As shown in Figure 3-2, viewing this in a browser supporting the `audio` tag will show a simple control and play bar representing the audio to play. When the user clicks the play button, the audio track starts as expected.

Figure 3-2. Simple audio controls

The **controls** attribute tells the browser to display common user controls for starting, stopping, and seeking in the media clip, as well as volume control. Leaving out the **controls** attribute hides them, and leaves the clip with no way for the user to start playing.

The content between the **audio** tags is text representation of what the browser will display if it does not support the media tag. This is what you and your users will see if they are running an older browser. It also gives the opportunity to include an alternate renderer for the media, such as a Flash player plugin or a direct link to the media file.

Using the Source

Finally, we come to the most important attribute: **src**. In the simplest setup, a single **src** attribute points to the file containing the media clip. But what if the browser in question does not support that container or codec (in this case, Ogg and Vorbis)? Then, an alternate declaration can be used that includes multiple sources from which the browser can choose (see the example file **audio_multisource.html**):

```
<audio controls>
    <source src="johann_sebastian_bach_air.ogg">
    <source src="johann_sebastian_bach_air.mp3">
    An audio clip from Johann Sebastian Bach.
</audio>
```

In this case, we include two new **source** elements instead of the **src** attribute on the **audio** tag. This allows the browser to choose which source best suits the playback capabilities it has and use the best fit as the actual media clip. Sources are processed in order, so a browser that can play multiple listed **source** types will use the first one it encounters.

■ **Note** Place the media source files with the best user experience or lowest server load highest in any source list.

Running this clip in a supported browser may not change what you see. But if a browser supports the MP3 format and not the Ogg Vorbis format, the media playback will now be supported. The beauty of this declaration model is that as you write code to interact with the media file, it doesn't matter to you which container or codec was actually used. The browser provides a unified interface for you to manipulate the media, no matter which source was matched for playback.

However, there is another way to give the browser hints about which media source to use. Recall that a container for media can support many different codec types, and you will understand that a browser may be misled into which types it does or does not support based on the extension of the declared source file. If you specify a type attribute that does not match your source, the browser may refuse to play the media. It may be wise to include the type only if you know it with certainty. Otherwise, it is better to omit this attribute and let the browser detect the encoding. Also note that the WebM format allows only one audio codec and one video codec. That means the `.webm` extension or the video/webm content-type tells you everything you need to know about the file. If a browser can play .webm, it should be able to play any valid `.webm` file, as shown in the following code example (and in the example file `audio_type.html`):

```
<audio controls>
    <source src="johann_sebastian_bach_air.ogg" type="audio/ogg; codecs=vorbis">
    <source src="johann_sebastian_bach_air.mp3" type="audio/mpeg">
    An audio clip from Johann Sebastian Bach.
</audio>
```

As you can see, the **type** attribute can declare both the container and codec type. The values here represent Ogg Vorbis and MP3, respectively. The full list is governed by RFC 4281, a document maintained by the Internet Engineering Task Force (IETF), but some common combinations are listed in Table 3-2.

Table 3-2. Media types and attribute values

Type	Attribute Value
Theora video and Vorbis audio in an Ogg container	`type='video/ogg; codecs="theora, vorbis"'`
Vorbis audio in an Ogg container	`type='audio/ogg; codecs=vorbis'`
Simple baseline H.264 video and low complexity AAC audio in an MP4 container	`type='video/mp4; codecs="avc1.42E01E, mp4a.40.2"'`
MPEG-4 visual simple profile and low complexity AAC audio in an MP4 container	`type='video/mp4; codecs="mp4v.20.8, mp4a.40.2"'`

Taking Control

You've already seen that the default playback controls can be displayed by using the `controls` attribute in the `video` or `audio` tag. As you might expect, leaving out this attribute will not display controls when the media is displayed, but it will also not show anything at all in the case of *audio* files, as the only visual representation of an audio element is its controls. (A video without controls still displays the video content.) Leaving out the `controls` attribute should not display any content that affects the normal rendering of the page. One way to cause the media to play is to set another attribute in the tag: `autoplay` (see the example file `audio_no_control.html`):

```
<audio autoplay>
    <source src="johann_sebastian_bach_air.ogg" type="audio/ogg; codecs=vorbis">
    <source src="johann_sebastian_bach_air.mp3" type="audio/mpeg">
    An audio clip from Johann Sebastian Bach.
</audio>
```

By including the `autoplay` attribute, the media file will play as soon as it is loaded, without any user interaction. However, most users will find this highly annoying, so use `autoplay` with caution. Playing audio without prompting may be intended to create an atmospheric effect or, worse, to force an advertisement on the user. But it also interferes with other audio playing on the user's machine, and can be quite detrimental to users who rely on audible screen readers to navigate web content.

If the built-in controls do not suit the layout of your user interface, or if you need to control the media element using calculations or behaviors that are not exposed in the default controls, there are many built-in JavaScript functions and attributes to help you, too. Table 3-3 lists some of the most common functions.

Table 3-3. Common control functions

Function	Behavior
load()	Loads the media file and prepares it for playback. Normally does not need to be called unless the element itself is dynamically created. Useful for loading in advance of actual playback.
play()	Loads (if necessary) and plays the media file. Plays from the beginning unless the media is already paused at another position.
pause()	Pauses playback if currently active.
canPlayType(type)	Tests to see whether the `video` element can play a hypothetical file of the given MIME type.

The `canPlayType(type)` function has a non-obvious use case: by passing in a MIME type of an arbitrary video clip to a dynamically created `video` element, you can use a simple script to determine whether the current browser supports that type. For example, the following code provides a quick way to determine whether the current browser can support playing videos with MIME type of `fooType` without displaying any visible content in the browser window:

```
var supportsFooVideo = !!(document.createElement('video').canPlayType('fooType'));
```

Table 3-4 shows a few of the read-only attributes on media elements.

Table 3-4. Read-only media attributes

Read-only attribute	Value
duration	The duration of the full media clip, in seconds. If the full duration is not known, NaN is returned.
paused	Returns true if the media clip is currently paused. Defaults to true if the clip has not started playing.
ended	Returns true if the media clip has finished playing.
startTime	Returns the earliest possible value for playback start time. This will usually be 0.0 unless the media clip is streamed and earlier content has left the buffer.
error	An error code, if an error has occurred.
currentSrc	Returns the string representing the file that is currently being displayed or loaded. This will match the source element selected by the browser.

Table 3-5 shows some of the attributes on the media elements that allow scripts to modify them and affect the playback directly. As such, they behave similar to functions.

Table 3-5. Scriptable attribute values

Attribute	Value
autoplay	Sets the media clip to play upon creation or query whether it is set to autoplay.
loop	Returns true if the clip will restart upon ending or sets the clip to loop (or not loop).
currentTime	Returns the current time in seconds that has elapsed since the beginning of the playback. Sets currentTime to seek to a specific position in the clip playback.
controls	Shows or hides the user controls, or queries whether they are currently visible.
volume	Sets the audio volume to a relative value between 0.0 and 1.0, or queries the value of the same.
muted	Mutes or unmutes the audio, or determines the current mute state.
autobuffer	Tells the player whether or not to attempt to load the media file before playback is initiated. If the media is set for auto-playback, this attribute is ignored.

Between the various functions and attributes, it is possible for a developer to create any media playback user interface and use it to control any audio or video clip that is supported by the browser.

Working with Audio

If you understand the shared attributes for both **audio** and **video** media elements, you've basically seen all that the **audio** tag has to offer. So let's look at a simple example that shows control scripting in action.

Audio Activation

If your user interface needs to play an audio clip for users, but you don't want to affect the display with a playback timeline or controls, you can create an invisible **audio** element—one with the **controls** attribute unset or set to **false**—and present your own controls for audio playback. Consider the following simple code, also available in the sample code file **audioCue.html**:

```
<!DOCTYPE html>
<html>
  <link rel="stylesheet" href="styles.css">
  <title>Audio cue</title>

  <audio id="clickSound">
    <source src="johann_sebastian_bach_air.ogg">
    <source src="johann_sebastian_bach_air.mp3">
  </audio>

  <button id="toggle" onclick="toggleSound()">Play</button>

  <script type="text/javascript">
    function toggleSound() {
        var music = document.getElementById("clickSound");
        var toggle = document.getElementById("toggle");

        if (music.paused) {
          music.play();
          toggle.innerHTML = "Pause";
        }
        else {
          music.pause();
          toggle.innerHTML ="Play";
        }
    }
  </script>
</html>
```

Once again, we are using an **audio** element to play our favorite Bach tune. However, in this example we hide user controls and don't set the clip to autoplay on load. Instead, we have created a toggle button to control the audio playback with script:

```
<button id="toggle" onclick="toggleSound()">Play</button>
```

Our simple button is initialized to inform the user that clicking it will start playback. And each time the button is pressed, the `toggleSound()` function is triggered. Inside the `toggleSound()` function, we first gain access to the `audio` and `button` elements in the DOM:

```
if (music.paused) {
    music.play();
    toggle.innerHTML = "Pause";
}
```

By accessing the `paused` attribute on the `audio` element, we can check to see whether the user has already paused playback. The attribute defaults to `true` if no playback is initiated, so this condition will be met on the first click. In that case, we call the `play()` function on the clip and change the text of the button to indicate that the next clip will pause:

```
else {
    music.pause();
    toggle.innerHTML ="Play";
}
```

Conversely, if the music clip is not paused (if it is playing), we will actively `pause()` it and change the button text to indicate that the next click will restart play. Seems simple, doesn't it? That's the point of the media elements in HTML5: to create simple display and control across media types where once a myriad of plugins existed. Simplicity is its own reward.

Working with Video

Enough with simplicity. Let's try something more complicated. The HTML5 `video` element is very similar to the `audio` element, but with a few extra attributes thrown in. Table 3-6 shows some of these attributes.

Table 3-6. Additional video attributes

Attribute	Value
poster	The URL of an image file used to represent the video content before it has loaded. Think "movie poster." This attribute can be read or altered to change the poster.
width, height	Read or set the visual display size. This may cause centering, letterboxing, or pillaring if the set width does not match the size of the video itself.
videoWidth, videoHeight	Return the intrinsic or natural width and height of the video. They cannot be set.

The `video` element has one other key feature that is not applicable to the `audio` element: it can be provided to many functions of the HTML5 Canvas. (See Chapter 2 for more information about HTML5 Canvas.)

Creating a Video Timeline Browser

In this more complex example, we'll show how a `video` element can have its frames grabbed and displayed in a dynamic canvas. To demonstrate this capability, we'll build a simple video timeline viewer. While the video plays, periodic image frames from its display will be drawn onto a nearby canvas. When the user clicks any frame displayed in the canvas, we'll jump the playback of the video to that precise moment in time. With only a few lines of code, we can create a timeline browser that users can use to jump around inside a lengthy video.

Our sample video clip is the tempting concession advert from the mid-20th century movie theaters, so let's all go to the lobby to get ourselves a treat (see Figure 3-3).

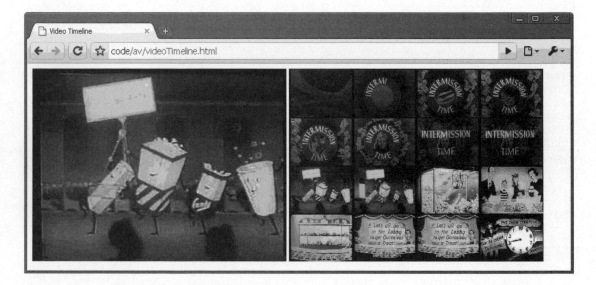

Figure 3-3. The video timeline application

Adding the Video and the Canvas Element

We start with a simple declaration to display our video clip:

```
<video id="movies" autoplay oncanplay="startVideo()" onended="stopTimeline()"
autobuffer="true" width="400px" height="300px">
    <source src="Intermission-Walk-in.ogv" type='video/ogg; codecs="theora, vorbis"'>
    <source src="Intermission-Walk-in_512kb.mp4"
            type='video/mp4; codecs="avc1.42E01E, mp4a.40.2"'>
</video>
```

As most of this markup will look familiar to you from the audio example, let's focus on the differences. Obviously, the `<audio>` element has been replaced with `<video>`, and the `<source>` elements point to the Ogg and MPEG movies that will be selected by the browser.

The video has, in this case, been declared to have `autoplay` so that it starts as soon as the page loads. Two additional event handler functions have been registered. When the video is loaded and ready to begin play, the `oncanplay` function will trigger and start our routine. Similarly, when the video ends, the `onended` callback will allow us to stop creating video frames.

Next, we'll add a canvas called `timeline` into which we will draw frames of our video at regular intervals.

```
<canvas id="timeline" width="400px" height="300px">
```

Adding Variables

In the next section of our demo, we begin our script by declaring some values that will let us easily tweak the demo and make the code more readable:

```
// # of milliseconds between timeline frame updates
var updateInterval = 5000;

// size of the timeline frames
var frameWidth = 100;
var frameHeight = 75;

// number of timeline frames
var frameRows = 4;
var frameColumns = 4;
var frameGrid = frameRows * frameColumns;
```

`updateInterval` controls how often we will capture frames of the video—in this case, every five seconds. The `frameWidth` and `frameHeight` set how large the small timeline video frames will be when displayed in the canvas. Similarly, the `frameRows`, `frameColumns`, and `frameGrid` determine how many frames we will display in our timeline:

```
// current frame
var frameCount = 0;

// to cancel the timer at end of play
var intervalId;

var videoStarted = false;
```

To keep track of which frame of video we are viewing, a `frameCount` is made accessible to all demo functions. (For the sake of our demo, a frame is one of our video samples taken every five seconds.) The `intervalId` is used to stop the timer we will use to grab frames. And finally, we add a `videoStarted` flag to make sure that we only create one timer per demo.

Adding the updateFrame Function

The core function of our demo—where the video meets the canvas—is where we grab a video frame and draw it onto our canvas:

```
// paint a representation of the video frame into our canvas
function updateFrame() {
    var video = document.getElementById("movies");
    var timeline = document.getElementById("timeline");

    var ctx = timeline.getContext("2d");

    // calculate out the current position based on frame
    // count, then draw the image there using the video
    // as a source
    var framePosition = frameCount % frameGrid;
    var frameX = (framePosition % frameColumns) * frameWidth;
    var frameY = (Math.floor(framePosition / frameRows)) * frameHeight;
    ctx.drawImage(video, 0, 0, 400, 300, frameX, frameY, frameWidth, frameHeight);

    frameCount++;
}
```

As you've seen in Chapter 2, the first thing to do with any canvas is to grab a two-dimensional drawing context from it:

```
var ctx = timeline.getContext("2d");
```

Because we want to populate our canvas grid with frames from left to right, top to bottom, we need to figure out exactly which of the grid slots will be used for our frame based on the number of the frame we are capturing. Based on the width and height of each frame, we can then determine exact X and Y coordinates at which to begin our drawing:

```
var framePosition = frameCount % frameGrid;
var frameX = (framePosition % frameColumns) * frameWidth;
var frameY = (Math.floor(framePosition / frameRows)) * frameHeight;
```

Finally, we reach the key call to draw an image onto the canvas. We've seen the position and scaling arguments before in our canvas demos, but instead of passing an image to the **drawImage** routine, we here pass the video object itself:

```
ctx.drawImage(video, 0, 0, 400, 300, frameX, frameY, frameWidth, frameHeight);
```

Canvas drawing routines can take video sources as images or patterns, which gives you a handy way to modify the video and redisplay it in another location.

■ **Note** When a canvas uses a video as an input source, it draws only the currently displayed video frame. Canvas displays will not dynamically update as the video plays. Instead, if you want the canvas content to update, you must redraw your images as the video is playing.

Adding the startVideo Function

Finally, we update `frameCount` to reflect that we've taken a new snapshot for our timeline. Now, all we need is a routine to regularly update our timeline frames:

```
function startVideo() {

    // only set up the timer the first time the
    // video is started
    if (videoStarted)
        return;

    videoStarted = true;

    // calculate an initial frame, then create
    // additional frames on a regular timer
    updateFrame();
    intervalId = setInterval(updateFrame, updateInterval);
```

Recall that the `startVideo()` function is triggered as soon as the video has loaded enough to begin playing. First, we make sure that we are going to handle the video start only once per page load, just in case the video is restarted:

```
    // only set up the timer the first time the
    // video is started
    if (videoStarted)
        return;

    videoStarted = true;
```

When the video starts, we will capture our first frame. Then, we will start an interval timer—a timer that repeats continuously at the specified update interval—which will regularly call our `updateFrame()` function. The end result is that a new frame will be captured every five seconds:

```
    // calculate an initial frame, then create
    // additional frames on a regular timer
    updateFrame();
    intervalId = setInterval(updateFrame, updateInterval);
```

Handling User Input

Now all we need to do is handle user clicks the individual timeline frames:

```
// set up a handler to seek the video when a frame
// is clicked
var timeline = document.getElementById("timeline");
timeline.onclick = function(evt) {
    var offX = evt.layerX - timeline.offsetLeft;
    var offY = evt.layerY - timeline.offsetTop;

    // calculate which frame in the grid was clicked
    // from a zero-based index
    var clickedFrame = Math.floor(offY / frameHeight) * frameRows;
    clickedFrame += Math.floor(offX / frameWidth);

    // find the actual frame since the video started
    var seekedFrame = (((Math.floor(frameCount / frameGrid)) *
                                frameGrid) + clickedFrame);

    // if the user clicked ahead of the current frame
    // then assume it was the last round of frames
    if (clickedFrame > (frameCount % 16))
        seekedFrame -= frameGrid;

        // can't seek before the video
        if (seekedFrame < 0)
            return;
```

Things get a little more complicated here. We retrieve the timeline canvas and set a click-handling function on it. The handler will use the event to determine which X and Y coordinates were clicked by the user:

```
var timeline = document.getElementById("timeline");
timeline.onclick = function(evt) {
    var offX = evt.layerX - timeline.offsetLeft;
    var offY = evt.layerY - timeline.offsetTop;
```

We then use the frame dimensions to figure out which of the 16 frames was clicked by the user:

```
    // calculate which frame in the grid was clicked
    // from a zero-based index
    var clickedFrame = Math.floor(offY / frameHeight) * frameRows;
    clickedFrame += Math.floor(offX / frameWidth);
```

The clicked frame should be only one of the most recent video frames, so determine the most recent frame that corresponds to that grid index:

```
// find the actual frame since the video started
var seekedFrame = (((Math.floor(frameCount / frameGrid)) *
                            frameGrid) + clickedFrame);
```

If the user clicks ahead of the current frame, jump back one complete cycle of grid frames to find the actual time:

```
// if the user clicked ahead of the current frame
// then assume it was the last round of frames
if (clickedFrame > (frameCount % 16))
    seekedFrame -= frameGrid;
```

And finally, we have to safeguard against any case in which the user clicks a frame that would be before the start of the video clip:

```
// can't seek before the video
if (seekedFrame < 0)
    return;
```

Now that we know what point in time the user wants to seek out, we can use that knowledge to change the current playback time. Although this is the key demo function, the routine itself is quite simple:

```
// seek the video to that frame (in seconds)
var video = document.getElementById("movies");
video.currentTime = seekedFrame * updateInterval / 1000;

// then set the frame count to our destination
frameCount = seekedFrame;
```

By setting the currentTime attribute on our video element, we cause the video to seek to the specified time and reset our current frame count to the newly chosen frame.

■ **Note** Unlike many JavaScript timers that deal with milliseconds, the currentTime of a video is specified in seconds.

Adding the stopTimeline Function

All that remains for our video timeline demo is to stop capturing frames when the video finishes playing. Although not required, if we don't take this step, the demo will continue capturing frames of the finished demo, blanking out the entire timeline after a while:

```
// stop gathering the timeline frames
function stopTimeline() {
    clearInterval(intervalId);
}
```

The `stopTimeline` handler will be called when another of our video handlers—**onended**—is triggered by the completion of video playback.

Our video timeline is probably not full-featured enough to satisfy power users, but it took only a short amount of code to accomplish. Now, on with the show.

Practical Extras

Sometimes there are techniques that don't fit into our regular examples, but which nonetheless apply to many types of HTML5 applications. We present to you some short, but common, practical extras here.

Background Noise in a Page

Many a web site has attempted to entertain its viewers by playing audio by default for any visitors. While we don't condone this practice, HTML5 audio support makes it quite easy to achieve this:

```
<!DOCTYPE html>
<html>
  <link rel="stylesheet" href="styles.css">
  <title>Background Music</title>

  <audio autoplay loop>
     <source src="johann_sebastian_bach_air.ogg">
     <source src="johann_sebastian_bach_air.mp3">
  </audio>

  <h1>You're hooked on Bach!</h1>

</html>
```

As you can see, playing a looping background sound is as easy as declaring a single `audio` tag with the `autoplay` and `loop` attributes set (see Figure 3-4).

Figure 3-4. *Using autoplay to play music when a page loads*

LOSING VIEWERS IN THE <BLINK> OF AN EYE

Brian says: "With great power comes great responsibility, and just because you *can*, doesn't mean you *should*. If you want an example, just remember the `<blink>` tag!"

Don't let the power of easy audio and video playback seduce you into using it where it isn't appropriate. If you have a compelling reason to enable media with `autoplay`—perhaps a media browser in which the user is expecting content to start on load—make sure to provide a clear means for disabling that feature. Nothing will turn users from your site faster than annoying content that they can't easily turn off."

Mouseover Video Playback

Another way to use simple scripting effectively with video clips is to trigger the `play` and `pause` routines, based on mouse movement over the video. This could be useful in a site that needs to display many video clips and let the user choose which ones to play. The video gallery can display short preview clips on when a user moves the mouse over them and a full video display when the user clicks. It is quite easy to achieve this affect using a code sample similar to the following (see the example file `mouseoverVideo.html`):

```
<!DOCTYPE html>
<html>
  <link rel="stylesheet" href="styles.css">
  <title>Mouseover Video</title>

  <video id="movies" onmouseover="this.play()" onmouseout="this.pause()"
        autobuffer="true"
    width="400px" height="300px">
    <source src="Intermission-Walk-in.ogv" type='video/ogg; codecs="theora, vorbis"'>
    <source src="Intermission-Walk-in_512kb.mp4" type='video/mp4; codecs="avc1.42E01E,
              mp4a.40.2"'>
  </video>
</html>
```

By simply setting a few extra attributes, the preview playback can trigger when a user points at the video, as shown in Figure 3-5.

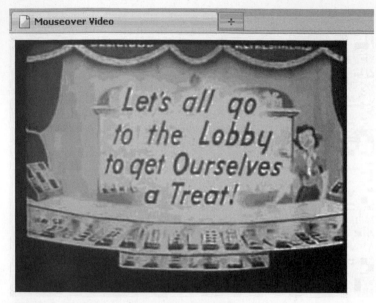

Figure 3-5. *Mouseover video playback*

Summary

In this chapter, we have explored what you can do with the two important HTML5 elements `audio` and `video`. We have shown you how they can be used to create compelling web applications. The `audio` and `video` elements add new media options to HTML5 applications that allow you to use audio and video without plugins, while at the same time providing a common, integrated, and scriptable API.

First, we discussed the audio and video container files and codecs and why we ended up with the codecs supported today. We then showed you a mechanism for switching to the most appropriate type of content for the browser to display.

Next, we showed you how you can use control audio and video programmatically using the APIs and finally we looked at how you can use of the HTML5 Audio and Video in your applications.

In the next chapter, we'll show how you can use geolocation to tailor your application's output to the whereabouts of your users with a minimal amount of code.

CHAPTER 4

■■■

Using the HTML5 Geolocation API

Let's say you want to create a web application that offers discounts and special deals on running shoes in stores that your application's users are within walking (or running) distance away from. Using the HTML5 Geolocation API, you can request users to share their location and, if they agree, you can provide them with instructions on how to get to a nearby store to pick up a new pair of shoes at a discounted rate.

Another example of the use of HTML5 Geolocation could be an application that tracks how far you have run (or walked). You can picture using an application in a browser on a mobile phone that you turn on when you start a run. While you're on the move, the application tracks how far you have run. The coordinates for the run can even be overlaid on a map, perhaps even with an elevation profile. If you're running a race against other competitors, the application might even show your opponents' locations.

Other HTML5 Geolocation application ideas could be turn-by-turn GPS-style navigation, social networking applications that allow you to see exactly where your friends are, so you can pick the coffee shop you want to visit, and many more unusual applications.

In this chapter, we'll explore what you can do with HTML5 Geolocation—an exciting API that allows users to share their location with web applications so that they can enjoy location-aware services. First, we'll take a look at the source of HTML5 Geolocation location information—the latitude, longitude and other attributes—and where they can come from (GPS, Wi-Fi, cellular triangulation, and so on). Then, we'll discuss the privacy concerns around using HTML5 Geolocation data and how browsers work with this data.

After that, we'll dive into a practical discussion about using the HTML5 Geolocation APIs. There are two types of position request APIs: the one-shot position request and the repeated position updates, and we'll show you how and when to use them. Next, we'll show you how to build a practical HTML5 Geolocation application using the same APIs, and we'll finish up with a discussion about a few additional use cases and tips.

About Location Information

Using the HTML5 Geolocation API is fairly straightforward. You request a position and, if the user agrees, the browser returns location information. The position is provided to the browser by the underlying device (for example, a laptop or a mobile phone) on which the HTML5 Geolocation–enabled browser is running. The location information is provided as a set of latitude and longitude coordinates along with additional metadata. Armed with this location information, you can then build a compelling, location-aware application.

Latitude and Longitude Coordinates

The location information consists primarily of a pair of latitude and longitude coordinates like the ones shown in the following example, which shows the coordinates for beautiful Tahoe City, located on the shore of Lake Tahoe, America's most beautiful mountain lake:

`Latitude: 39.17222, Longitude: -120.13778`

In the preceding example, the latitude (the numerical value indicating distance north or south of the equator is 39.17222) and the longitude (the numerical value indicating distance east or west of Greenwich, England) is -120.13778.

Latitude and longitude coordinates can be expressed in different ways:

- Decimal format (for example, 39.17222)

- Degree Minute Second (DMS) format (for example, 39° 10' 20')

■ **Note** When you use the HTML5 Geolocation API, coordinates are always returned in decimal degrees.

In addition to latitude and longitude coordinates, HTML5 Geolocation always provides the *accuracy* of the location coordinates. Additional metadata may also be provided, depending on the device that your browser is running on. These include *altitude, altitudeAccuracy, heading,* and *speed.* If this additional metadata is not available it will be returned as a null value.

Where Does Location Information Come From?

The HTML5 Geolocation API does not specify which underlying technology a device has to use to locate the application's user. Instead, it simply exposes an API for retrieving location information. What is exposed, however, is the level of accuracy with which the location was pinpointed. There is no guarantee that the device's actual location returns an accurate location.

LOCATION, LOCATION

Peter says: "Here is a funny example of that. At home, I use a wireless network. I opened the HTML5 Geolocation example application shown in this chapter in Firefox and it figured out that I was in Sacramento (about 75 miles from my actual physical location). Wrong, but not too surprising, because my Internet Service Provider (ISP) is located in downtown Sacramento.

Then, I asked my sons, Sean and Rocky, to browse to the same page on their iPod Touch (using the same Wi-Fi network). In Safari, it looked like they were located in Marysville, California—a town that is located 30 miles from Sacramento. Go figure!"

A device can use any of the following sources:

- IP address
- Coordinate triangulation
    - Global Positioning System (GPS)
    - Wi-Fi with MAC addresses from RFID, Wi-Fi, and Bluetooth
    - GSM or CDMA cell phone IDs
- User defined

Many devices use a combination of one or more sources to ensure an even higher accuracy. Each of these methods has its own pros and cons, as explained in the next sections.

IP Address Geolocation Data

In the past, IP address–based geolocation was the only way to get a possible location, but the returned locations often proved unreliable. IP address–based geolocation works by automatically looking up a user's IP address and then retrieving the registrant's physical address. Therefore, if you have an ISP that provides you with an IP address, your location is often resolved to the physical address of your service provider that could be miles away. Table 4-1 shows the pros and cons of IP address–based geolocation data.

Table 4-1.Pros and cons of IP address–based geolocation data

Pros	Cons
Available everywhere	Not very accurate (wrong many times, but also accurate only to the city level)
Processed on the server side	Can be a costly operation

Many websites advertise based on IP address locations. You can see this in action when you travel to another country and suddenly see advertisements for local services (based on the IP address of the country or region you are visiting).

GPS Geolocation Data

As long as you can see the sky, GPS can provide very accurate location results. A GPS fix is acquired by acquiring the signal from multiple GPS satellites that fly around the earth. However, it can take awhile to get a fix, which does not lend itself particularly well for applications that must start up rapidly.

Because it can take a long time to get a GPS location fix, you might want to query for the user's location asynchronously. To show your application's users that a fix is being acquired, you can add a status bar. Table 4-2 shows the pros and cons of GPS–based geolocation data.

CHAPTER 4 ■ USING THE HTML5 GEOLOCATION API

Table 4-2.Pros and cons of GPS–based geolocation data

Pros	Cons
Very accurate	It can take a long time getting a location fix, which can drain a user's device's batteries
	Does not work well indoors
	May require additional hardware

Wi-Fi Geolocation Data

Wi-Fi–based geolocation information is acquired by triangulating the location based on the user's distance from a number of known Wi-Fi access points, mostly in urban areas. Unlike GPS, Wi-Fi is very accurate indoors as well as in urban areas. Table 4-3 shows the pros and cons of Wi-Fi–based geolocation data.

Table 4-3. Pros and cons of Wi-Fi–based geolocation data

Pros	Cons
Accurate	Not good in rural areas with few wireless access points
Works indoors	
Can get fix quickly and cheaply	

Cell Phone Geolocation Data

Cell phone–based geolocation information is acquired by triangulating the location based on the user's distance from a number of cell phone towers. This method provides a general location result that is fairly accurate. This method is often used in combination with Wi-Fi– and GPS–based geolocation information. Table 4-4 shows the pros and cons of cell phone–based geolocation data.

Table 4-4. Pros and cons of cell phone–based geolocation data

Pros	Cons
Fairly accurate	Requires a device with access to a cell phone or cell modem
Works indoors	Not good in rural areas with fewer cell phone towers
Can get fix quickly and cheaply	

User–Defined Geolocation Data

Instead of programmatically figuring out where the user is, you can also allow users to define their location themselves. An application may allow users to enter their address, ZIP code, or some other details; your application can then use that information to provide location-aware services. Table 4-5 shows the pros and cons of user–defined geolocation data.

Table 4-5. Pros and cons of user–defined geolocation data

Pros	Cons
Users may have more accurate location data than programmatic services	Can also be very inaccurate, especially if the location changes
Allows geolocation services for alternate locations	
User entry might be faster than detection	

Browser Support for HTML5 Geolocation

Browser support for HTML5 Geolocation is at varying stages and will continue to evolve. The good news is that HTML5 Geolocation was one of the first HTML5 features to be fully embraced and implemented. The specification is in a very advanced stage and is unlikely to change a whole lot. As shown in Table 4-6, HTML5 Geolocation is already supported in many browsers at the time of this writing.

Table 4-6. Browser support for HTML5 Geolocation

Browser	Details
Chrome	Supported in Google Chrome version 2 with Gears
Firefox	Supported in version 3.5 and greater
Internet Explorer	Supported via the Gears plugin
Opera	Planned support version 10, experimental support in nightly builds
Safari	Supported in version 4 for the iPhone

Due to the varying levels of support, it is a good idea to first see whether HTML5 Geolocation is supported before you use the APIs. The section "Checking for Browser Support" later in this chapter will show you how you can programmatically check for browser support.

Privacy

The HTML5 Geolocation specification mandates that a mechanism is provided to protect the user's privacy. Furthermore, location information should not be made available unless the application's users grant their express permission.

This makes sense and addresses the "big brother" concerns users often raise about HTML5 Geolocation applications. However, as you can see from some of the possible use cases for HTML 5 Geolocation applications, there is usually an incentive for the user to share this information. For example, users might be OK with sharing their location if this could let them know about a rare 50% discount on a pair of running shoes that are ready to be picked up in a store located just a few blocks away from where they happen to be drinking coffee. Let's take a closer look at the browser and device privacy architecture shown in Figure 4-1.

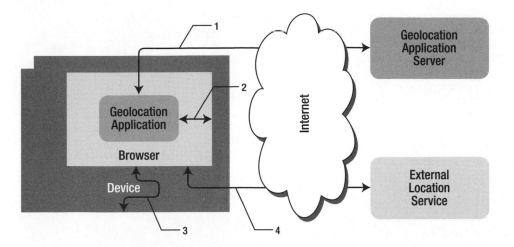

Figure 4-1. HTML5 Geolocation browser and device privacy architecture

The following steps are shown in the diagram:

1.   A user navigates to a location-aware application in the browser.

2.   The application web page loads and requests coordinates from the browser by making a Geolocation function call. The browser intercepts this and requests user permission. Let's assume that the permission is granted.

3.   The browser retrieves coordinate information from the device it is running on. For example, the IP address, Wi-Fi, or GPS coordinates. This is an internal function of the browser.

4.   The browser sends these coordinates to a trusted external location service, which returns a detailed location that can now be sent back to the host of the HTML5 Geolocation application.

■ **Important**: The application does *not* have direct access to the device; it can only query the browser to access the device on its behalf.

Triggering the Privacy Protection Mechanism

When you access a web page that uses the HTML5 Geolocation APIs, the privacy protection mechanism should kick in. Figure 4-2 shows what this looks like in Firefox 3.5.

Figure 4-2. The notification bar is triggered in Firefox when the HTML5 Geolocation APIs are used

The mechanism is triggered when the HTML5 Geolocation code is executed. Simply adding HTML5 Geolocation code that is not called anywhere (as, for example, in an `onload` method) does not do anything. If, however, the HTML5 Geolocation code is executed, for example, in a call to `navigator.geolocation.getCurrentPosition` (explained in more detail later on), the user is prompted to share their location with the application. Figure 4-3 shows what happens on Safari, running on an iPhone.

Figure 4-3. The notification dialog box is triggered in Safari when the HTML5 Geolocation APIs are used

Apart from providing the necessary mechanism to request permission to share your location, some implementations (Firefox, for example) also allow you to remember the permission granted to the site for the next time you enter. This is similar to how you can remember passwords for certain sites in your browser.

■ **Note** If you've given permission to always give your location to a site in Firefox and later change your mind, you can easily revoke that permission by going back to the site and selecting **Page Info** from the **Tools** menu. Then change the setting for **Share Location** on the **Permissions** tab.

Dealing with Location Information

Location data is sensitive information, so when you receive it, you must be careful about handling, storing, and retransmitting the data. Unless users give permission to store data, you should always dispose of the data after the task for which it was required is complete.

Therefore, if you retransmit the location data, it is recommended that you first encrypt the data. Regarding the collection of geolocation data, your application should prominently show the following:

- That you are collecting location data

- Why you are collecting location data

- How long the location data is kept

- How you are securing the data

- How the location data is shared (if it is)

- How users can check and update their location data

Using the HTML5 Geolocation API

In this section, we'll explore the use of the HTML5 Geolocation API in more detail. For the sake of illustration, we've created a simple browser page—`geolocation.html`. Remember that you can download all the code from the book's page on `apress.com`.

Checking for Browser Support

Before you call the HTML5 Geolocation API functions, you will want to make sure that there is support in the browser for what you're about to do. This way, you can provide some alternate text, prompting the users of your application to dump their dinosaur-like browsers or install a plugin such as Gears, which augments the existing browser functionality! Listing 4-1 shows one way you can use to test for browser support.

Listing 4-1. Checking for browser support

```
function loadDemo() {
  if(navigator.geolocation) {
    document.getElementById("support").innerHTML = "HTML5 Geolocation supported.";

} else {
     document.getElementById("support").innerHTML = "HTML5 Geolocation is not supported in
                                     your browser.";
   }
}
```

In this example, you test for browser support in the `loadDemo` function, which might be called when the application's page is loaded. A call to `navigator.geolocation` will return the Geolocation object if it exists, or trigger the failure case if it does not. In this case, the page is updated to reflect whether there is browser support or not by updating a previously defined `support` element on the page with a suitable message.

Position Requests

There are two types of position requests:

- One-shot position request

- Repeated position updates

One-Shot Position Requests

In many applications, it will be acceptable to retrieve the user's location only once, or only by request. For example, if someone is looking for the nearest movie theater showing today's popular movie in the next hour, the simplest form of the HTML5 Geolocation API shown in Listing 4-2 can be used.

Listing 4-2. One-shot position request

```
void getCurrentPosition(in PositionCallback successCallback,
                        in optional PositionErrorCallback errorCallback,
                        in optional PositionOptions options);
```

Let's take a look at this core function call in more detail.

First, this is a function that is available on the `navigator.geolocation` object, so you will need to have already retrieved this object in your script. As noted previously, make sure that you have a good fallback handler if your browser does not support HTML5 Geolocation.

The function takes one required parameter, and two optional ones.

- The `successCallback` function parameter tells the browser which function you want called when the location data is made available. This is important because operations such as fetching location data may take a long time to complete. No user wants the browser to be locked up while the location is retrieved, and no developer wants his program to pause indefinitely—especially because fetching the location data will often be waiting on a user to grant permission. The successCallback is where you will receive the actual location information and act on it.

- However, as in most programming scenarios, it is good to plan for failure cases. It is quite possible that the request for location information may not complete for reasons beyond your control, and for those cases you will want to provide an `errorCallback` function that can present the user with an explanation, or perhaps make an attempt to try again. While optional, it is recommended that you provide one.

- Finally, an `options` object can be provided to the HTML5 Geolocation service to fine-tune the way it gathers data. This is an optional parameter that we will examine later.

Let's say that you've created a JavaScript function on our page named `updateLocation()` in which you update the contents of the page with the new location data. Similarly, you've created a `handleLocationError()` function to handle the error cases. We'll examine the details of those functions next, but that means that your core request to access the user's position would be the code shown in the following example:

```
navigator.geolocation.getCurrentPosition(updateLocation, handleLocationError);
```

The updateLocation() Function

So, what happens in the `updateLocation()` call? It's actually quite simple. As soon as the browser has access to the location information, it will call `updateLocation()` with a single parameter: a position object. The position will contain coordinates—as the attribute `coords`—and a timestamp for when the location data was gathered. While you may or may not need the timestamp, the `coords` attribute contains the crucial values for the location.

The coordinates always have multiple attributes on them, but it is up to the browser and the hardware of the user's device whether they will have meaningful values. The following are the first three attributes:

- `latitude`

- `longitude`

- `accuracy`

These attributes are guaranteed to have values and are fairly self-explanatory. `latitude` and `longitude` will contain the HTML5 Geolocation service's best determined value of the user's location specified in decimal degrees. `accuracy` will contain a value in meters which specifies how close the latitude and longitude values are to the actual location, with a 95% confidence level. Due to the nature of HTML5 Geolocation implementations, approximation will be common and coarse. Make sure to check the accuracy of the returned values before you present them with any certainty. Recommending a user to visit a "nearby" shoe store that is actually hours away could have unintended consequences.

The other attributes of the coordinates are not guaranteed to be supported, but they will return a null value if they are not:

- altitude—the height of the user's location, in meters

- altitudeAccuracy—once again in meters, or null if no altitude is provided

- heading—direction of travel, in degrees relative to true north

- speed—ground speed in meters per second

Unless you are sure that your users have devices with access to such information, it is recommended that you not rely on them as critical to your application. While global positioning devices are likely to provide this level of detail, network triangulation will not.

Now let's take a look at a simple code implementation of our updateLocation() function that performs some trivial updates with the coordinates (see Listing 4-3).

Listing 4-3. Example of using the updateLocation() function

```
function updateLocation(position) {
  var latitude = position.coords.latitude;
  var longitude = position.coords.longitude;
  var accuracy = position.coords.accuracy;

  document.getElementById("latitude").innerHTML = latitude;
  document.getElementById("longitude").innerHTML = longitude;
  document.getElementById("accuracy").innerHTML = "This location is accurate within " +

accuracy + " meters."
}
```

In this example, the updateLocation() callback is used to update the text in three elements of our HTML page; coincidentally, we put the value of the longitude attribute in the longitude element, and the latitude attribute in the latitude element.

The handleLocationError() Function

Handling errors will be very important for an HTML5 Geolocation application because there are many possibilities for the location calculation services to go awry. Fortunately, the API defines error codes for all the cases you will need to handle, and it sets them on the error object passed to your error handler as the code attribute. Let's look at them in turn:

- UNKNOWN_ERROR (error code 0)—An error occurred that is not covered by the other error codes. You will want to check the message attribute for more details on what went wrong.

- PERMISSION_DENIED (error code 1)—The user chose not to let the browser have access to the location information.

- **POSITION_UNAVAILABLE** (error code 2)—The technique used to determine the user's location was attempted, but failed.

- **TIMEOUT** (error code 3)—A timeout value was set as an option, and the attempt to determine the location exceeded that limit.

In these cases, you will probably want to let the user know that something went wrong. You may want to retry getting the values in the case of an unavailable or timed-out request.

Listing 4-4 shows an example of an error handler in action.

Listing 4-4. Using an error handler

```
function handleLocationError(error) {
    switch(error.code){
    case 0:
            updateStatus("There was an error while retrieving your location: " +
            error.message);
    break;

    case 1:
    updateStatus("The user prevented this page from retrieving a location.");
    break;

    case 2:
    updateStatus("The browser was unable to determine your location: " +
                            error.message);
    break;

    case 3:
    updateStatus("The browser timed out before retrieving the location.");
    break;
    }
}
```

The error codes are accessed from the **code** attribute of the provided **error** object, while the **message** attribute will give access to a more detailed description of what went wrong. In all cases, we call our own routine to update the status of the page with the necessary info.

Optional Geolocation Request Attributes

With both the normal and error cases handled, you should turn your attention to the three optional attributes that you can pass to the HTML5 Geolocation service in order to fine-tune how it gathers its data. Note that these three attributes can be passed using shorthand object notation, making it trivial to add them to your HTML5 Geolocation request calls.

- **enableHighAccuracy**—This is a hint to the browser that, if available, you would like the HTML5 Geolocation service to use a higher accuracy-detection mode. This defaults to false, but when turned on, it may not cause any difference, or it may cause the machine to take more time or power to determine location. Use with caution.

■ **Note** Curiously, the high accuracy setting is only a toggle switch: `true` or `false`. The API was not created to allow the accuracy to be set to various values or a numeric range. Perhaps this will be addressed in future versions of the specification.

- `timeout`—This optional value, provided in milliseconds, tells the browser the maximum amount of time it is allowed to calculate the current location. If the calculation does not complete in this amount of time, the error handler is called instead. This defaults the value of Infinity, or no limit.

- `maximumAge`—This value indicates how old a location value can be before the browser must attempt to recalculate. Again, it is a value in milliseconds. This value defaults to zero, meaning that the browser must attempt to recalculate a value immediately.

■ **Note** You might be wondering what the difference is between the `timeout` and `maximumAge` options. Although similarly named, they do have distinct uses. The `timeout` value deals with the *duration* needed to calculate the location value, while `maximumAge` refers to the *frequency* of the location calculation. If any single calculation takes longer than the `timeout` value, an error is triggered. However, if the browser does not have an up-to-date location value that is younger than `maximumAge`, it must refetch another value. Special values apply here: setting the `maximumAge` to "0" requires the value to always be re-fetched, while setting it to `Infinity` means it should never be refetched.

However, note that the API does not allow us to tell the browser how often to recalculate the position. This is left entirely up to the browser implementation. All we can do is tell the browser what the `maximumAge` is of the value it returns. The actual frequency is a detail we cannot control.

Let's update our location request to include an optional parameter using shorthand notation, as shown in the following example:

```
navigator.geolocation.getCurrentPosition(updateLocation,handleLocationError,
                              {timeout:10000});
```

This new call tells HTML5 Geolocation that any request for location that takes longer than 10 seconds (10000 milliseconds) should trigger an error, in which case the `handleLocationError` function will be called with the `TIMEOUT` error code.

Repeated Position Updates

Sometimes once is not enough. Thankfully, the designers of the Geolocation service made it trivial to switch from an application that requests a user location one time to one that requests the location at regular intervals. In fact, it's largely as trivial as switching the request call, as shown in the following examples:

```
navigator.geolocation.getCurrentPosition(updateLocation, handleLocationError);
navigator.geolocation.watchPosition(updateLocation, handleLocationError);
```

This simple change will cause the Geolocation service to call your `updateLocation` handler repeatedly as the user's location changes, rather than one time. It acts as though your program is *watching* the location and will let you know whenever the location changes.

Why would you want to do this?

Consider a web page that gives turn-by-turn directions as the viewer moves around town. Or a page that constantly updates to show you the nearest gas station as you drive down the highway. Or even a page that records and sends your location so that you can retrace your steps. All these services become easy to build once the location updates flow into your application right as they are changing.

Turning off the updates is also simple. Should your application no longer need to receive regular updates about the user's location, you need merely make a call to the `clearWatch()` function, as shown in the following example:

```
navigator.geolocation.clearWatch(watchId);
```

This function will inform the Geolocation service that you no longer want to receive updates on a user's location. But what is the `watchID` and where did it come from? It is actually the return value from the `watchPosition()` call. It identifies the unique monitor request in order to allow us to cancel it later. So, if your application ever needs to stop receiving location updates, you would write some code, as shown in Listing 4-5.

Listing 4-5. Using watchPostion

```
var watchId = navigator.geolocation.watchPosition(updateLocation,
                                                   handleLocationError);
// do something fun with the location updates!

// ...

// OK, now we are ready to stop receiving location updates
navigator.geolocation.clearWatch(watchId);
```

Building a Real-Time Application with HTML5 Geolocation

So far, we've mainly focused on single-shot location requests. Let's see how powerful the HTML5 Geolocation API can really be by using its multirequest feature to build a small but useful application: a web page with a distance tracker.

If you've ever wanted a quick way to determine how far you've traveled in a certain amount of time, you would normally use a dedicated device such as a GPS navigation system or a pedometer. Using the power of the HTML5 Geolocation service, you can create a web page that tracks how far you have traveled from where the page was originally loaded. Although less useful on a desktop computer, this page is ideal for the millions of web-enabled phones that ship with geolocation support today. Simply point your phone browser to this example page, grant the page permission to access your location, and every few seconds it will update with the distance you just traveled and add it to a running total (see Figure 4-4).

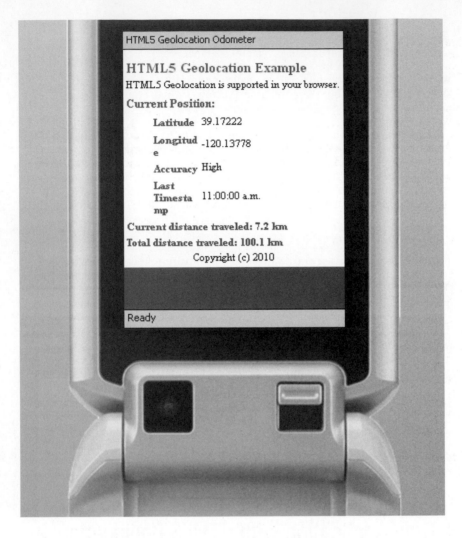

Figure 4-4. *The HTML5 Geolocation example application in action*

This sample works by using the `watchPosition()` capability we discussed in the last section. Every time a new position is sent to us, we will compare it to the last known position and calculate the distance traveled. This is accomplished using a well-known calculation known as the Haversine formula, which allows us to calculate distance between two longitude and latitude positions on a sphere. As shown in Listing 4-6, the Haversine formula tells us the following:

Listing 4-6. The Haversine formula

$$\Delta\hat{\sigma} = 2\arcsin\left(\sqrt{\sin^2\left(\frac{\Delta\phi}{2}\right) + \cos\phi_s\cos\phi_f\sin^2\left(\frac{\Delta\lambda}{2}\right)}\right)$$

If you're hoping to learn how the Haversine formula works, you'll be sorely disappointed. Instead, we'll present you a JavaScript implementation of the formula, which allows anyone to use it to calculate the distance between two positions (see Listing 4-7).

Listing 4-7. A JavaScript Haversine implementation

```
function toRadians(degree) {
    return degree * Math.PI / 180;
    }

    function distance(latitude1, longitude1, latitude2, longitude2) {
    // R is the radius of the earth in kilometers
var R = 6371;

    var deltaLatitude = toRadians(latitude2-latitude1);
var deltaLongitude = toRadians(longitude2-longitude1);
    latitude1 =toRadians(latitude1);
 latitude2 =toRadians(latitude2);

var a = Math.sin(deltaLatitude/2) *
Math.sin(deltaLatitude/2) +
            Math.cos(latitude1) *
            Math.cos(latitude2) *
Math.sin(deltaLongitude/2) *
Math.sin(deltaLongitude/2);

    var c = 2 * Math.atan2(Math.sqrt(a),
Math.sqrt(1-a));
    var d = R * c;
    return d;
}
```

If you want to know why or how this formula works, consult a teenager's math textbook. For our purposes, we have written a conversion from degrees to radians, and we provided a `distance()` function to calculate the distance between two latitude and longitude position values.

If we check the user's position and calculate the distance traveled at frequent and regular intervals, it gives a reasonable approximation of distance traveled over time. This assumes that the user is moving in a straight direction during each interval, but we'll make that assumption for the sake of our example.

Writing the HTML Display

Let's start with the HTML display. We kept it quite simple for this exercise because the real interest is in the script driving the data. We display a simple table with rows for latitude, longitude, accuracy, and a timestamp in milliseconds since our last update. In addition, we'll put a few status text indicators in place so that the user can see the summary of distance traveled (see Listing 4-8).

Listing 4-8. Code for the Distance Tracker HTML page

```
<h1>HTML5 Geolocation Distance Tracker</h1>

<p id="status">HTML5 Geolocation is <strong>not</strong> supported in your browser.</p>

<h2>Current Position:</h2>
<table border="1">
<tr>
<th width="40" scope="col">Latitude</th>
<td width="114" id="latitude">?</td>
</tr>
<tr>
<td> Longitude</td>
<td id="longitude">?</td>
</tr>
<tr>
<td>Accuracy</td>
<td id="accuracy">?</td>
</tr>
<tr>
<td>Last Timestamp</td>
<td id="timestamp">?</td>
</tr>
</table>

<h4 id="currDist">Current distance traveled: 0.0 km</h4>
<h4 id="totalDist">Total distance traveled: 0.0 km</h4>
```

These table values are all defaulted for now and are populated once data starts flowing into the application.

Processing the Geolocation Data

Our first JavaScript code section should look familiar. We've set a handler—`loadDemo()`—that will execute as soon as the page completes loading. This script will detect if HTML5 Geolocation is supported in the browser and use a handy utility to change the status message on the page to indicate what it finds. It will then request a watch of the user's position, as shown in Listing 4-9.

Listing 4-9. Adding the loadDemo() function

```
var totalDistance = 0.0;
var lastLat;
    var lastLong;

function updateStatus(message) {
        document.getElementById("status").innerHTML = message;
    }

    function loadDemo() {
        if(navigator.geolocation) {
            updateStatus("HTML5 Geolocation is supported in your browser.");
            navigator.geolocation.watchPosition(updateLocation,
                                        handleLocationError,
                                        {maximumAge:20000});
        }
    }

    window.addEventListener("load", loadDemo, true);
```

For error handling, we'll use the same routine we identified earlier, as it is generic enough to work for our distance tracker. In it we'll check the error code of any error we receive and update the status message on the page accordingly as shown in Listing 4-10.

Listing 4-10. Adding the error handling code

```
function handleLocationError(error) {
  switch (error.code) {
    case 0:
    updateStatus("There was an error while retrieving your location: " +
                    error.message);
    break;

    case 1:
    updateStatus("The user prevented this page from retrieving a location.");
    break;

    case 2:
    updateStatus("The browser was unable to determine your location: " +
                    error.message);
    break;

    case 3:
    updateStatus("The browser timed out before retrieving the location.");
    break;
  }
}
```

Note also that we are setting a `maximumAge` option on our position watch: `{maximumAge:20000}`. This will tell the location service that we don't want any cached location values that are greater than 20 seconds (or 20000 milliseconds) old. Setting this option will keep our page updating at regular intervals, but feel free to adjust this number and experiment with larger and smaller cache sizes.

The bulk of our work will be done in our `updateLocation()` function. Here we will update the page with our most recent values and calculate the distance traveled, as shown in Listing 4-11.

Listing 4-11. Adding the updateLocation() function

```
function updateLocation(position) {
        var latitude = position.coords.latitude;
        var longitude = position.coords.longitude;
        var accuracy = position.coords.accuracy;
        var timestamp = position.timestamp;

        document.getElementById("latitude").innerHTML = latitude;
        document.getElementById("longitude").innerHTML = longitude;
        document.getElementById("accuracy").innerHTML = accuracy;
        document.getElementById("timestamp").innerHTML = timestamp;
```

As you might expect, the first thing we will do when we receive an updated set of position coordinates is to record all the information. We gather the latitude, longitude, accuracy, and timestamp, and then update the table values with the new data.

You might not choose to display a timestamp in your own application. The timestamp number used here is in a form primarily useful to computers, which won't be meaningful to an end user. Feel free to replace it with a more user-friendly time indicator or remove it altogether.

The accuracy value is given to us in meters and might at first seem unnecessary. However, any data depends on its accuracy. Even if you don't present the user with the accuracy values, you should take them into account in your own code. Presenting inaccurate values could give the user a skewed idea of his or her location. Therefore, we will throw out any position updates with an unreasonably low accuracy, as shown in Listing 4-12.

Listing 4-12. Ignoring inaccurate accuracy updates

```
        // sanity test... don't calculate distance if accuracy
        // value too large
        if (accuracy >= 500) {
            updateStatus("Need more accurate values to calculate distance.");
            return;
        }
}
```

THE EASIEST WAY TO TRAVEL

Brian says: "Keeping track of position accuracy is vital. As a developer, you won't have access to the methodologies a browser uses to calculate position, but you will have access to the accuracy attribute. Use it!

Sitting here in my backyard hammock on a lazy afternoon, I monitored my position on a geolocation–enabled cell phone browser. I was surprised to see that over the course of only a few minutes, my reclined body was reported to travel half a kilometer in distance at varying speeds. As exciting as this might sound, it is a reminder that data is only as accurate as its source permits."

Finally, we will calculate the distance traveled, assuming that we have already received at least one accurate position value before. We will update the totals of travel distance and display them for the user, and we will store the current values for future comparison. To keep our interface a little less cluttered, it is a good idea to round or truncate the calculated values, as shown in Listing 4-13.

Listing 4-13. Adding the distance calculation code

```
// calculate distance

if ((lastLat !== null) && (lastLong !== null)) {
        var currentDistance = distance(latitude, longitude, lastLat, lastLong);
        document.getElementById("currDist").innerHTML =
          "Current distance traveled: " + currentDistance.toFixed(4) + " km";

        totalDistance += currentDistance;

        document.getElementById("totalDist").innerHTML =
          "Total distance traveled: " + totalDistance.toFixed(4) + " km";
    }


    lastLat = latitude;
    lastLong = longitude;

    updateStatus("Location successfully updated.");
}
```

That's it. In fewer than 200 lines of HTML and script, we've created a sample application that monitors the viewer's position over time and demonstrated nearly the entire Geolocation API, complete with error handling. Although this example is inherently less interesting when viewed on a desktop computer, try it out on your favorite geolocation–enabled phone or device and see how mobile you truly are during the course of a day.

The Final Code

The full code sample is shown in Listing 4-14.

Listing 4-14. Complete distance tracker code

```html
<!DOCTYPE html>
<html>
<title>HTML5 Geolocation Odometer</title>
<h1>HTML5 Geolocation Distance Tracker</h1>

<p id="status">HTML5 Geolocation is <strong>not</strong> supported in your browser.</p>

<h2>Current Position:</h2>
<table border="1">
<tr>
<th width="40" scope="col">Latitude</th>
<td width="114" id="latitude">?</td>
</tr>
<tr>
<td> Longitude</td>
<td id="longitude">?</td>
</tr>
<tr>
<td>Accuracy</td>
<td id="accuracy">?</td>
</tr>
<tr>
<td>Last Timestamp</td>
<td id="timestamp">?</td>
</tr>
</table>

<h4 id="currDist">Current distance traveled: 0.0 km</h4>
<h4 id="totalDist">Total distance traveled: 0.0 km</h4>

<script type="text/javascript">

    var totalDistance = 0.0;
    var lastLat;
    var lastLong;

    function toRadians(degree) {
      return degree * Math.PI / 180;
    }

    function distance(latitude1, longitude1, latitude2, longitude2) {
      // R is the radius of the earth in kilometers
      var R = 6371;
```

```
    var deltaLatitude = toRadians(latitude2-latitude1);
    var deltaLongitude = toRadians(longitude2-longitude1);
    latitude1 = toRadians(latitude1);
    latitude2 = toRadians(latitude2);

    var a = Math.sin(deltaLatitude/2) *
    Math.sin(deltaLatitude/2) +
    Math.cos(latitude1) *
    Math.cos(latitude2) *
    Math.sin(deltaLongitude/2) *
    Math.sin(deltaLongitude/2);

    var c = 2 * Math.atan2(Math.sqrt(a),
    Math.sqrt(1-a));
    var d = R * c;
    return d;
}


function updateStatus(message) {
    document.getElementById("status").innerHTML = message;
}

function loadDemo() {
    if(navigator.geolocation) {
        updateStatus("HTML5 Geolocation is supported in your browser.");
        navigator.geolocation.watchPosition(updateLocation,
                                            handleLocationError,
                                            {maximumAge:20000});
    }
}

window.addEventListener("load", loadDemo, true);

function updateLocation(position) {
    var latitude = position.coords.latitude;
    var longitude = position.coords.longitude;
    var accuracy = position.coords.accuracy;
    var timestamp = position.timestamp;

    document.getElementById("latitude").innerHTML = latitude;
    document.getElementById("longitude").innerHTML = longitude;
    document.getElementById("accuracy").innerHTML = accuracy;
    document.getElementById("timestamp").innerHTML = timestamp;

    // sanity test... don't calculate distance if accuracy
    // value too large
    if (accuracy >= 500) {
        updateStatus("Need more accurate values to calculate distance.");
        return;
    }
```

```
        // calculate distance

        if ((lastLat !== null) && (lastLong !== null)) {
            var currentDistance = distance(latitude, longitude, lastLat, lastLong);
            document.getElementById("currDist").innerHTML =
               "Current distance traveled: " +
                currentDistance.toFixed(4) + " km";

            totalDistance += currentDistance;

            document.getElementById("totalDist").innerHTML =
               "Total distance traveled: " + totalDistance.toFixed(4) + " km";
        }


        lastLat = latitude;
        lastLong = longitude;

        updateStatus("Location successfully updated.");
    }

    function handleLocationError(error) {
      switch (error.code) {
        case 0:
        updateStatus("There was an error while retrieving your location: " +
                    error.message);
        break;

        case 1:
        updateStatus("The user prevented this page from retrieving a location.");
        break;

        case 2:
        updateStatus("The browser was unable to determine your location: " +
                    error.message);
        break;

        case 3:
        updateStatus("The browser timed out before retrieving the location.");
        break;
      }
    }
</script>
</html>
```

Practical Extras

Sometimes there are techniques that don't fit into our regular examples, but which nonetheless apply to many types of HTML5 applications. We present to you some short, common, and practical extras here.

What's My Status?

You might have already noticed that a large portion of the HTML5 Geolocation API pertains to timing values. This should not be too surprising. Techniques for determining location—cell phone triangulation, GPS, IP lookup, and so on—can take a notoriously long time to complete, if they complete at all. Fortunately, the APIs give a developer plenty of information to create a reasonable status bar for the user.

If a developer sets the optional `timeout` value on a position lookup, she is requesting that the geolocation service notify her with an error if the lookup takes longer than the `timeout` value. The side effect of this is that it is entirely reasonable to show the user a status message in the user interface while the request is underway. The start of the status begins when the request is made, and the end of the status should correspond to the timeout value, whether or not it ends in success or failure.

In Listing 4-15, we'll kick off a JavaScript interval timer to regularly update the status display with a new progress indicator value.

Listing 4-15. Adding a status bar

```
function updateStatus(message) {
    document.getElementById("status").innerHTML = message;
}

function endRequest() {
  updateStatus("Done.");
}

function updateLocation(position) {
  endRequest();
  // handle the position data
}

function handleLocationError(error) {
  endRequest();

  // handle any errors
}

navigator.geolocation.getCurrentPosition(updateLocation,
                                         handleLocationError,
                                         {timeout:10000});
                                         // 10 second timeout value

updateStatus("Requesting location data…");
```

Let's break that example down a little. As before, we've got a function to update our status value on the page, as shown in the following example.

```
function updateStatus(message) {
        document.getElementById("status").innerHTML = message;
}
```

Our status here will be a simple text display, although this approach applies equally well for more compelling graphical status displays (see Listing 4-16).

Listing 4-16. Showing the status

```
navigator.geolocation.getCurrentPosition(updateLocation,
                                         handleLocationError,
                                         {timeout:10000});
                                         // 10 second timeout value

updateStatus("Requesting location data…");
```

Once again, we use the Geolocation API to get the user's current position, but with a set timeout of ten seconds. Once ten seconds have elapsed, we should either have a success or failure due to the timeout option.

We immediately update the status text display to indicate that a position request is in progress. Then, once the request completes or ten seconds elapses—whichever comes first—you use the callback method to reset the status text, as shown in Listing 4-17.

Listing 4-17. Resetting the status text

```
    function endRequest() {
                    updateStatus("Done.");
    }
    function updateLocation(position) {
      endRequest();

      // handle the position data
    }
```

A simple extra, but easy to extend.

This technique works well for one-shot position lookups because it is easy for the developer to determine when a position lookup request starts. The request starts as soon as the developer calls `getCurrentPosition()`, of course. However, in the case of a repeated position lookup via `watchPosition()`, the developer is not in control of when each individual position request begins.

Furthermore, the timeout does not begin until the user grants permission for the geolocation service to access position data. For this reason, it is impractical to implement a precise status display because the page is not informed during the instant when the user grants permission.

Show Me on a Google Map

One very common request for geolocation data is to show a user's position on a map, such as the popular Google Maps service. In fact, this is so popular that Google itself built support for HTML5 Geolocation into its user interface. Simply press the Show My Location button (see Figure 4-5); Google Maps will use the Geolocation API (if it is available) to determine and display your location on the map.

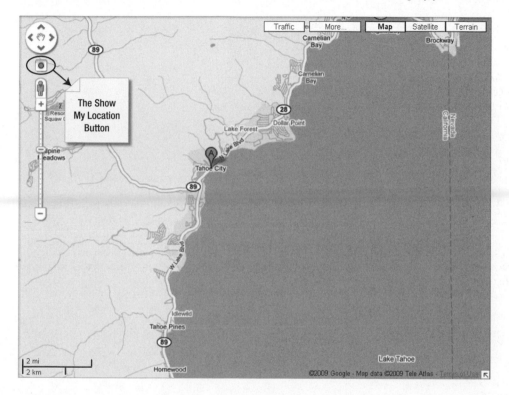

Figure 4-5. Google Map's Show My Location button

However, it is also possible to do this yourself. Although the Google Map API is beyond the scope of this book, it has (not coincidentally) been designed to take decimal latitude and longitude locations. Therefore, you can easily pass the results of your position lookup to the Google Map API, as shown in Listing 4-18. You can read more on this subject in *Beginning Google Maps Applications*, Second Edition (Apress, 2010).

Listing 4-18. Passing a position to the Google Map API

```
// Create a Google Map... see Google API for more detail
var map = new google.maps.Map(document.getElementById("map"));

function updateLocation(position) {
  //pass the position to the Google Map and center it
  map.setCenter(new google.maps.LatLng(position.coords.latitude,
                                       position.coords.longitude);
}

navigator.geolocation.getCurrentPosition(updateLocation,
                                         handleLocationError);
```

Summary

This chapter discussed HTML5 Geolocation. You learned the HTML5 Geolocation location information—latitude, longitude, and other attributes—and where they can come from. You also learned about the privacy concerns that accompany HTML5 Geolocation and you've seen how the HTML5 Geolocation APIs can be used to create compelling, location–aware web applications.

In the next chapter, we'll demonstrate how HTML5 lets you communicate between tabs and windows as well as between pages and servers with different domains.

CHAPTER 5

∎∎∎

Using the Communication APIs

In this chapter, we'll explore what you can do with two of the important building blocks for real-time, cross-origin communication: *Cross Document Messaging* and *XMLHttpRequest Level 2* and we'll show you how they can be used to create compelling applications. Both of these building blocks add new communication options to HTML5 applications and allow applications served from different domains to safely communicate with each other.

First, we'll discuss the `postMessage` API and the origin security concept—two key elements of HTML5 communication—and then we'll show you how the `postMessage` API can be used to communicate between iframes, tabs, and windows.

Next, we'll discuss XMLHttpRequest Level 2—an improved version of XMLHttpRequest. We'll show you in which areas XMLHttpRequest has been improved. Specifically, we'll show you how you can use XMLHttpRequest to make cross-origin requests and how to use the new progress events.

Cross Document Messaging

Until recently, communications between frames, tabs, and windows in a running browser was entirely restricted due to security concerns. For instance, while it might be handy for certain sites to share information from inside the browser, it would also open up the possibility for malicious attacks. If browsers granted the ability to programmatically access the content loaded into other frames and tabs, sites would be able to steal whatever information they could get from another site's content using scripting. Wisely, the browser vendors restricted this access; attempting to retrieve or modify content loaded from another source raises a security exception and prevents the operation.

However, there are some legitimate cases for content from different sites to be able to communicate inside the browser. The classic example is the "mashup", a combination of different applications such as mapping, chat, and news from different sites, all combined together to form a new meta-application. In these cases, a well-coordinated set of applications would be served by direct communication channels inside the browser itself.

To meet this need, the browser vendors and standards bodies agreed to introduce a new feature: Cross Document Messaging. Cross Document Messaging enables secure cross-origin communication across iframes, tabs, and windows. It defines the `postMessage` API as a standard way to send messages. As shown in the following example, it is very simple to send a message with the `postMessage` API.

```
chatFrame.contentWindow.postMessage('Hello, world', 'http://www.example.com/');
```

To receive messages, you just have to add an event handler to your page. When a message arrives, you can check its origin and decide whether or not to do something with the message. Listing 5-1 shows an event listener that passes the message to a `messageHandler` function.

Listing 5-1. An event listener for message events

```
window.addEventListener("message", messageHandler, true);
function messageHandler(e) {
    switch(e.origin) {
        case "friend.example.com":
        // process message
        processMessage(e.data);
        break;
        default:
        // message origin not recognized
        // ignoring message
    }
}
```

A message event is a DOM event with `data` and `origin` properties. The `data` property is the actual message that the sender passed along and the `origin` property is the sender's origin. Using the `origin` property, it is easy for the receiving side to ignore messages from untrusted sources; the origin can simply be checked against a list of allowed origins.

As shown in Figure 5-1, the `postMessage` API provides a way to communicate between a chat widget iframe hosted at `http://chat.example.net` and an HTML page that contains the chat widget iframe hosted at `http://portal.example.com` (two different origins).

Figure 5-1. postMessage communication between an iframe and a main HTML page

In this example, the chat widget is contained in an iframe, so it does not have direct access to the parent window. When the chat widget receives a chat message, it can use postMessage to send a message to the main page so that the page can alert the user of the chat widget that a new message has been received. Similarly, the page can send messages about the user's status to the chat widget. Both the page and the widget can listen for messages from each other by adding the respective origins to a white list of allowed origins.

Before the introduction of postMessage, communicating between iframes could sometimes be accomplished by direct scripting. A script running in one page would attempt to manipulate another document. This might not be allowed due to security restrictions. Instead of direct programmatic access, postMessage provides asynchronous message passing between JavaScript contexts. As shown in Figure 5-2, without postMessage, cross origin communication would result in security errors, enforced by browsers to prevent cross-site scripting attacks.

Figure 5-2. Cross-site scripting error in earlier version of Firefox and Firebug

The postMessage API can be used for communicating between documents with the same origin, but it is particularly useful when communication might otherwise be disallowed by the same-domain policy, which is enforced by browsers. However, there are reasons to use postMessage for messaging between same-origin documents as well because it provides a consistent, easy-to-use API. The postMessage API is used whenever there is communication between JavaScript contexts, such as with HTML5 Web Workers.

Understanding Origin Security

HTML5 clarifies and refines domain security by introducing the concept of an *origin*. An origin is a subset of an address used for modeling trust relationships on the Web. Origins are made up of a scheme, a host, and a port. For example, a page at https://www.example.com has a different origin than one at http://www.example.com because the scheme differs (https vs. http). The path is not considered in the origin value, so a page at http://www.example.com/index.html has the same origin as a page at http://www.example.com/page2.html because only the paths differ.

HTML5 defines the serialization of origins. In string form, origins can be referred to in APIs and protocols. This is essential for cross-origin HTTP requests using XMLHttpRequest, as well as for WebSockets.

Cross-origin communication identifies the sender by origin. This allows the receiver to ignore messages from origins it does not trust or does not expect to receive messages from. Furthermore, applications must opt-in to receiving messages by adding an event listener for message events. Because of this, there is no risk of messages interfering with an unsuspecting application.

Security rules for `postMessage` ensure that messages cannot be delivered to pages with unexpected—and possibly undesired—origins. When sending a message, the sender specifies the receiver's origin. If the window on which the sender is calling `postMessage` does not have that specific origin (for instance, if the user has navigated to another site) the browser will not transmit that message.

Likewise, when receiving a message, the sender's origin is included as part of the message. The message's origin is provided by the browser and cannot be spoofed. This allows the receiver to decide which messages to process and which to ignore. You can keep a white list and process only messages from documents with trusted origins.

BE CAREFUL WITH EXTERNAL INPUT

Frank says: "Applications that process cross-origin messages should always verify the source origin of every message. Furthermore, message data should be treated with caution. Even if a message comes from a trusted source, it should be treated with the same caution as any other external input. The following two examples show a method of injecting content that can lead to trouble, as well as a safer alternative.

```
// Dangerous: e.data is evaluated as markup!
element.innerHTML = e.data;

// Better
element.textContent = e.data;
```

As a best practice, *never* evaluate strings received from third parties. Furthermore, avoid using `eval` with strings originating from your own application. Instead, you can use JSON with `window.JSON` or the json.org parser. JSON is a data language that is meant to be safely consumed by JavaScript, and the json.org parser is designed to be paranoid."

Browser Support for Cross Document Messaging

As shown in Table 5-1, HTML5 Cross Document Messaging is already supported in many browsers at the time of this writing.

Table 5-1. Browser support for HTML5 Cross Document Messaging

Browser	Details
Chrome	Supported in version 2.0 and greater
Firefox	Supported in version 3.0 and greater
Internet Explorer	Supported in version 8.0 and greater
Opera	Supported in version 9.6 and greater
Safari	Supported in version 4.0 and greater

It is always a good idea to first test if HTML5 Cross Document Messaging is supported, before you use it. The section "Checking for Browser Support" later in this chapter will show you how you can programmatically check for browser support.

Using the postMessage API

In this section, we'll explore the use of the HTML5 `postMessage` API in more detail.

Checking for Browser Support

Before you call `postMessage`, it is a good idea to check if the browser supports it. The following example shows one way to check for `postMessage` support:

```
if (typeof window.postMessage === "undefined") {
    // postMessage not supported in this browser
}
```

Sending Messages

To send messages, invoke `postMessage` on the target window object, as shown in the following example:

```
window.postMessage("Hello, world", "portal.example.com");
```

The first argument contains the data to send, and the second argument contains the intended target. To send messages to iframes, you can invoke `postMessage` on the iframe's contentWindow, as shown in the following example:

```
document.getElementsByTagName("iframe")[0].contentWindow.postMessage("Hello, world",
"chat.example.net");
```

Listening for Message Events

A script receives messages by listening for events on the window object, as shown in Listing 5-2. In the event listener function, the receiving application can decide to accept or ignore the message.

Listing 5-2. Listening for message events and comparing origins against a white list

```
var originWhiteList = ["portal.example.com", "games.example.com", "www.example.com"];

function checkWhiteList(origin) {
    for (var i=0; i<originWhiteList.length; i++) {
        if (origin === originWhiteList[i]) {
          return true;
        }
    }
    return false;
}
```

```
function messageHandler(e) {
    if(checkWhiteList(e.origin)) {
        processMessage(e.data);
    } else {
        // ignore messages from unrecognized origins
    }
}
window.addEventListener("message", messageHandler, true);
```

■ **Note** The MessageEvent interface defined by HTML5 is also part of HTML5 WebSockets and HTML5 Web Workers. The communication features of HTML5 have consistent APIs for receiving messages. Other communication APIs, such as the EventSource API and Web Workers, also use MessageEvent to deliver messages.

Building an Application Using the postMessage API

Let's say that you wanted to build the aforementioned portal application with its cross-origin chat widget. You can use Cross Document Messaging to communicate between the portal page and the chat widget, as shown in Figure 5-3.

Cross-Origin Portal

Origin: http://portal.example.com:9999

Status [Out for a run!] [Change Status]

This uses postMessage to send a status update to the widget iframe contained in the portal page.

Widget iframe

Origin: http://chat.example.net:9999

Status set to: **Out for a run!** by containing portal.

[Runtime] [Send Notification]

This will ask the portal to notify the user. The portal does this by flashing the title. If the message comes from an origin other than http://chat.example.net:9999, the portal page will ignore it.

[Stop Blinking Title]

Figure 5-3. Portal page with cross-origin chat widget iframe

In this example, we show how a portal might embed widgets from third parties in iframes. Our example shows a single widget from `chat.example.net`. The portal page and widget then communicate using `postMessage`. In this case, the iframe represents a chat widget that wants to notify the user by blinking the title text. This is a common UI technique found in applications that receive events in the background. However, because the widget is isolated in an iframe served from a different origin than the parent page, changing the title would be a security violation. Instead, the widget uses `postMessage` to request that the parent page perform the notification on its behalf.

The example portal also sends messages to the iframe to inform the widget that the user has changed his or her status. Using `postMessage` in this way allows a portal such as this to coordinate with widgets across the combined application. Of course, because the target origin is checked when the message is sent, and the event origin is checked when it is received, there is no chance that data leaks out accidentally or is spoofed.

■ **Note** In this example application, the chat widget is not connected to a live chat system, and notifications are driven by the application's users clicking **Send Notification**. A working chat application could use Web Sockets, as described in Chapter 6.

For the sake of illustration, we created a few simple HTML pages: `postMessagePortal.html` and `postMessageWidget.html`. The following steps highlight the important parts of building the portal page and the chat widget page. The sample code for the following examples is located in the `code/communication` folder.

Building the Portal Page

First, add the chat widget iframe hosted at the different origin:

```
<iframe id="widget" src="http://chat.example.net:9999/postMessageWidget.html"></iframe>
```

Next, add an event listener `messageHandler` to listen for message events coming from the chat widget. As shown in the following example code, the widget will ask the portal to notify the user, which can be done by flashing the title. To make sure the message comes from the chat widget, the message's origin is verified; if it does not come from `http://chat.example.net:9999`, the portal page simply ignores it.

```
var targetOrigin = "http://chat.example.net:9999";

function messageHandler(e) {
    if (e.origin == targetOrigin) {
        notify(e.data);
    } else {
        // ignore messages from other origins
    }
}
```

Next, add a function to communicate with the chat widget. It uses **postMessage** to send a status update to the widget iframe contained in the portal page. In a live chat application, it could be used to communicate the user's status (available, away, and so on).

```
function sendString(s) {
    document.getElementById("widget").contentWindow.postMessage(s, targetOrigin);
}
```

Building the Chat Widget Page

First, add an event listener **messageHandler** to listen for message events coming from the portal page. As shown in the following example code, the chat widget listens for incoming status-change messages. To make sure the message comes from the portal page, the message's origin is verified; if it does not come from **http://portal.example.com:9999**, the widget simply ignores it.

```
var targetOrigin = "http://portal.example.com:9999";
function messageHandler(e) {
    if (e.origin === "http://portal.example.com:9999") {
        document.getElementById("status").textContent = e.data;
    } else {
        // ignore messages from other origins
    }
}
```

Next, add a function to communicate with the portal page. The widget will ask the portal to notify the user on its behalf and uses **postMessage** to send a message to the portal page when a new chat message is received, as shown in the following example:

```
function sendString(s) {
    window.top.postMessage(s, targetOrigin);
}
```

The Final Code

Listing 5-3 shows the complete code for the Portal page **postMessagePortal.html**.

Listing 5-3. Contents of postMessagePortal.html

```
<!DOCTYPE html>
<title>Portal [http://portal.example.com:9999]</title>
<link rel="stylesheet" href="styles.css">
<style>
    iframe {
        height: 400px;
        width: 800px;
    }
</style>
<link rel="icon" href="http://apress.com/favicon.ico">
<script>
```

```
var defaultTitle = "Portal [http://portal.example.com:9999]";
var notificationTimer = null;

var targetOrigin = "http://chat.example.net:9999";

function messageHandler(e) {
    if (e.origin == targetOrigin) {
        notify(e.data);
    } else {
        // ignore messages from other origins
    }
}

function sendString(s) {
    document.getElementById("widget").contentWindow.postMessage(s, targetOrigin);
}


function notify(message) {
    stopBlinking();
    blinkTitle(message, defaultTitle);
}

function stopBlinking() {
    if (notificationTimer !== null) {
        clearTimeout(notificationTimer);
    }
    document.title = defaultTitle;
}

function blinkTitle(m1, m2) {
    document.title = m1;
    notificationTimer = setTimeout(blinkTitle, 1000, m2, m1)
}

function sendStatus() {
var statusText = document.getElementById("statusText").value;
            sendString(statusText);
}

function loadDemo() {
    document.getElementById("sendButton").addEventListener("click", sendStatus, true);
    document.getElementById("stopButton").addEventListener("click", stopBlinking, true);
    sendStatus();
}
window.addEventListener("load", loadDemo, true);
window.addEventListener("message", messageHandler, true);

</script>
```

```
<h1>Cross-Origin Portal</h1>
<p><b>Origin</b>: http://portal.example.com:9999</p>
Status <input type="text" id="statusText" value="Online">
<button id="sendButton">Change Status</button>
<p>
This uses postMessage to send a status update to the widget iframe contained in the portal
page.
</p>
<iframe id="widget" src="http://chat.example.net:9999/postMessageWidget.html"></iframe>
<p>
    <button id="stopButton">Stop Blinking Title</button>
</p>
```

Listing 5-4 shows the code for the portal page postMessageWidget.html.

Listing 5-4. Contents of postMessageWidget.html

```
<!DOCTYPE html>
<title>widget</title>
<link rel="stylesheet" href="styles.css">
<script>

var targetOrigin = "http://portal.example.com:9999";

function messageHandler(e) {
    if (e.origin === "http://portal.example.com:9999") {
        document.getElementById("status").textContent = e.data;
    } else {
        // ignore messages from other origins
    }
}

function sendString(s) {
    window.top.postMessage(s, targetOrigin);
}

function loadDemo() {
    document.getElementById("actionButton").addEventListener("click",
        function() {
            var messageText = document.getElementById("messageText").value;
            sendString(messageText);
        }, true);

}
window.addEventListener("load", loadDemo, true);
window.addEventListener("message", messageHandler, true);

</script>
<h1>Widget iframe</h1>
<p><b>Origin</b>: http://chat.example.net:9999</p>
<p>Status set to: <strong id="status"></strong> by containing portal.<p>
```

```
<div>
    <input type="text" id="messageText" value="Widget notification.">
    <button id="actionButton">Send Notification</button>
</div>

<p>
This will ask the portal to notify the user. The portal does this by flashing the title. If
the message comes from an origin other than http://chat.example.net:9999, the portal page
will ignore it.
</p>
```

The Application in Action

To see this example in action, there are two prerequisites: the pages have to be served up by a web server and the pages have to be served up from two different domains. If you have access to multiple web servers (for example, two Apache HTTP servers) on separate domains, you can host the example files on those servers and run the demo. Another way to accomplish this on your local machine is to use Python SimpleHTTPServer, as shown in the following steps.

1. Update the path to the Windows hosts file (C:\Windows\system32\drivers\etc\hosts) and the Linux version (/etc/hosts) by adding two entries pointing to your localhost (IP address 127.0.0.1), as shown in the following example:

    ```
    127.0.0.1 chat.example.net
    127.0.0.1 portal.example.com
    ```

■ **Note** You must restart your browser after modifying the host file to ensure that the DNS entries take effect.

---

2. Install Python, which includes the lightweight SimpleHTTPServer web server.

3. Navigate to the directory that contains the two example files (postMessageParent.html and postMessageWidget.html).

4. Start Python as follows:

    ```
    python -m SimpleHTTPServer 9999
    ```

5. Open a browser and navigate to http://portal.example.com:9999/postMessagePortal.html. You should now see the page shown in Figure 5.3

XMLHttpRequest Level 2

XMLHttpRequest is the API that made Ajax possible. There are many books about XMLHttpRequest and Ajax. You can read more about XMLHttpRequest programming in John Resig's *Pro JavaScript Techniques*, (Apress, 2006).

XMLHttpRequest Level 2—the new version of XMLHttpRequest—has been significantly enhanced. In this chapter, we will be covering the improvements introduced in XMLHttpRequest Level 2. These improvements are centered on the following areas:

- Cross-origin XMLHttpRequests
- Progress events

Cross-Origin XMLHttpRequest

In the past, XMLHttpRequest was limited to same-origin communication. XMLHttpRequest Level 2 allows for cross-origin XMLHttpRequests using Cross Origin Resource Sharing (CORS), which uses the *origin* concept discussed in the earlier *Cross Document Messaging* section.

Cross-origin HTTP requests have an `Origin` header. This header provides the server with the request's origin. This header is protected by the browser and cannot be changed from application code. In essence, it is the network equivalent of the `origin` property found on message events used in Cross Document Messaging. The origin header differs from the older referer [*sic*] header in that the referer is a complete URL including the path. Because the path may contain sensitive information, the referer is sometimes not sent by browsers attempting to protect user privacy. However, the browser will always send the required `Origin` headers when necessary.

Using cross-origin XMLHttpRequest, you can build web applications that use services hosted on different origins. For example, if you wanted to host a web application that used static content from one origin and Ajax services from another, you could use cross-origin XMLHttpRequest to communicate between the two. Without cross-origin XMLHttpRequest, you would be limited to same-origin communication. This would constrain your deployment options. For example, you might have to deploy the web application on a single domain or set up a subdomain.

As shown in Figure 5-4, cross-origin XMLHttpRequest allows you to aggregate content from different origins on the client side. Additionally, you can access secured content with the user's credentials if the target server allows it, providing users with direct access to personalized data. Server-side aggregation, on the other hand, forces all content to be funneled through a single server-side infrastructure, which can create a bottleneck.

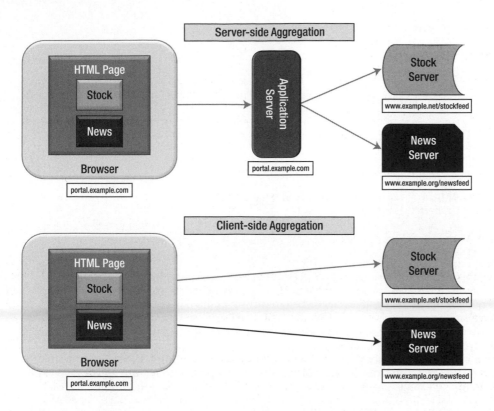

Figure 5-4. Difference between client-side and server-side aggregation

The CORS specification dictates that, for sensitive actions—for example, a request with credentials, or a request other than GET or POST—an OPTIONS preflight request must be sent to the server by the browser to see whether the action is supported and allowed. This means that successful communication may require a CORS-capable server. Listings 5-5 and 5-6 show the HTTP headers involved in a cross-origin exchange between a page hosted on www.example.com and a service hosted on www.example.net.

Listing 5-5. Example request headers

```
POST /main HTTP/1.1
Host: www.example.net
User-Agent: Mozilla/5.0 (X11; U; Linux x86_64; en-US; rv:1.9.1.3) Gecko/20090910 Ubuntu/9.04
(jaunty) Shiretoko/3.5.3
Accept: text/html,application/xhtml+xml,application/xml;q=0.9,*/*;q=0.8
Accept-Language: en-us,en;q=0.5
Accept-Encoding: gzip,deflate
Accept-Charset: ISO-8859-1,utf-8;q=0.7,*;q=0.7
Keep-Alive: 300
Connection: keep-alive
Referer: http://www.example.com/
```

```
Origin: http://www.example.com
Pragma: no-cache
Cache-Control: no-cache
Content-Length: 0
```

Listing 5-6. Example response headers

```
HTTP/1.1 201 Created
Transfer-Encoding: chunked
Server: Kaazing Gateway
Date: Mon, 02 Nov 2009 06:55:08 GMT
Content-Type: text/plain
Access-Control-Allow-Origin: http://www.example.com
Access-Control-Allow-Credentials: true
```

Progress Events

One of the most important API improvements in XMLHttpRequest has been the changes related to progressive responses. In the previous version of XMLHttpRequest, there was only a single readystatechange event. On top of that, it was inconsistently implemented across browsers. For example, readyState 3 (progress) never fires in Internet Explorer. Furthermore, the readyState change event lacked a way to communicate upload progress. Implementing an upload progress bar was not a trivial task and involved server-side participation.

XMLHttpRequest Level 2 introduces progress events with meaningful names. Table 5-2 shows the new progress event names. You can listen for each of these events by setting a callback function for the event handler attribute. For example, when the loadstart event fires, the callback for the onloadstart property is called.

Table 5-2. New XMLHttpRequest Level 2 progress event names

Progress Event Name
loadstart
progress
abort
error
load
loadend

The old readyState property and readystatechange events will be retained for backward compatibility.

"SEEMINGLY ARBITRARY" TIMES

In the XMLHttpRequest Level 2 specification's description for the `readystatechange` event (maintained for backward compatibility), the `readyState` attribute is described as changing at, get this, "*some seemingly arbitrary times for historical reasons.*"

Browser Support for HTML5 XMLHttpRequest Level 2

As shown in Table 5-3, HTML5 XMLHttpRequest is already supported in many browsers at the time of this writing.

Table 5-3. Browser support for HTML5 XMLHttpRequest

Browser	Details
Chrome	Supported in version 2.0 and greater
Firefox	Supported in version 3.5 and greater
Internet Explorer	Not supported
Opera	Not supported
Safari	Supported in version 4.0 and greater

Due to the varying levels of support, it is a good idea to first test if HTML5 XMLHttpRequest is supported, before you use these elements. The section "*Checking for Browser Support*" later in this chapter will show you how you can programmatically check for browser support.

Using the XMLHttpRequest API

In this section, we'll explore the use of the XMLHttpRequest in more detail. For the sake of illustration, we've created a simple HTML page—**crossOriginUpload.html**. The sample code for the following examples is located in the **code/communication** folder.

Checking for Browser Support

Before you try to use XMLHttpRequest Level 2 functionality—such as cross-origin support—it is a good idea to check if it is supported. You can do this by checking whether the new `withCredentials` property is available on an XMLHttpRequest object as shown in Listing 5-7.

Listing 5-7. Checking if cross-origin support is available in XMLHttpRequest

```
var xhr = new XMLHttpRequest()
if (typeof xhr.withCredentials === undefined) {
    document.getElementById("support").innerHTML =
        "Your browser <strong>does not</strong> support cross-origin XMLHttpRequest";
} else {
    document.getElementById("support").innerHTML =
        "Your browser <strong>does</strong>support cross-origin XMLHttpRequest";
}
```

Making Cross-Origin Requests

To make a cross-origin XMLHttpRequest, you must first create a new XMLHttpRequest object, as shown in the following example.

```
var crossOriginRequest = new XMLHttpRequest()
```

Next, make the cross-origin XMLHttpRequest by specifying an address on a different origin as shown in the following example.

```
crossOriginRequest.open("GET", "http://www.example.net/stockfeed", true);
```

Make sure, you listen for errors. There are many reasons why this request might not succeed. For example, network failure, access denied, and lack of CORS support on the target server.

Using Progress Events

Instead of numerical states representing different stages of the request and response, XMLHttpRequest Level 2 provides named progress events. You can listen for each of these events by setting a callback function for the event handler attribute.

Listing 5-8 shows how callback functions are used to handle progress events. Progress events have fields for the total amount of data to transfer, the amount that has already transferred, and a Boolean value indicating whether the total is known (it may not be in the case of streaming HTTP). `XMLHttpRequest.upload` dispatches events with the same fields.

Listing 5-8. Using the onprogress event

```
crossOriginRequest.onprogress = function(e) {
    var total = e.total;
    var loaded = e.loaded;

    if (e.lengthComputable) {
        // do something with the progress information
    }
}
```

```
crossOriginRequest.upload.onprogress = function(e) {
    var total = e.total;
    var loaded = e.loaded;

    if (e.lengthComputable) {
        // do something with the progress information
    }
}
```

Building an Application Using XMLHttpRequest

In this example, we'll look at uploading race geolocation coordinates to a web server hosted on a different origin. We use the new progress events to monitor the status of the HTTP request including the upload percentage. Figure 5-5 shows the application in action.

XMLHttpRequest Level 2

Your browser **does** support cross-origin XMLHttpRequest

Geolocation Data to upload:

```
[[39.080018, 39.112557, 39.135261, 39.150458,
39.170653, 39.190128, 39.204511, 39.226759,
39.238483, 39.228154, 39.2494, 39.249533,
39.225277, 39.191253, 39.167993, 39.145686,
39.121621, 39.095761, 39.080593, 39.053132,
39.02619, 39.002929, 38.982886, 38.954035,
```

Upload

Status: finished

Figure 5-5. A web application that uploads geolocation data

For the sake of illustration, we've created the HTML file `crossOrignUpload.html`. The following steps highlight the important parts of building the cross-origin upload page shown in Figure 5-5. The sample code for the following examples is located in the `code/communication` folder.

First, create a new `XMLHttpRequest` object, as shown in the following example.

```
var xhr = new XMLHttpRequest();
```

Next, do check if cross-origin XMLHttpRequest is supported in the browser, as shown in the following example.

```
if (typeof xhr.withCredentials === undefined) {
  document.getElementById("support").innerHTML =
          "Your browser <strong>doesnot</strong> support cross-origin XMLHttpRequest";
} else {
    document.getElementById("support").innerHTML =
            "Your browser <strong>does</strong> support cross-origin XMLHttpRequest";
}
```

Next, set callback functions to handle the progress events and calculate the uploaded and downloaded ratios.

```
xhr.upload.onprogress = function(e) {
  var ratio = e.loaded / e.total;
  setProgress(ratio + "% uploaded");
}

xhr.onprogress = function(e) {
  var ratio = e.loaded / e.total;
  setProgress(ratio + "% downloaded");
}


xhr.onload = function(e) {
  setProgress("finished");
}

xhr.onerror = function(e) {
  setProgress("error");
}
```

Finally, open the request and send the string containing the encoded geolocation data. This will be a cross-origin request because the target location is a URL with a different origin than the page.

```
var targetLocation = "http://geodata.example.net:9999/upload";
xhr.open("POST", targetLocation, true);

geoDataString = dataElement.textContent;
xhr.send(geoDataString);
```

The Final Code

Listing 5-9 shows the complete application code—the contents of the crossOriginUpload.html file.

Listing 5-9. Contents of crossOriginUpload.html

```
<!DOCTYPE html>
<title>Upload Geolocation Data</title>
<link rel="stylesheet" href="styles.css">
<link rel="icon" href="http://apress.com/favicon.ico">
<script>
```

```
function loadDemo() {
    var dataElement = document.getElementById("geodata");
    dataElement.textContent = JSON.stringify(geoData).replace(",", ", ", "g");

    var xhr = new XMLHttpRequest()
    if (typeof xhr.withCredentials === undefined) {
        document.getElementById("support").innerHTML =
            "Your browser <strong>does not</strong> support cross-origin XMLHttpRequest";
    } else {
        document.getElementById("support").innerHTML =
            "Your browser <strong>does</strong> support cross-origin XMLHttpRequest";
    }

    var targetLocation = "http://geodata.example.net:9999/upload";

    function setProgress(s) {
        document.getElementById("progress").innerHTML = s;
    }

    document.getElementById("sendButton").addEventListener("click",
        function() {
            xhr.upload.onprogress = function(e) {
                var ratio = e.loaded / e.total;
                setProgress(ratio + "% uploaded");
            }

            xhr.onprogress = function(e) {
                var ratio = e.loaded / e.total;
                setProgress(ratio + "% downloaded");
            }

            xhr.onload = function(e) {
                setProgress("finished");
            }

            xhr.onerror = function(e) {
                setProgress("error");
            }

            xhr.open("POST", targetLocation, true);

            geoDataString = dataElement.textContent;
            xhr.send(geoDataString);
        }, true);

}
window.addEventListener("load", loadDemo, true);

</script>
```

```
<h1>XMLHttpRequest Level 2</h1>
<p id="support"></p>

<h4>Geolocation Data to upload:</h4>
<textarea id="geodata">
</textarea>
</div>

<button id="sendButton">Upload</button>

<script>
geoData = [[39.080018000000003, 39.112557000000002, 39.135261, 39.150458,
39.170653000000001, 39.190128000000001, 39.204510999999997, 39.226759000000001,
39.238483000000002, 39.228154000000004, 39.249400000000001, 39.249533, 39.225276999999998,
39.191253000000003, 39.167993000000003, 39.145685999999998, 39.121620999999998,
39.095761000000003, 39.080593, 39.053131999999998, 39.02619, 39.002929000000002,
38.982886000000001, 38.954034999999998, 38.944926000000002, 38.919960000000003,
38.925261999999996, 38.934922999999998, 38.949373000000001, 38.950133999999998,
38.952649000000001, 38.969692000000002, 38.988512999999998, 39.010652, 39.033088999999997,
39.053493000000003, 39.072752999999999], [-120.15724399999999, -120.15818299999999, -
120.15600400000001, -120.14564599999999, -120.141285, -120.10889900000001, -
120.09528500000002, -120.077596, -120.045428, -120.0119, -119.98897100000002, -
119.95124099999998, -119.93270099999998, -119.927131, -119.92685999999999, -
119.926362000000001, -119.92844600000001, -119.911036, -119.942834, -119.94413000000002, -
119.94555200000001, -119.95411000000001, -119.941327, -119.94605900000001, -
119.97527599999999, -119.99445, -120.028998, -120.066335, -120.07867300000001, -120.089985,
-120.112227, -120.09790700000001, -120.10881000000001, -120.116692, -120.117847, -
120.11727899999998, -120.14398199999999]];
</script>

<p>
    <b>Status: </b> <span id="progress">ready</span>
</p>
```

The Application in Action

To see this example in action, there are two prerequisites: the pages have to be served up from different domains, and the target page has to be served up by a web server that understands CORS headers. A CORS-compliant Python script that can handle incoming cross-origin XMLHttpRequests is included in the example code for this chapter. You can run the demo on your local machine by performing the following steps:

1. Update your hosts file (C:\Windows\system32\drivers\etc\hosts on Windows or /etc/hosts on Unix/Linux) by adding two entries pointing to your localhost (IP address 127.0.0.1) as shown in the following example:

    ```
    127.0.0.1 geodata.example.net
    127.0.0.1 portal.example.com
    ```

---

2. Install Python, which includes the lightweight `SimpleHTTPServer` web server, if you did not do so for the previous example.

3. Navigate to the directory that contains the example file (`crossOrignUpload.html`) and the Python CORS server script (`CORSServer.py`).

4. Start Python in this directory as follows:
   `python CORSServer.py 9999`

5. Open a browser and navigate to `http://portal.example.com:9999/crossOriginUpload.html`. You should now see the page shown in Figure 5.5.

Practical Extras

Sometimes there are techniques that don't fit into our regular examples, but that nonetheless apply to many types of HTML5 applications. We present to you some short, but common, practical extras here.

Structured Data

Early versions of `postMessage` only supported strings. Later revisions allowed other types of data including JavaScript objects, canvas imageData, and files. Support for different object types will vary by browser as the specification develops.

In some browsers, the limitations on JavaScript objects that can be sent with `postMessage` are the same as those for JSON data. In particular, data structures with cycles may not be allowed. An example of this is a list containing itself.

Framebusting

Framebusting is a technique for ensuring that your content is not loaded in an iframe. An application can detect that its window is not the outermost window (`window.top`) and subsequently break out of its containing frame, as shown in the following example.

```
if (window !== window.top) {
    window.top.location = location;
}
```

However, there may be certain partner pages that you want to allow to frame your content. One solution is to use `postMessage` to handshake between cooperating iframes and containing pages, as shown in the Listing 5-11.

Listing 5-10. Using postMessage in an iframe to handshake with a trusted partner page

```
var framebustTimer;
var timeout = 3000; // 3 second framebust timeout

if (window !== window.top) {
    framebustTimer = setTimeout(
        function() {
            window.top.location = location;
        }, timeout);
}

window.addEventListener("message", function(e) {
    switch(e.origin) {
        case trustedFramer:
            clearTimeout(framebustTimer);
            break;
    }
), true);
```

Summary

In this chapter, you have seen how HTML5 Cross Document Messaging and XMLHttpRequest Level 2 can be used to create compelling applications that can securely communicate cross-origin.

First, we discussed **postMessage** and the origin security concept—two key elements of HTML5 communication—and then we showed you how the **postMessage** API can be used to communicate between iframes, tabs, and windows.

Next, we discussed XMLHttpRequest Level 2—an improved version of XMLHttpRequest. We showed you in which areas XMLHttpRequest has been improved; most importantly in the readystatechange events area. We then showed you how you can use XMLHttpRequest to make cross-origin requests and how to use the new progress events.

Finally, we wrapped up the chapter with a few practical examples. In the next chapter, we'll demonstrate how HTML5 WebSockets enables you to stream real-time data to an application with incredible simplicity and minimal overhead.

■■■

## CHAPTER 6

Using the HTML5 WebSocket API

In this chapter, we'll explore what you can do with the most powerful communication feature in the HTML5 specification: *HTML5 WebSockets*, which defines a full-duplex communication channel that operates through a single socket over the web. Websocket is not just another incremental enhancement to conventional HTTP communications; it represents a large advance, especially for real-time, event-driven web applications.

HTML5 WebSockets provide such an improvement from the old, convoluted "hacks" that are used to simulate a full-duplex connection in a browser that it prompted Google's Ian Hickson—the HTML5 specification lead—to say:

> *"Reducing kilobytes of data to 2 bytes…and reducing latency from 150ms to 50ms is far more than marginal. In fact, these two factors alone are enough to make WebSockets seriously interesting to Google."*
>
> —www.ietf.org/mail-archive/web/hybi/current/msg00784.html

We'll show you in detail just why HTML5 WebSockets provide such a dramatic improvement and you'll see how—in one fell swoop—HTML5 WebSockets makes all the old Comet and Ajax polling, long-polling, and streaming solutions obsolete.

Overview of HTML5 WebSockets

Let's take a look at how HTML5 WebSockets can offer a reduction of unnecessary network traffic and latency by comparing HTTP solutions to full duplex "real time" browser communication with WebSockets.

Real-Time and HTTP

Normally when a browser visits a web page, an HTTP request is sent to the web server that hosts that page. The web server acknowledges this request and sends back the response. In many cases—for example, for stock prices, news reports, ticket sales, traffic patterns, medical device readings, and so on—the response could be stale by the time the browser renders the page. If you want to get the most up-to-date real-time information, you can constantly refresh that page manually, but that's obviously not a great solution.

Current attempts to provide real-time web applications largely revolve around polling and other server-side push technologies, the most notable of which is "Comet", which delays the completion of an HTTP response to deliver messages to the client.

With polling, the browser sends HTTP requests at regular intervals and immediately receives a response. This technique was the first attempt for the browser to deliver real-time information. Obviously, this is a good solution if the exact interval of message delivery is known, because you can synchronize the client request to occur only when information is available on the server. However, real-time data is often not that predictable, making unnecessary requests inevitable and as a result, many connections are opened and closed needlessly in low-message-rate situations.

With long-polling, the browser sends a request to the server and the server keeps the request open for a set period of time. If a notification is received within that period, a response containing the message is sent to the client. If a notification is not received within the set time period, the server sends a response to terminate the open request. It is important to understand, however, that when you have a high message-volume, long-polling does not provide any substantial performance improvements over traditional polling.

With streaming, the browser sends a complete request, but the server sends and maintains an open response that is continuously updated and kept open indefinitely (or for a set period of time). The response is then updated whenever a message is ready to be sent, but the server never signals to complete the response, thus keeping the connection open to deliver future messages. However, since streaming is still encapsulated in HTTP, intervening firewalls and proxy servers may choose to buffer the response, increasing the latency of the message delivery. Therefore, many streaming solutions fall back to long-polling in case a buffering proxy server is detected. Alternatively, TLS (SSL) connections can be used to shield the response from being buffered, but in that case the setup and tear down of each connection taxes the available server resources more heavily.

Ultimately, all of these methods for providing real-time data involve HTTP request and response headers, which contain lots of additional, unnecessary header data and introduce latency. On top of that, full-duplex connectivity requires more than just the downstream connection from server to client. In an effort to simulate full-duplex communication over half-duplex HTTP, many of today's solutions use two connections: one for the downstream and one for the upstream. The maintenance and coordination of these two connections introduces significant overhead in terms of resource consumption and adds lots of complexity. Simply put, HTTP wasn't designed for real-time, full-duplex communication as you can see in the Figure 5-1, which shows the complexities associated with building a web application that displays real-time data from a back-end data source using a publish/subscribe model over half-duplex HTTP.

Figure 6-1. *The complexity of real-time HTTP applications*

It gets even worse when you try to scale out those solutions. Simulating bi-directional browser communication over HTTP is error-prone and complex and all that complexity does not scale. Even though your end users might be enjoying something that looks like a real-time web application, this "real-time" experience has a high price tag. It's a price that you will pay in additional latency, unnecessary network traffic and a drag on CPU performance.

Understanding HTML5 WebSockets

HTML5 WebSocket was first defined as "TCPConnection" in the Communications section of the HTML5 specification by Ian Hickson (lead writer of the HTML5 specification). The specification evolved and changed to WebSocket, which is now an independent specification (just like Geolocation, Web Workers and so on), to keep the discussion focused.

WHAT DO WEBSOCKETS AND MODEL TRAINS HAVE IN COMMON?

Peter says: "Ian Hickson is quite the model train enthusiast; he has been planning ways to control trains from computers ever since 1984 when Marklin first came out with a digital controller, long before the web even existed.

At the that time, Ian added TCPConnection to the HTML5 specification, he was working on a program to control a model train set from a browser and he was using the prevalent pre-WebSocket "hanging GET" and XHR techniques to achieve browser to train communication. The train-controller program would have been a lot easier to build if there was a way to have socket communication in a browser—much like traditional asynchronous client/server communication model that is found in "fat" clients. So, inspired by what *could* be possible, the (train) wheels had been set in motion and the WebSocket train had left the station. Next stop: the real-time web."

139

The WebSocket Handshake

To establish a WebSocket connection, the client and server upgrade from the HTTP protocol to the WebSocket protocol during their initial handshake, as shown in Listing 6-1. Note that this connection description represents draft 76 of the protocol; the connection handshake may change during future specification revisions.

Listing 6-1. The WebSocket Upgrade handshake

```
From client to server:
GET /demo HTTP/1.1
Host: example.com
Connection: Upgrade
Sec-WebSocket-Key2: 12998 5 Y3 1 .P00
Sec-WebSocket-Protocol: sample
Upgrade: WebSocket
Sec-WebSocket-Key1: 4@1 46546xW%0l 1 5
Origin: http://example.com

[8-byte security key]

From server to client:
HTTP/1.1 101 WebSocket Protocol Handshake
Upgrade: WebSocket
Connection: Upgrade
WebSocket-Origin: http://example.com
WebSocket-Location: ws://example.com/demo
WebSocket-Protocol: sample

[16-byte hash response]
```

Once established, WebSocket messages can be sent back and forth between the client and the server in full-duplex mode. This means that text-based messages can be sent full-duplex, in either direction at the same time. On the network each message starts with a **0x00** byte, ends with a **0xFF** byte, and contains UTF-8 data in between.

The WebSocket Interface

Along with the definition of the WebSocket protocol, the specification also defines the WebSocket interface for use in JavaScript applications. Listing 6-2 shows the **WebSocket** interface.

Listing 6-2. The WebSocket interface

```
[Constructor(in DOMString url, in optional DOMString protocol)]
interface WebSocket {
  readonly attribute DOMString URL;

  // ready state
  const unsigned short CONNECTING = 0;
  const unsigned short OPEN = 1;
  const unsigned short CLOSED = 2;
  readonly attribute unsigned short readyState;
  readonly attribute unsigned long bufferedAmount;

  // networking
  attribute Function onopen;
  attribute Function onmessage;
  attribute Function onclose;
  boolean send(in DOMString data);
  void close();
};
WebSocket implements EventTarget;
```

Using the `WebSocket` interface is straightforward. To connect a remote host, just create a new `WebSocket` instance, providing the new object with a URL that represents the end-point to which you wish to connect. Note that a `ws://` and `wss://` prefix indicate a WebSocket and a secure WebSocket connection, respectively.

A WebSocket connection is established by upgrading from the HTTP protocol to the WebSocket protocol during the initial handshake between the client and the server, over the same underlying TCP/IP connection. Once established, WebSocket data frames can be sent back and forth between the client and the server in full-duplex mode. The connection itself is exposed via the `message` event and `send` method defined by the `WebSocket` interface. In your code, you use asynchronous event listeners to handle each phase of the connection life cycle.

```
myWebSocket.onopen = function(evt) { alert("Connection open ..."); };
myWebSocket.onmessage = function(evt) { alert( "Received Message: "  + evt.data); };
myWebSocket.onclose = function(evt) { alert("Connection closed."); };
```

A Dramatic Reduction in Unnecessary Network Traffic and Latency

So how efficient can WebSockets be? Let's compare a polling application and a WebSocket application side by side. To illustrate polling, we will examine a simple web application in which a web page requests real-time stock data from a RabbitMQ message broker using a traditional publish/subscribe model. It does this by polling a Java Servlet that is hosted on a web server. The RabbitMQ message broker receives data from a fictitious stock price feed with continuously updating prices. The web page connects and subscribes to a specific stock channel (a topic on the message broker) and uses an XMLHttpRequest to poll for updates once per second. When updates are received, some calculations are performed and the stock data is shown in a table as shown in Figure 6-2.

COMPANY	SYMBOL	PRICE	CHANGE	SPARKLINE	OPEN	LOW	HIGH
THE WALT DISNEY COMPANY	DIS	27.65	0.56		27.09	24.39	29.80
GARMIN LTD.	GRMN	35.14	0.35		34.79	31.31	38.27
SANDISK CORPORATION	SNDK	20.11	-0.13		20.24	18.22	22.26
GOODRICH CORPORATION	GR	49.99	-2.35		52.34	47.11	57.57
NVIDIA CORPORATION	NVDA	13.92	0.07		13.85	12.47	15.23
CHEVRON CORPORATION	CVX	67.77	-0.53		68.30	61.49	75.11
THE ALLSTATE CORPORATION	ALL	30.88	-0.14		31.02	27.92	34.12
EXXON MOBIL CORPORATION	XOM	65.66	-0.86		66.52	59.87	73.17
METLIFE INC.	MET	35.58	-0.15		35.73	32.16	39.30

Figure 6-2. A JavaScript stock ticker application

It all looks great, but a look under the hood reveals there are some serious issues with this application. For example, in Mozilla Firefox with Firebug, you can see that GET requests hammer the server at one-second intervals. Turning on the Live HTTP Headers add-on reveals the shocking amount of header overhead that is associated with each request. Listings 6-3 and 6-4 show the HTTP header data for just a single request and response.

Listing 6-3. HTTP request header

```
GET /PollingStock//PollingStock HTTP/1.1
Host: localhost:8080
User-Agent: Mozilla/5.0 (Windows; U; Windows NT 5.1; en-US; rv:1.9.1.5) Gecko/20091102
 Firefox/3.5.5
Accept: text/html,application/xhtml+xml,application/xml;q=0.9,*/*;q=0.8
Accept-Language: en-us
Accept-Encoding: gzip,deflate
Accept-Charset: ISO-8859-1,utf-8;q=0.7,*;q=0.7
Keep-Alive: 300
Connection: keep-alive
Referer: http://www.example.com/PollingStock/
Cookie: showInheritedConstant=false; showInheritedProtectedConstant=false;
 showInheritedProperty=false; showInheritedProtectedProperty=false;
 showInheritedMethod=false; showInheritedProtectedMethod=false;
 showInheritedEvent=false; showInheritedStyle=false; showInheritedEffect=false
```

Listing 6-4. HTTP response header

```
HTTP/1.x 200 OK
X-Powered-By: Servlet/2.5
Server: Sun Java System Application Server 9.1_02
Content-Type: text/html;charset=UTF-8
Content-Length: 21
Date: Sat, 07 Nov 2009 00:32:46 GMT
```

Just for fun (ha!), we can count all the characters. The total HTTP request and response header information overhead contains 871 bytes and that does not even include any data. Of course, this is just an example and you can have less than 871 bytes of header data, but there are also common cases where the header data exceeded 2,000 bytes. In this example application, the data for a typical stock topic message is only about 20 characters long. As you can see, it is effectively drowned out by the excessive header information, which was not even required in the first place.

So, what happens when you deploy this application to a large number of users? Let's take a look at the network overhead for just the HTTP request and response header data associated with this polling application in three different use cases.

- **Use case A**: 1,000 clients polling every second: Network traffic is $(871 \times 1,000) =$ 871,000 bytes = 6,968,000 bits per second (6.6 Mbps)

- **Use case B**: 10,000 clients polling every second: Network traffic is $(871 \times 10,000) =$ 8,710,000 bytes = 69,680,000 bits per second (66 Mbps)

- **Use case C**: 100,000 clients polling every 1 second: Network traffic is $(871 \times 100,000) = 87,100,000$ bytes = 696,800,000 bits per second (665 Mbps)

That's an enormous amount of unnecessary network overhead. Consider if we rebuilt the application to use HTML5 WebSockets, adding an event handler to the web page to asynchronously listen for stock update messages from the message broker (more on that in just a little bit). Each of these messages is a WebSocket frame that has just two bytes of overhead (instead of 871). Take a look at how that affects the network overhead in our three use cases.

- **Use case A**: 1,000 clients receive 1 message per second: Network traffic is $(2 \times 1,000) = 2,000$ bytes = 16,000 bits per second (0.015 Mbps)

- **Use case B**: 10,000 clients receive 1 message per second: Network traffic is $(2 \times 10,000) = 20,000$ bytes = 160,000 bits per second (0.153 Mbps)

- **Use case C**: 100,000 clients receive 1 message per second: Network traffic is $(2 \times 100,000) = 200,000$ bytes = 1,600,000 bits per second (1.526 Mbps)

As you can see in Figure 6-3, HTML5 WebSockets provide a dramatic reduction of unnecessary network traffic compared to the polling solution.

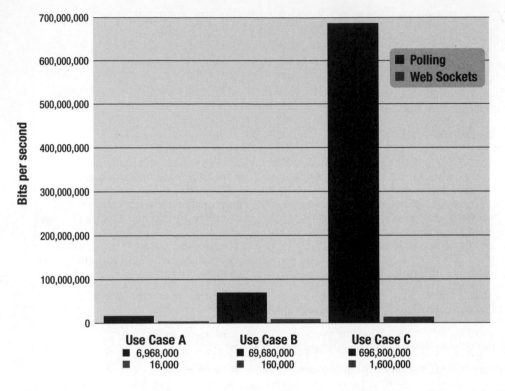

Figure 6-3. Comparison of the unnecessary network overhead between the polling and the WebSocket applications

And what about the reduction in latency? Take a look at Figure 6-4. In the top half, you can see the latency of the half-duplex polling solution. If we assume, for this example, that it takes 50 milliseconds for a message to travel from the server to the browser, then the polling application introduces a lot of extra latency, because a new request has to be sent to the server when the response is complete. This new request takes another 50ms and during this time the server cannot send any messages to the browser, resulting in additional server memory consumption.

In the bottom half of the figure, you see the reduction in latency provided by the WebSocket solution. Once the connection is upgraded to WebSocket, messages can flow from the server to the browser the moment they arrive. It still takes 50 ms for messages to travel from the server to the browser, but the WebSocket connection remains open so there is no need to send another request to the server.

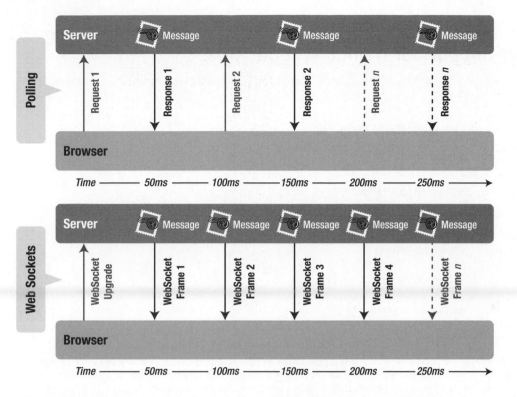

Figure 6-4. Latency comparison between the polling and WebSocket applications

HTML5 WebSockets provides an enormous step forward in the scalability of the real-time web. As you have seen in this chapter, HTML5 WebSockets can provide a 500:1 or—depending on the size of the HTTP headers—even a 1000:1 reduction in unnecessary HTTP header traffic and 3:1 reduction in latency.

Browser Support for HTML5 WebSockets

As shown in Table 6-1, HTML5 WebSockets is supported and planned in various browsers at the time of this writing.

Table 6-1. *Browser support for HTML5 WebSocket*

Browser	Details
Chrome	Supported in version 4+
Firefox	Supported in version 4+
Internet Explorer	Not supported yet
Opera	Not supported yet
Safari	Supported in version 5+

Due to the varying levels of support, it is a good idea to first test if HTML5 WebSockets are supported, before you use these elements. The section "*Checking for Browser Support*" later in this chapter will show you how you can programmatically check for browser support.

Writing a Simple Echo WebSocket Server

Before you can use the WebSocket API, you need a server that supports WebSockets. In this section we'll take a look at how a simple WebSocket "echo" server is written. To run the examples for this chapter, we have included a simple WebSocket server written in Python. The sample code for the following examples is located in the WebSockets section of the book web site.

There are lots of WebSocket server implementations out there already and even more under development. The following are just a couple of the existing WebSocket servers:

- **Kaazing WebSocket Gateway**—a Java-based WebSocket Gateway

- **mod_pywebsocket**—a Python-based extension for the Apache HTTP Server

- **Netty**—a Java network framework which includes WebSocket support

- **node.js**—a server-side JavaScript framework on which multiple WebSocket servers have been written

Kaazing's WebSocket Gateway includes full client-side WebSocket emulation support for browsers without native implementation of WebSocket, which allows you to code against the WebSocket API today and have your code work in all browsers.

To run the Python WebSocket echo server accepting connections at `ws://localhost:8080/echo`, open a command prompt, navigate to the folder that contains the file, and issue the following command:

```
python websocket.py
```

We have also included a *broadcast* server that accepts connections at `ws://localhost:8080/broadcast`. Contrary to the echo server, any WebSocket message sent to this particular server implementation will bounce back to *everyone* that is currently connected. It's a very simple way to broadcast messages to multiple listeners. To run the broadcast server, open a command prompt, navigate to the folder that contains the file, and issue the following command:

```
python broadcast.py
```

Both scripts make use of the example WebSocket protocol library in `websocket.py`. You can add handlers for other paths that implement additional server- side behavior.

■ **Note** This is only a server for the WebSocket protocol and it cannot respond to HTTP requests. Because WebSocket connections begin with a subset of legal HTTP and rely on the Upgrade header, other servers can serve both WebSocket and HTTP on the same port.

Let's see what happens when a browser tries to communicate with this server. When the browser makes a request to the WebSocket URL, the server sends back the headers that finish the WebSocket handshake. A WebSocket handshake response must begin with *exactly* the line `HTTP/1.1 101 WebSocket`

`Protocol Handshake`. In fact, the order and content of the handshake headers are more strictly defined than HTTP headers.

■ **Note** If you are implementing a WebSocket server, you should refer to the protocol draft at the IETF at `http://tools.ietf.org/html/draft-hixie-thewebsocketprotocol` or the latest specification.

```
# write out response headers
self.send_bytes("HTTP/1.1 101 Web Socket Protocol Handshake\r\n")
self.send_bytes("Upgrade: WebSocket\r\n")
self.send_bytes("Connection: Upgrade\r\n")
self.send_bytes("Sec-WebSocket-Origin: %s\r\n" % headers["Origin"])
self.send_bytes("Sec-WebSocket-Location: %s\r\n" % headers["Location"])

if "Sec-WebSocket-Protocol" in headers:
    protocol = headers["Sec-WebSocket-Protocol"]
    self.send_bytes("Sec-WebSocket-Protocol: %s\r\n" % protocol)

self.send_bytes("\r\n")
# write out hashed response token
self.send_bytes(response_token)
```

After the handshake, the client and server can send messages at any time. Each connection is represented on the server by a `WebSocketConnection` instance. The `WebSocketConnection`'s `send` function, shown below, transforms a string for the WebSocket protocol. The `0x00` and `0xFF` bytes surrounding the UFT-8 encoded string mark the frame boundary. In this server, each WebSocket connection is an `asyncore.dispatcher_with_send`, which is an asynchronous socket wrapper with support for buffered sends.

■ **Note** There are many other asynchronous I/O frameworks for Python and other languages. Asyncore was chosen because it is included in the Python standard library. Note also that both version 75 and 76 of the WebSocket protocol are supported in this implementation. Strictly speaking, supporting both versions at the same time is not allowed. This is a simple example designed for testing and illustation.

`WebSocketConnection` inherits from `asyncore.dispatcher_with_send` and overrides the `send` method to UTF-8 encode strings and add WebSocket string framing.

```
def send(self, s):
  if self.readystate == "open":
    self.send_bytes("\x00")
    self.send_bytes(s.encode("UTF8"))
    self.send_bytes("\xFF")
```

Handlers for `WebSocketConnections` in `websocket.py` follow a simplified dispatcher interface. The handler's `dispatch()` method is called with the payload of each frame the connection receives. The `EchoHandler` sends back each message to the sender.

```python
class EchoHandler(object):
    """
    The EchoHandler repeats each incoming string to the same WebSocket.
    """

    def __init__(self, conn):
        self.conn = conn

    def dispatch(self, data):
        self.conn.send("echo: " + data)
```

The basic broadcast server `broadcast.py` works in much the same way, but in this case when the broadcast handler receives a string, it sends it back on all connected WebSockets as shown in the following example.

```python
class BroadcastHandler(object):
    """
    The BroadcastHandler repeats incoming strings to every connected
    WebSocket.
    """

    def __init__(self, conn):
        self.conn = conn

    def dispatch(self, data):
        for session in self.conn.server.sessions:
            session.send(data)
```

The handler in `broadcast.py` provides a lightweight message broadcaster that simply sends and receives strings. This is sufficient for the purposes of our example. Be aware that this broadcast service does not perform any input verification as would be desirable in a production message server. A production WebSocket server should, at the very least, verify the format of incoming data.

For completeness, Listings 6-5 and 6-6 provide the complete code for `websocket.py` and `broadcast.py`. Note that this is just an example server implementation; it is not suited for production deployment.

Listing 6-5. complete code for websocket.py

```python
#!/usr/bin/env python

import asyncore
import socket
import struct
import time
import hashlib

class WebSocketConnection(asyncore.dispatcher_with_send):
```

```python
    def __init__(self, conn, server):
        asyncore.dispatcher_with_send.__init__(self, conn)

        self.server = server
        self.server.sessions.append(self)
        self.readystate = "connecting"
        self.buffer = ""

    def handle_read(self):
        data = self.recv(1024)
        self.buffer += data
        if self.readystate == "connecting":
            self.parse_connecting()
        elif self.readystate == "open":
            self.parse_frametype()

    def handle_close(self):
        self.server.sessions.remove(self)
        self.close()

    def parse_connecting(self):
        header_end = self.buffer.find("\r\n\r\n")
        if header_end == -1:
            return
        else:
            header = self.buffer[:header_end]
            # remove header and four bytes of line endings from buffer
            self.buffer = self.buffer[header_end+4:]
            header_lines = header.split("\r\n")
            headers = {}

            # validate HTTP request and construct location
            method, path, protocol = header_lines[0].split(" ")
            if method != "GET" or protocol != "HTTP/1.1" or path[0] != "/":
                self.terminate()
                return

            # parse headers
            for line in header_lines[1:]:
                key, value = line.split(": ")
                headers[key] = value

            headers["Location"] = "ws://" + headers["Host"] + path

            self.readystate = "open"
            self.handler = self.server.handlers.get(path, None)(self)

            if "Sec-WebSocket-Key1" in headers.keys():
                self.send_server_handshake_76(headers)
            else:
                self.send_server_handshake_75(headers)
```

```python
def terminate(self):
    self.ready_state = "closed"
    self.close()

def send_server_handshake_76(self, headers):
    """
    Send the WebSocket Protocol v.76 handshake response
    """

    key1 = headers["Sec-WebSocket-Key1"]
    key2 = headers["Sec-WebSocket-Key2"]
    # read additional 8 bytes from buffer
    key3, self.buffer = self.buffer[:8], self.buffer[8:]

    response_token = self.calculate_key(key1, key2, key3)

    # write out response headers
    self.send_bytes("HTTP/1.1 101 Web Socket Protocol Handshake\r\n")
    self.send_bytes("Upgrade: WebSocket\r\n")
    self.send_bytes("Connection: Upgrade\r\n")
    self.send_bytes("Sec-WebSocket-Origin: %s\r\n" % headers["Origin"])
    self.send_bytes("Sec-WebSocket-Location: %s\r\n" % headers["Location"])

    if "Sec-WebSocket-Protocol" in headers:
        protocol = headers["Sec-WebSocket-Protocol"]
        self.send_bytes("Sec-WebSocket-Protocol: %s\r\n" % protocol)

    self.send_bytes("\r\n")
    # write out hashed response token
    self.send_bytes(response_token)

def calculate_key(self, key1, key2, key3):
    # parse keys 1 and 2 by extracting numerical characters
    num1 = int("".join([digit for digit in list(key1) if digit.isdigit()]))
    spaces1 = len([char for char in list(key1) if char == " "])
    num2 = int("".join([digit for digit in list(key2) if digit.isdigit()]))
    spaces2 = len([char for char in list(key2) if char == " "])

    combined = struct.pack(">II", num1/spaces1, num2/spaces2) + key3
    # md5 sum the combined bytes
    return hashlib.md5(combined).digest()

def send_server_handshake_75(self, headers):
    """
    Send the WebSocket Protocol v.75 handshake response
    """

    self.send_bytes("HTTP/1.1 101 Web Socket Protocol Handshake\r\n")
    self.send_bytes("Upgrade: WebSocket\r\n")
    self.send_bytes("Connection: Upgrade\r\n")
    self.send_bytes("WebSocket-Origin: %s\r\n" % headers["Origin"])
    self.send_bytes("WebSocket-Location: %s\r\n" % headers["Location"])
```

```python
        if "Protocol" in headers:
            self.send_bytes("WebSocket-Protocol: %s\r\n" % headers["Protocol"])

        self.send_bytes("\r\n")

    def parse_frametype(self):
        while len(self.buffer):
            type_byte = self.buffer[0]
            if type_byte == "\x00":
                if not self.parse_textframe():
                    return

    def parse_textframe(self):
        terminator_index = self.buffer.find("\xFF")
        if terminator_index != -1:
            frame = self.buffer[1:terminator_index]
            self.buffer = self.buffer[terminator_index+1:]
            s = frame.decode("UTF8")
            self.handler.dispatch(s)
            return True
        else:
            # incomplete frame
            return false

    def send(self, s):
        if self.readystate == "open":
            self.send_bytes("\x00")
            self.send_bytes(s.encode("UTF8"))
            self.send_bytes("\xFF")

    def send_bytes(self, bytes):
        asyncore.dispatcher_with_send.send(self, bytes)


class EchoHandler(object):
    """
    The EchoHandler repeats each incoming string to the same Web Socket.
    """

    def __init__(self, conn):
        self.conn = conn

    def dispatch(self, data):
        self.conn.send("echo: " + data)


class WebSocketServer(asyncore.dispatcher):

    def __init__(self, port=80, handlers=None):
        asyncore.dispatcher.__init__(self)
        self.handlers = handlers
```

```
        self.sessions = []
        self.port = port
        self.create_socket(socket.AF_INET, socket.SOCK_STREAM)
        self.set_reuse_addr()
        self.bind(("", port))
        self.listen(5)

    def handle_accept(self):
        conn, addr = self.accept()
        session = WebSocketConnection(conn, self)

if __name__ == "__main__":
    print "Starting WebSocket Server"
    WebSocketServer(port=8080, handlers={"/echo": EchoHandler})
    asyncore.loop()
```

You may have noticed an unusual key calculation in the WebSocket handshake. This is intended to prevent cross-protocol attacks. In short, this should stop malicious WebSocket client code from spoofing connections to non-WebSocker servers. This part of the handshake design is still undergoing discussion as of draft-76.

Listing 6-6. complete code for broadcast.py

```
#!/usr/bin/env python

import asyncore
from websocket import WebSocketServer

class BroadcastHandler(object):
    """
    The BroadcastHandler repeats incoming strings to every connected
    WebSocket.
    """

    def __init__(self, conn):
        self.conn = conn

    def dispatch(self, data):
        for session in self.conn.server.sessions:
            session.send(data)

    if __name__ == "__main__":
        print "Starting WebSocket broadcast server"
        WebSocketServer(port=8000, handlers={"/broadcast": BroadcastHandler})
            asyncore.loop()
```

Now that we've got a working echo server, we need to write the client side.

Using the HTML5 WebSocket API

In this section, we'll explore the use of HTML5 WebSocket in more detail.

Checking for Browser Support

Before you use the HTML5 WebSocket API, you will want to make sure there is support in the browser for what you're about to do. This way, you can provide some alternate text, prompting the users of your application to upgrade to a more up-to-date browser. Listing 6-9 shows one way you can test for browser support.

Listing 6-7. Checking for browser support

```
function loadDemo() {
  if (window.WebSocket) {
    document.getElementById("support").innerHTML = "HTML5 WebSocket is supported in your
                                  browser.";
  } else {
    document.getElementById("support").innerHTML = "HTML5 WebSocket is not supported in
                                  your browser.";
  }
}
```

In this example, you test for browser support in the `loadDemo` function, which might be called when the application's page is loaded. A call to `window.WebSocket` will return the `WebSocket` object if it exists, or trigger the failure case if it does not. In this case, the page is updated to reflect whether there is browser support or not by updating a previously defined `support` element on the page with a suitable message.

Another way to see if HTML5 WebSocket is supported in your browser, is to use the browser's console (Firebug or Chrome Developer Tools for example). Figure 6-5 shows how you can test whether WebSockets is supported natively in Google Chrome (if it is not, the `window.WebSocket` command returns "undefined.")

Figure 6-5. Testing WebSocket support in Google Chrome Developer Tools

Basic API Usage

The sample code for the following examples is located on the book web site in the WebSockets section. This folder contains a websocket.html file and a broadcast.html file (and a tracker.html file used in the following section) as well as the WebSocket server code shown previously that can be run in Python.

Creating a WebSocket object and Connecting to a WebSocket Server

Using the WebSocket interface is straight-forward. To connect to an end-point, just create a new WebSocket instance, providing the new object with a URL that represents the end-point to which you wish to connect. You can use the ws:// and wss:// prefixes are to indicate a WebSocket and a WebSocket Secure connection, respectively.

```
url = "ws://localhost:8080/echo";
w = new WebSocket(url);
```

Adding Event Listeners

WebSocket programming follows an asynchronous programming model; once you have an open socket, you simply wait for events. You don't have to actively poll the server anymore. To do this, you add callback functions to the WebSocket object to listen for events.

A WebSocket object dispatches three events: open, close, and message. The open event fires when a connection is established, the message event fires when messages are received, and the close event fires when the WebSocket connection is closed. As in most JavaScript APIs, there are corresponding callbacks (onopen, onmessage, and onclose) that are called when the events are dispatched.

```
w.onopen = function() {
  log("open");
  w.send("thank you for accepting this websocket request");
}
w.onmessage = function(e) {
  log(e.data);
}
w.onclose = function(e) {
  log("closed");
}
```

Sending Messages

While the socket is open (that is, after the onopen listener is called and before the onclose listener is called), you can use the send method to send messages. After sending the message, you can also call close to terminate the connection, but you can also leave the connection open.

```
document.getElementById("sendButton").onclick = function() {
  w.send(document.getElementById("inputMessage").value);
}
```

That's it. Bi-directional browser communication made simple. For completeness, Listing 6-8 shows the entire HTML page with the WebSocket code.

Listing 6-8. websocket.html code

```html
<!DOCTYPE html>
<title>WebSocket Test Page</title>
<script>

    var log = function(s) {
        if (document.readyState !== "complete") {
            log.buffer.push(s);
        } else {
            document.getElementById("output").innerHTML += (s + "\n");
        }
    }
    log.buffer = [];

    url = "ws://localhost:8080/echo";
    w = new WebSocket(url);
    w.onopen = function() {
        log("open");
        w.send("thank you for accepting this WebSocket request");
    }
    w.onmessage = function(e) {
        log(e.data);
    }
    w.onclose = function(e) {
        log("closed");
    }

    window.onload = function() {
        log(log.buffer.join("\n"));
        document.getElementById("sendButton").onclick = function() {
            w.send(document.getElementById("inputMessage").value);
        }
    }
</script>

<input type="text" id="inputMessage" value="Hello, WebSocket!"><button
 id="sendButton">Send</button>
<pre id="output"></pre>
```

Running the WebSocket Page

To test the websocket.html page that contains the WebSocket code, open a command prompt, navigate to the folder that contains the WebSocket code, and issue the following command to host the HTML file:

```
python -m SimpleHTTPServer 9999
```

Next, open another command prompt, navigate to the folder that contains the WebSocket code, and issue the following command to run thc Python WebSocket server:

```
python websocket.py
```

Finally, open a browser that supports WebSockets natively and navigate to `http://localhost:9999/websocket.html`.

Figure 6-6 shows the web page in action.

Figure 6-6. *websocket.html in action*

The example code folder also contains a web page that connects to the broadcast service that was created in the previous section. To see that action, close the command prompt that is running the WebSocket server and navigate to the folder that contains the WebSocket code, and issue the following command to run the python WebSocket server.

```
python broadcast.py
```

Open two separate browsers that supports WebSockets natively and navigate (in each browser) to `http://localhost:9999/broadcast.html`.

Figure 6-7 shows the broadcast WebSocket server in action on two separate web pages.

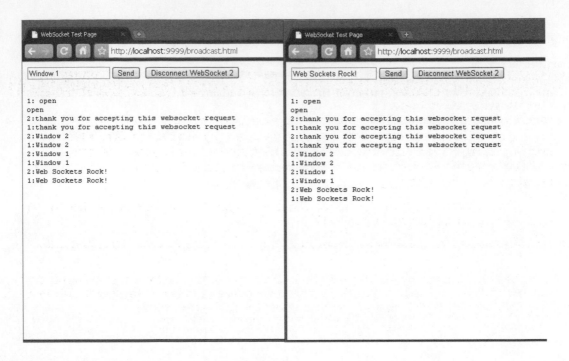

Figure 6-7. broadcast.html in action in two browsers

Building an Application with HTML5 WebSockets

Now that we've seen the basics of WebSocket, it's time to tackle something a little more substantial. Previously, we used the HTML5 Geolocation API to build an application that allowed us to calculate distance traveled directly inside our web page. We can utilize those same Geolocation techniques, mixed together with our new support for WebSockets, and create a simple application that keeps multiple participants connected: a location tracker.

■ **Note** We'll be using the broadcast WebSocket server described above, so if you aren't familiar with it you should consider taking some time to learn its basics.

In this application, we'll combine the WebSocket and Geolocation support by determining our location and broadcasting it to all available listeners. Everyone who loads this application and connects to the same broadcast server will regularly send their geographic location using the WebSocket. At the same time, the application will listen for any messages from the server and update in real-time display entries for everyone it hears about. In a race scenario, this sort of application could keep runners informed of the location of all their competitors and prompt them to run faster (or slow down).

This tiny application does not include any personal information other than latitude and longitude location. Name, date of birth, and favorite ice cream flavor are kept strictly confidential.

YOU WERE WARNED!

Brian says: "This application is all about sharing your personal information. Granted, only a location is shared. However, if you (or your users) didn't understand the browser warning that was offered when the Geolocation API was first accessed, this application should be a stark lesson in how easy it will be to transmit sensitive data to remote locations. Make sure your users understand the consequences of agreeing to submit location data.

When in doubt, go above and beyond in your application to let the user know how their sensitive data can be used. Make opting out the easiest path of action."

But that's enough warnings… Let's dig into the code. As always, the entire code sample is located online for your perusal. We'll focus on the most important parts here. The finished application will look like Figure 6-8. Although ideally, this would be enhanced by overlaying it on a map.

HTML5 WebSocket / Geolocation Tracker

Geolocation:
Location updated at Sun Jan 17 2010 23:37:04 GMT-0800 (Pacific Standard Time)

WebSocket:
Updated location from Me

Me \ Lat: 37.3993806 \ Lon: -122.0763057

Figure 6-8. The Location Tracker application

Coding the HTML File

The HTML markup for this application will be kept deliberately simple so that we can focus on the data at hand. How simple?

```
<body onload="loadDemo()">

<h1>HTML5 WebSocket / Geolocation Tracker</h1>

<div><strong>Geolocation</strong>: <p id="geoStatus">HTML5 Geolocation is
 <strong>not</strong> supported in your browser.</p></div>
<div><strong>WebSocket</strong>: <p id="socketStatus">WebSockets are <strong>not</strong>
 supported in your browser.</p></div>

</body>
```

Simple enough that we only include a title and a few status areas: one status area for Geolocation updates, and another to log any WebSocket activity. The actual visuals for location data will be inserted into the page as messages are received in real-time.

By default, our status messages indicate that a viewer's browser does not support either Geolocation or WebSockets. Once we detect support for the two HTML5 technologies, we'll update the status with something a little friendlier.

```
<script>

    // reference to the WebSocket
    var socket;

    // a semi-unique random ID for this session
    var myId = Math.floor(100000*Math.random());

    // number of rows of data presently displayed
    var rowCount = 0;
```

The meat of this application is once again accomplished via the script code. First, we will establish a few variables:

- A global reference to our socket so that functions have easy access to it later.

- A random myId number between 0 and 100,000 to identify our location data online. This number is merely used to correlate changes in location over time back to the same source without using more personal information such as names. A sufficiently large pool of numbers makes it unlikely that more than one user will have the same identifier.

- A rowCount which holds how many unique users have transmitted their location data to us. This is largely used for visual formatting.

The next two functions should look familiar. As in other example applications, we've provided utilities to help us update our status message. This time, there are two status messages to update.

```
function updateSocketStatus(message) {
    document.getElementById("socketStatus").innerHTML = message;
}

function updateGeolocationStatus(message) {
    document.getElementById("geoStatus").innerHTML = message;
}
```

It is always helpful to include a user-friendly set of error messages whenever something goes wrong with location retrieval. If you need more information on the error handling associated with Geolocation, consult Chapter 4.

```
function handleLocationError(error) {
    switch(error.code)
    {
    case 0:
      updateGeolocationStatus("There was an error while retrieving your location: " +
                  error.message);
      break;
    case 1:
      updateGeolocationStatus("The user prevented this page from retrieving a
                  location.");
      break;
    case 2:
      updateGeolocationStatus("The browser was unable to determine your location: " +
                  error.message);
      break;
    case 3:
      updateGeolocationStatus("The browser timed out before retrieving the location.");
      break;
    }
}
```

Adding the WebSocket Code

Now, let's examine something more substantial. The loadDemo function is called on the initial load of our page, making it the starting point of the application.

```
function loadDemo() {
    // test to make sure that sockets are supported
    if (window.WebSocket) {

        // the location of our broadcast WebSocket server
        url = "ws://localhost:8080";
        socket = new WebSocket(url);
        socket.onopen = function() {
            updateSocketStatus("Connected to WebSocket tracker server");
        }
        socket.onmessage = function(e) {
            updateSocketStatus("Updated location from " + dataReturned(e.data));
        }
    }
}
```

The first thing we do here is set up our WebSocket connection. As with any HTML5 technology, it is wise to check for support before jumping right in, so we test to make sure that window.WebSocket is a supported object in this browser.

Once that is verified, we make a connection to the remote broadcast server using the connect string format described above. The connection is stored in our globally declared socket variable.

Finally, we declare two handlers to take action when our WebSocket receives updates. The onopen handler will merely update the status message to let the user know that we made a successful connection. The onmessage will similarly update the status to let the user know that a message has arrived. It will also call our upcoming `dataReturned` function to show the arriving data in the page, but we'll tackle that later.

Adding the Geolocation Code

The next section should be familiar to you from Chapter 4. Here, we verify support for the Geolocation service and update the status message appropriately.

```
var geolocation;
if(navigator.geolocation) {
    geolocation = navigator.geolocation;
    updateGeolocationStatus("HTML5 Geolocation is supported in your browser.");
}

// register for position updates using the Geolocation API
geolocation.watchPosition(updateLocation,
                          handleLocationError,
                          {maximumAge:20000});
}
```

As before, we watch our current location for changes and register that we want the `updateLocation` function called when they occur. Errors are sent to the `handleLocationError` function, and the location data is set to expire every twenty seconds.

The next section of code is the handler which is called by the browser whenever a new location is available.

```
function updateLocation(position) {
    var latitude = position.coords.latitude;
    var longitude = position.coords.longitude;
    var timestamp = position.timestamp;

    updateGeolocationStatus("Location updated at " + timestamp);

    // Send my location via WebSocket
    var toSend = JSON.stringify([myId, latitude, longitude]);
    sendMyLocation(toSend);
}
```

This section is similar to, but simpler than, the same handler in Chapter 4. Here, we grab the latitude, longitude, and timestamp from the position provided by the browser. Then, we update the status message to indicate that a new value has arrived.

Putting It All Together

The final section calculates a message string to send to the remote broadcast WebSocket server. The string here will be JSON encoded:

```
"[<id>, <latitude>, <longitude>]"
```

The ID will be the randomly calculated value already created to identify this user. The latitude and longitude are provided by the geolocation position object. We send the message directly to the server as a JSON encoded string.

The actual code to send the position to the server resides in the `sendMyLocation()` function.

```
function sendMyLocation(newLocation) {
    if (socket) {
        socket.send(newLocation);
    }
}
```

If a socket was successfully created—and stored for later access—then it is safe to send the message string passed into this function to the server. Once it arrives, the WebSocket message broadcast server will distribute the location string to every browser currently connected and listening for messages. Everyone will know where you are. Or, at least, a largely anonymous "you" identified only by a random number.

Now that we're sending messages, let's see how those same messages should be processed when they arrive at the browser. Recall that we registered an `onmessage` handler on the socket to pass any incoming data to a `dataReturned()` function. Next, we will look at that final function in more detail.

```
function dataReturned(locationData) {
    // break the data into ID, latitude, and longitude
    var allData = JSON.parse(locationData);
    var incomingId   = allData[1];
    var incomingLat  = allData[2];
    var incomingLong = allData[3];
```

The `dataReturned` function serves two purposes. It will create (or update) a display element in the page showing the position reflected in the incoming message string, and it will return a text representation of the user this message originated from. The user name will be used in the status message at the top of the page by the calling function, the `socket.onmessage` handler.

The first step taken by this data handler function is to break the incoming message back down into its component parts using `JSON.parse`. Although a more robust application would need to check for unexpected formatting, we will assume that all messages to our server are valid, and therefore our string separates cleanly into a random ID, a latitude, and a longitude.

```
    // locate the HTML element for this ID
    // if one doesn't exist, create it
    var incomingRow = document.getElementById(incomingId);
    if (!incomingRow) {
        incomingRow = document.createElement('div');
        incomingRow.setAttribute('id', incomingId);
```

Our demonstration user interface will create a visible `<div>` for every random ID for which it receives a message. This includes the user's ID itself; in other words, the user's own data will also be displayed only after it is sent and returned from the WebSocket broadcast server.

Accordingly, the first thing we do with the ID from our message string is use it to locate the display row element matching it. If one does not exist, we create one and set its `id` attribute to be the id returned from our socket server for future retrieval.

```
        incomingRow.userText = (incomingId == myId) ?
                                    'Me'                :
                                    'User ' + rowCount;

        rowCount++;
```

The user text to be displayed in the data row is easy to calculate. If the ID matches the user's ID, it is simply 'me'. Otherwise, the username is a combination of a common string and a count of rows, which we will increment.

```
        document.body.appendChild(incomingRow);
    }
```

Once the new display element is ready, it is inserted into the end of the page. Regardless of whether the display element is newly created or if it already existed—due to the fact that a location update was not the first for that particular user—the display row needs to be updated with the current text information.

```
    // update the row text with the new values
    incomingRow.innerHTML = incomingRow.userText + " \\ Lat: " +
                            incomingLat + "  \\ Lon: " +
                            incomingLong;

    return incomingRow.userText;
}
```

In our case, we will separate the user text name from the latitude and longitude values using a backslash (properly escaped, of course). Finally, the display name is returned to the calling function for updating the status row.

Our simple WebSocket and Geolocation mashup is now complete. Try it out, but keep in mind that unless there are multiple browsers accessing the application at the same time, you won't see many updates. As an exercise to the reader, consider updating this example to display the incoming locations on a global Google Map to get an idea of where HTML5 interest is flourishing at this very moment.

The Final Code

For completeness, the Listing 6-9 provides the entire `tracker.html` file.

Listing 6-9. The tracker.html code

```
<!DOCTYPE html>
<html lang="en">

<head>
<title>HTML5 WebSocket / Geolocation Tracker</title>
<link rel="stylesheet" href="styles.css">
</head>

<body onload="loadDemo()">
```

```
<h1>HTML5 WebSocket / Geolocation Tracker</h1>

<div><strong>Geolocation</strong>: <p id="geoStatus">HTML5 Geolocation is
 <strong>not</strong> supported in your browser.</p></div>
<div><strong>WebSocket</strong>: <p id="socketStatus">WebSockets are <strong>not</strong>
 supported in your browser.</p></div>

<script>

    // reference to the WebSocket
    var socket;

    // a semi-unique random ID for this session
    var myId = Math.floor(100000*Math.random());

    // number of rows of data presently displayed
    var rowCount = 0;

    function updateSocketStatus(message) {
        document.getElementById("socketStatus").innerHTML = message;
    }

    function updateGeolocationStatus(message) {
        document.getElementById("geoStatus").innerHTML = message;
    }

    function handleLocationError(error) {
        switch(error.code)
        {
        case 0:
          updateGeolocationStatus("There was an error while retrieving your location: " +
                                  error.message);
          break;
        case 1:
          updateGeolocationStatus("The user prevented this page from retrieving a
                                  location.");
          break;
        case 2:
          updateGeolocationStatus("The browser was unable to determine your location: " +
                                  error.message);
          break;
        case 3:
          updateGeolocationStatus("The browser timed out before retrieving the location.");
          break;
        }
    }

    function loadDemo() {
        // test to make sure that sockets are supported
        if (window.WebSocket) {
```

```
        // the location where our broadcast WebSocket server is located
        url = "ws://localhost:8080";
        socket = new WebSocket(url);
        socket.onopen = function() {
            updateSocketStatus("Connected to WebSocket tracker server");
        }
        socket.onmessage = function(e) {
            updateSocketStatus("Updated location from " + dataReturned(e.data));
        }
    }

    var geolocation;
    if(navigator.geolocation) {
        geolocation = navigator.geolocation;
        updateGeolocationStatus("HTML5 Geolocation is supported in your browser.");
    }

    // register for position updates using the Geolocation API
    geolocation.watchPosition(updateLocation,
                              handleLocationError,
                              {maximumAge:20000});
}

function updateLocation(position) {
    var latitude = position.coords.latitude;
    var longitude = position.coords.longitude;
    var timestamp = position.timestamp;

    updateGeolocationStatus("Location updated at " + timestamp);

    // Send my location via WebSocket
    var toSend = JSON.stringify([myId, latitude, longitude]);
    sendMyLocation(toSend);
}

function sendMyLocation(newLocation) {
    if (socket) {
        socket.send(newLocation);
    }
}

function dataReturned(locationData) {
    // break the data into ID, latitude, and longitude
    var allData = JSON.parse(locationData)
    var incomingId   = allData[1];
    var incomingLat  = allData[2];
    var incomingLong = allData[3];

    // locate the HTML element for this ID
    // if one doesn't exist, create it
    var incomingRow = document.getElementById(incomingId);
    if (!incomingRow) {
```

```
        incomingRow = document.createElement('div');
        incomingRow.setAttribute('id', incomingId);

        incomingRow.userText = (incomingId == myId) ?
                                    'Me'                :
                                    'User ' + rowCount;

        rowCount++;

        document.body.appendChild(incomingRow);
    }

    // update the row text with the new values
    incomingRow.innerHTML = incomingRow.userText + " \\ Lat: " +
                            incomingLat + " \\ Lon: " +
                            incomingLong;

    return incomingRow.userText;
  }

</script>
</body>
</html>
```

Summary

In this chapter, you have seen how HTML5 WebSockets provide a simple, yet powerful mechanism for creating compelling, real-time applications.

First we looked at the nature of the protocol itself, and how it interoperates with existing HTTP traffic. We compared the network overhead demands of current polling-based communcation strategies versus the limited overhead of a native WebSocket.

To illustrate WebSockets in action, we explored a simple implementation of a WebSocket server to show how simple it is to implement this protocol in practice. Similary, we examined the client-side WebSocket API, noting the ease of integration it provides with existing JavaScript programming.

Finally, we walked through a more complex sample application which combined the power of Geolocation with WebSockets to demonstrate how well the two technologies can work together.

Now that we've seen how HTML5 brings socket-style network programming to the browser, we'll turn our attention to gathering more interesting data than just a user's current location. In the next chapter, we look at the enhancements made to form controls in HTML5.

CHAPTER 7

■ ■ ■

Using the HTML5 Forms API

In this chapter, we'll explore all the new capabilities at your command with a longstanding technology: HTML Forms. Forms have been the backbone of the explosion of the Web since they first appeared. Without form controls, web business transactions, social discussions, and efficient searches would simply not be possible.

Sadly, HTML5 Forms is one of the areas in greatest flux in both specification and implementation, in spite of having been in design for many years. There's good and bad news. The good news is that the progress in this area, while incremental, is increasing fairly rapidly. The bad news is that you'll need to tread carefully to find the subset of new form controls that will work in all your target browsers. The forms specification details a large set of APIs, and it is not uncommon to find that each major new release of an HTML5-compliant web browser adds support for one or more form controls and some of the helpful validation features.

Regardless, we'll use this chapter to help you navigate through the virtual sea of controls and find which ones are ready to use today, and which are nearing release.

Overview of HTML5 Forms

If you are already familiar with forms in HTML—and we assume you are if you are interested in pro HTML programming—then you will find the new additions in HTML5 to be a comfortable fit on a solid foundation. If you aren't yet familiar with the basics of form usage, we recommend any of the numerous books and tutorials on creating and handling form values. The topic is well covered at this point, and you will be happy to know that:

- Forms should still be encapsulated in a `<form>` element where the basic submission attributes are set.

- Forms still send the values of the controls to the server when the user or the application programmer submits the page.

- All of the familiar form controls—text fields, radio buttons, check boxes, and so on—are still present and working as before (albeit with some new features).

- Form controls are still fully scriptable for those who wish to write their own modifiers and handlers.

HTML Forms vs. XForms

You may have heard references to XForms in the last few years, long before the HTML5 effort gained much traction. XForms is an XML-centric, powerful, and somewhat complex, standard for specifying client-side form behavior that has been developed in its own W3C working group for nearly ten years. XForms harnesses the full power of XML Schema to define precise rules for validation and formatting. Unfortunately, no current major browser supports XForms without additional plugins.

Functional Forms

HTML5 Forms has instead focused on evolving the existing, simple HTML Forms to encompass more types of controls and address the practical limitations that web developers face today. There is an important note to keep in mind, especially as you compare form implementations across different browsers.

■ **Note** The most important concept to grasp about HTML5 Forms is that the specification deals with functional behavior and semantics, not appearances or displays.

For example, while the specification details the functional APIs for elements such as color and date pickers, number selectors, and email address entry, the specification does not state how browsers should render these elements to end users. This is a great choice on multiple levels. It allows browsers to compete on innovate ways to provide user interaction; it separates styling from semantics; and it allows future or specialized user input devices to interact in ways that are natural to their operation. However, until your targeted browser platforms support all the form controls in your application, make sure you provide enough contextual information for the user to know how to interact with a fallback rendering. With the right tips and descriptions, users will have no trouble with your application, even if it falls back to alternate content when presented with unknown input types.

HTML5 Forms encompasses a great number of new APIs and elements types, and support for them is all over the map now. In order to wrap our heads around all the new functionality, we will address it by breaking it into two categories

- New input types

- New functions and attributes

However, before we even start with that, let's take a quick assessment of how the HTML5 Form specifications are supported in today's browsers.

Browser Support for HTML5 Forms

Browser support for HTML5 Forms is growing, but limited. It appears that many browser vendors besides Opera have not put significant effort into their new form controls yet. However, the WebKit browsers have recently increased support for forms, perhaps because of the introduction of the iPhone and its virtual keyboard display, as we will see shortly. More advanced features such as validation are just being introduced. Table 7-1 summarizes the current state of HTML5 Forms support today.

Table 7-1. Browser support for HTML5 Forms

Browser	Details
Chrome	5.0.x supports input types email, number, tel, url, search, and range. Most validation.
Firefox	Not supported in 3.6. Initial support coming in 4.0.Unsupported input types such as `url`, `email`, and `range` will fall back to a text field.
Internet Explorer	Not supported, but new types will fall back to a text field rendering.
Opera	Strong support for initial specifications in current versions, including validation.
Safari	4.0.x supports input types email, number, tel, url, search, and range. Most validation. Some types supported better in mobile Safari.

Checking for browser support is less useful in the context of the new HTML5 Forms, as they have been designed to degrade gracefully in older browsers. Largely, this means that it is safe for you to use the new elements today, because older browsers will fall back to simple text field displays for any input types that they do not understand. However, as we'll see later in this chapter, this raises the importance of multi-tier form validation, as it is not sufficient to rely on the presence of browser validators to enforce the data types for your form controls, even if you assume full modern-browser support.

Now that we have surveyed the browser landscape, let's take a look at the new form controls added in the HTML5 specification.

An Input Catalog

One of the best places to get a catalog of all the new and changed elements in HTML5 is the markup list maintained at the W3C site itself. The W3C keeps a catalog page file at `http://dev.w3.org/html5/markup/`

This page denotes all the current and future elements in an HTML page. New and changed elements are noted in the catalog list. However, "new" in this list only means that the element has been added since the HTML4 specification—not that the element is implemented in browsers or in a final specification yet. With that warning in place, let's take a look at the new form elements arriving with HTML5, starting with the ones that are being implemented today. Table 7-2 lists the new `type` attributes. For example, many HTML developers will be intimately familiar with `<input type="text">` and `<input type="checkbox">`. The new input types follow a similar model to the existing ones.

Table 7-2. New HTML5 Form elements appearing in browsers

Type	Purpose
tel	Telephone number
email	Email address text field
url	Web location URL
search	Term to supply to a search engine. For example, the search bar atop a browser.
range	Numeric selector within a range of values, typically visualized as a slider

What do these new input types provide? In terms of programmatic APIs… not a lot. In fact, in the case of the types for tel, email, url, and search, there are no attributes distinguishing them from the simplest input type of text.

So, what do you get exactly by specifying that an input is of a specialized type? You get specialized input controls. (Restrictions may apply. Offer void in many desktop browsers.)

Let's illustrate with an example. By specifying that an input is of type email:

```
<input type="email">
```

rather than using the conventional standard which states that a field is merely of type text:

```
<input type="text">
```

you provide a hint to the browser to present a different user interface or input where applicable. You also provide the browser the ability to further validate the field before submission, but we'll cover that topic later in this chapter.

Mobile device browsers have been some of the quickest to take up support for these new form controls types, and they do so by displaying a different input interface based on the type declared. In the Apple iPhone, the standard onscreen keyboard display for an input with type text appears as it does in Figure 7-1.

Figure 7-1. Onscreen keyboard display for an input with type text

However, when an input field is marked as being of type e-mail, the iPhone presents a different keyboard layout customized for e-mail entry, as shown in Figure 7-2.

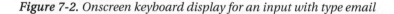

Figure 7-2. Onscreen keyboard display for an input with type email

Note the subtle tweaks to the space bar area of the keyboard to allow for the @ symbol and easy access to the period. Similar tweaks to the keyboard layout are done for type URL and type search. However, in the desktop version of the Safari browser—and in any browser that does not explicitly support the types for e-mail, URL, search, and tel—only the normal text input field will be displayed. Future browsers, even the desktop versions, may provide visual hints or cues to the user to indicate that the field is of a certain subtype. Opera, for example, will display a small envelope icon next to a field to indicate that it is expecting an e-mail address. However, it is safe to use these types in your web applications today, as any browser will either optimize for the type or simply do nothing at all.

Another specialized type that is gaining traction in browsers now is the <input type="range">. This specialized input control is designed to let users pick from within a range of numbers. For example, a range control could be used in a form to select an age from a range that limits access to minors under the age of, say, 18. By creating a range input and setting its special min and max values, a developer can request that a page display a constrained numerical picker that only operates within the specified bounds. In the Opera browser, for example, the control:

```
<input type="range" min="18" max="120">
```

gives a convenient way to pick a suitable value for age-restricted material. In the latest Opera browser, it displays as follows:

Unfortunately, the range input itself doesn't display a numerical representation of the browser. Moreover, without one, it is practically impossible for the user to know what the currently selected value happens to be. To fix this, one can easily add an onchange handler to update a display field based on changes to the current range value as shown in Listing 7-1.

Listing 7-1. onchange handler to update a display field

```
<script type="text/javascript">

function showValue(newVal) {
  document.getElementById("ageDisplay").innerHTML = newVal;
}
</script>

<label for="age">Age</label>
<input id="age" type="range" min="18" max="120" value="18" onchange="showValue(this.value)">
<span id="ageDisplay">18</span>
```

This gives a nice display to our range input, as follows:

Opera and the WebKit-based browsers—Safari and Chrome—have now added support for the type range element. Firefox support is planned, but not yet scheduled as of this writing. Firefox will fall back to a simple text element when presented with a range input type.

HERE BE DRAGONS

Brian says: "The phrase 'Here be dragons' is said to have been used in history to denote dangerous areas on maps where unknown perils lurk. The same could be said for the following form elements. Although they are specified, and have been for lengths of time now, most are lacking in actual implementation.

As such, expect large changes between now and the time that browser developers have had a chance to play with the designs, smooth the rough edges, and respond with feedback and changes. Rather than rely on the following components as inevitable, take them as a sign of the direction in which HTML5 forms are moving. If you attempt to use them today, the risk you take is your own…"

Additional form elements which are planned, but not widely supported yet include the ones listed in Table 7-3:

Table 7-3. Future HTML5 Form elements

Type	Purpose
`number`	A field containing a numeric value only
`color`	Color selector, which could be represented by a wheel or swatch picker
`datetime`	Full date and time display, including a time zone, as shown in Figure 7-3
`datetime-local`	Date and time display, with no setting or indication for time zones
`time`	Time indicator and selector, with no time zone information
`date`	Selector for calendar date
`week`	Selector for a week within a given year
`month`	Selector for a month within a given year

Although some early implementations of these elements are beginning to appear in leading edge browsers (for example, the datetime display in Opera as shown in Figure 7-3), we won't focus on them in this chapter as they are likely to undergo significant change. Stay tuned to future revisions!

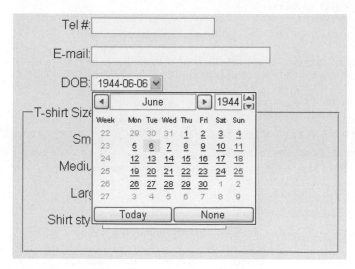

Figure 7-3. Display for an input of type datetime

Using the HTML5 Forms APIs

Now that we've spent some time familiarizing ourselves with the new form element types, let's turn to the attributes and APIs that are present on both the old and new form controls. Many of them are designed to reduce the amount of scripting needed to create a powerful web application user interface. You may find that the new attributes give you the power to enhance your user interface in ways that you had not considered. Or, at the very least, you may be able to remove blocks of script in your existing pages.

New form attributes and functions

First, we'll consider new attributes, functions, and a few elements that did not previously exist in earlier versions of HTML. Like the new input types, it is generally safe to use these attributes today, whether or not your target browser supports them. This is because the attributes will be safely ignored by any browser on the market today if the browser does not understand them.

The placeholder Attribute

The `placeholder` attribute gives input controls an easy way to provide descriptive, alternate hint text which is shown only when the user has not yet entered any values. This is common in many modern user interface frameworks, and popular JavaScript frameworks have also provided emulation of this feature. However, modern browsers have it built-in.

To use this attribute, simply add it to an input with a text representation. This includes the basic text type, as well as the semantic types such as `email`, `number`, `url`, etc.

```
<label>Runner: <input name="name" placeholder="First and last name" required></label>
```

In a supporting browser, such as Google Chrome, this causes the field to display a faint version of the placeholder text which will disappear whenever the user or application puts focus into the field, or whenever there is a value present.

The same attribute, when running in a non-supporting browser, will just be ignored, causing the default field behavior to display.

Similarly, whenever a value is entered in the field, the placeholder text will not appear.

The autocomplete Attribute

The `autocomplete` attribute, introduced in Internet Explorer 5.5, has finally been standardized. Hooray! (Browsers have been supporting the attribute for nearly as long as its inception, but having a specified behavior helps everyone.)

The `autocomplete` attribute tells the browser whether or not the value of this input should be saved for future. For example:

```
<input type="text" name="creditcard" autocomplete="off">
```

The `autocomplete` attribute should be used to protect sensitive user data from insecure storage in the local browser files. Table 7-4 shows the different behavior types.

Table 7-4. Autocomplete behavior in input controls

Type	Purpose
on	The field is not secure, and its value can be saved and restored.
off	The field is secure, and its value should not be saved.
unspecified	Default to the setting on the containing `<form>`. If not contained in a form, or no value is set on the form, then behave as if on.

The autofocus Attribute

The `autofocus` attribute lets a developer specify that a given form element should take input focus immediately when the page loads. Only one attribute per page should specify the `autofocus` attribute. Behavior is undefined if more than one control is set to autofocus.

■ **Note** Only one autofocus control per page is difficult to achieve if your content is being rendered into a portal or shared content page. Do not rely on autofocus if you are not in complete control of the page.

To set the focus automatically to a control such as a search text field, simply set the `autofocus` attribute on that element alone:

```
<input type="search" name="criteria" autofocus>
```

Like other boolean attributes, no value needs to be specified for the true case.

■ **Note** Autofocus can annoy users if they are not expecting a focus change. Many users utilize keystrokes for navigation, and switching focus to a form control subverts that ability. Use it only when it is a given that a form control should take all default keys.

The list Attribute and the datalist Element

The list attribute and datalist element combine to let a developer specify a list of possible values for an input. To use this combination:

1.   Create a datalist element in your document with its id set to a unique value. The datalist can be located anywhere in the document.

2.   Populate the datalist with as many option elements as needed to represent the full set of suggestions for values of a control. For example, a datalist representing e-mail contacts should contain all of the contact e-mail addresses as individual option children.

```
<datalist id="contactList">
    <option value="x@example.com" label="Racer X">
    <option value="peter@example.com" label="Peter">
</datalist>
```

3.   Link the input element to the datalist by setting the list attribute to a value which is the id of the associated datalist.

```
<input type="email" id="contacts" list="contactList">
```

On a supporting browser, like Opera, this produces a customized list control like the following:

The min and max Attributes

As seen before in our example for <input type="range">, the min and max attributes allow a numerical input to be constrained to minimum and maximum values. One, both, or neither of these attributes can be provided as necessary, and the input control should adjust accordingly to increase or decrease the range of acceptable values. For example, to create a range control representing a level of confidence in ability from zero% to 100%, the following code could be used as follows:

```
<input id="confidence" name="level" type="range" min="0" max="100" value="0">
```

This would create a range control with a minimum zero value and maximum of 100, which, coincidentally, are the default values for the same.

The step Attribute

Also, for input types which expect numerical values, the `step` attribute specifies the granularity of increments or decrements in value as the range is adjusted. For example, our confidence level range control listed above can be set up with a `step` attribute of five as follows:

```
<input id="confidence" name="level" type="range" min="0" max="100" step="5" value="0">
```

This would limit the acceptable values to be increments of five from the starting value. In other words, only 0, 5, 10, 15, … 100 would be allowed either through typed input or through a slider control, depending on the browser representation of the input.

The default `step` value is dependent on the type of control to which it is applied. For a `range` input, the default step is one. To accompany the `step` attribute, HTML5 introduces two functions on the input element that allow the value to be controlled: `stepUp` and `stepDown`.

As you might expect, these functions increment or decrement the current value, respectively. As you might also expect, the amount by which the value is increased or decreased is the value of the step. As such, the value of a numeric input control can be tweaked without direct input from the user.

The valueAsNumber Function

The new `valueAsNumber` function is a handy way to convert the value of a control from text to number… and back! That is the case because the `valueAsNumber` is both a getter and a setter function. When called as a getter, the `valueAsNumber` function converts the text value of an input field into a number type upon which calculations are allowed. If the text value does not cleanly convert into a `number` type, then the `NaN` value (Not-a-Number) is returned.

The `valueAsNumber` can also be used to set the value of an input to a numeric type. For example, our confidence range could be set using a call such as:

```
document.getElementById("confidence").valueAsNumber(65);
```

Make sure the number meets the requirements of the `min`, `max`, and `step`, or an error will be thrown.

The required Attribute

If any input control has the `required` attribute set, then a value must be set on it before its form can be submitted. For example, to set a text input field as required, simply add the attribute as shown here:

```
<input type="text" id="firstname" name="first" required>
```

If no value is set on this field, either programmatically or by the user, the ability to submit this form is blocked. The `required` attribute is the simplest type of form validation, but the capabilities of validation are vast. Let's discuss form validation in more detail now.

Checking forms with validation

Before we get too deep into specifics, let's review what form validation really entails. At its core, form validation is a system for detecting invalid control data and flagging those errors for end users. In other words, form validation is a series of checks and notifications that let a user correct the controls of a form before submitting it to the server.

But what is form validation, really?

It is an optimization.

Form validation is an optimization because it alone is not sufficient to guarantee that forms submitted to the server are correct and valid. It is an optimization because it is designed to help a web application fail fast. In other words, it is better to notify a user that a page contains invalid form controls right inside the page, using the browser's built-in processing. Why bother with the expense of a network round trip just so the server can inform a user that there was a typo in the data entry? If the browser has all the knowledge and capability to catch errors before they leave the client, we should take advantage of that.

However, browser form checking is not sufficient to handle all errors.

MALICIOUS OR MISUNDERSTOOD?

Brian says: "Even though the HTML5 specification goes a long way in improving the ability to check forms within the browser, it is still not a replacement for server validation. It may never be.

Obviously, there are many error conditions that require server interaction to verify, such as whether or not a credit card is authorized to make a purchase, or even basic authentication. However, even mundane validation cannot rely solely on clients. Some users may be using browsers that don't support the form validation features. A few may turn off scripting altogether, which can end up disabling all but the simplest attribute-based validators. Yet other users can utilize an assortment of tools such as the Firefox Greasemonkey addon to modify a page's content to their…. err, content. This could include removing all form validation checks. Ultimately, it is not sufficient to rely on client-side validation as the sole means of checking any important data. If it exists on the client, it can be manipulated.

HTML5 Form validation lets users get important feedback fast, but don't rely on it for absolute correctness!"

That being said, HTML5 does introduce eight handy ways to enforce correctness on form control entry. Let's examine them in turn, starting with the object that gives us access to their status: the `ValidityState`.

The `ValidityState` can be accessed from any form control in a browser that supports HTML5 Form validation:

```
var valCheck = document.myForm.myInput.validity;
```

This simple command grabs a reference to the `ValidityState` object of a form element conspicuously named `myInput`. This object contains handy references to each of the eight possible validity statuses, as well as an overall validity summary check.

You can do this by calling:

`valCheck.valid`

we can get a Boolean value which informs us whether or not all validity constraints are currently met on this particular form control. Think of the `valid` flag as a summary: if all eight constraints are passing, the `valid` flag will be true. Otherwise, if any of the validity constraints fail, the `valid` attribute will be false.

■ **Note** The `ValidityState` object is a live object. Once you grab a reference to it, you can keep a hold of it and the validity checks it returns will update as needed when changes occur.

As mentioned before, there are eight possible validity constraints on any given form element. Each can be accessed from the `ValidityState` by accessing the field with the appropriate name. Let's look at what they mean, how they can be enforced on a form control, and how you can use the `ValidityState` to check for them:

The valueMissing Constraint

Purpose: Ensure that some value is set on this form control

Usage: Set the `required` attribute on the form control to true

Usage example: `<input type="text" name="myText" `**`required`**`>`

Details: If the `required` attribute is set on a form control, the control will be in an invalid state unless the user or a programmatic call sets some value to the field. For example, a blank text field will fail a required check, but will pass as soon as any text is entered. When blank, the `valueMissing` will return true.

typeMismatch

Purpose: Guarantee that the type of the value matches expectations (number, email, URL, and so on)

Usage: Specify one of the appropriate `type` attributes on the form control

Usage example: `<input type="email" name="myEmail">`

Details: Special form control types aren't just for customized phone keyboards! If your browser can determine that the value entered into a form control doesn't conform to the rules for that type—for example, an email address without an @ symbol—the browser can flag this control as having a type mismatch. Another example would be a number field that cannot parse to a valid number. In either case, the `typeMismatch` will return `true`.

patternMismatch

Purpose: Enforce any pattern rule set on a form control which details specific valid formats

Usage: Set the `pattern` attribute on the form control with the appropriate pattern

Usage example: `<input type="text" name="creditcardnumber" `**`pattern="[0-9]{16}"`**` title="A credit card number is 16 digits with no spaces or dashes">`

Details: The `pattern` attribute gives developers a powerful and flexible way of enforcing a regular expression pattern on the value of a form control. When a pattern is set on a control, the `patternMismatch` will return true whenever the value does not conform to the rules of the pattern. To assist users and assistive technology, you should set the `title` on any pattern-controlled field to describe the rules of the format.

tooLong

Purpose: Make sure that a value does not contain too many characters

Usage: Put a `maxLength` attribute on the form control

Usage example: `<input type="text" name="limitedText" maxLength="140">`

Details: This humorously-named constraint will return true if the value length exceeds the `maxLength`. While form controls will generally try to enforce the maximum length during user entry, certain situations including programmatic settings can cause the value to exceed the maximum.

rangeUnderflow

Purpose: Enforce the minimum value of a numeric control

Usage: Set a `min` attribute with the minimum allowed value

Usage example: `<input type="range" name="ageCheck" min="18">`

Details: In any form controls that do numeric-range checking, it is possible for the value to get temporarily set below the allowable range. In these cases, the `ValidityState` will return true for the `rangeUnderflow` field.

rangeOverflow

Purpose: Enforce the maximum value of a numeric control

Usage: Set a `max` attribute with the maximum allowed value

Usage example: `<input type="range" name="kidAgeCheck" max="12">`

Details: Similar to its counterpart `rangeUnderflow`, this validity constraint will return `true` if the value of a form control becomes greater than the `max` attribute.

stepMismatch

Purpose: Guarantee that a value conforms to the combination of `min`, `max`, and `step`

Usage: Set a step attribute to specify the granular steps of a numeric value

Usage example: `<input type="range" name="confidenceLevel" min="0" max="100" step="5">`

Details: This constraint enforces the sanity of the combinations of `min`, `max`, and `step`. Specifically, the current value must be a multiple of the step added to the minimum value. For example, a range from 0 to 100 with steps at every 5 would not allow a value of 17 without `stepMismatch` returning true.

customError

Purpose: Handle errors explicitly calculated and set by the application code

Usage: Call `setCustomValidity(message)` to put a form control into the `customError` state

Usage example: `passwordConfirmationField.setCustomValidity("Password values do not match.");`

Details: For those cases where the built-in validity checks don't apply, the custom validity errors can suffice. Application code should set a custom validity message whenever a field does not conform to semantic rules.

One common use case for custom validity is when consistency between controls is not achieved, for example if password confirmation fields don't match. (We'll delve into this specific example in the "Practical Extras" section.) Whenever a custom validity message is set, the control will be invalid and return the `customError` constraint as `true`. To clear the error, simply call `setCustomValidity("")` on the control with an empty string value.

Validation Fields and Functions

Together, these eight constraints allow a developer to find out exactly why a given form control is failing a validation check. Or, if you don't care which specific reason is causing the failure, simply access the Boolean value `valid` on the `ValidityState`; it is an aggregate of the other eight constraints. If all eight constraints return `false`, then the `valid` field will return `true`. There are a few other helpful fields and functions on the form controls which can assist you in programming for validation checking.

The willValidate Attribute

The `willValidate` attribute simply indicates whether validation will be checked on this form control at all. If any of the above constraints—e.g. the `required` attribute, `pattern` attribute, etc.—are set on the control, the `willValidate` field will let you know that validation checking is going to be enforced.

The checkValidity Function

The `checkValidity` function allows you to check validation on the form without any explicit user input. Normally, a form's validation is checked whenever the user or script code submits the form. This function allows validation to be done at any time.

■ **Note** Calling `checkValidity` on a form control doesn't just check validation, it causes all resulting events and UI triggers to occur just as if the form had been submitted.

The validationMessage Attribute

This attribute isn't yet supported by any current browser versions, but it might be by the time you read this. The `validationMessage` attribute lets you query programmatically a localized error message that the browser would display based on the current state of validation. For example, if a `required` field has no value, the browser might present an error message to the user that "This field requires a value." Once supported, this is the text string that would be returned by the `validationMessage` field, and it would adjust according to the current state of validation on the control.

Validation feedback

On the subject of validation feedback... one topic we've avoided thus far is how and when the browser should present the user with feedback on a validation error. The specification does not dictate the terms of how the user interface is updated to present an error message, and existing implementations differ fairly significantly. Consider the case for Opera. In Opera 10.5, the browser indicates that a validation error has occurred by marking the field in error with a popup message and a flashing red field.

In contrast, the Google Chrome browser only navigates to the offending field and puts the focus there when an error is found. What is the correct behavior?

Neither is specified. However, if you would like to take control of the feedback shown to the user when a validation error occurs, there is an appropriate handler for you to do so: the `invalid` event.

Whenever a form is checked for validity—either due to the form being submitted, or due to the `checkValidity` function being called directly—any form in an invalid state will be delivered an `invalid` event. This event can be ignored, observed, or even cancelled. To add an event handler to a field which will receive this notification, add some code similar to Listing 7-2:

Listing 7-2. Adding event handlers for invalid events

```
// event handler for "invalid" events
function invalidHandler(evt) {
  var validity = evt.srcElement.validity;

  // check the validity to see if a particular constraint failed
  if (validity.valueMissing) {
    // present a UI to the user indicating that the field is missing a value
  }

  // perhaps check additional constraints here...

  // If you do not want the browser to provide default validation feedback,
  // cancel the event as shown here
  evt.preventDefault();
}

// register an event listener for "invalid" events
myField.addEventListener("invalid", invalidHandler, false);
```

Let's break that code snippet down a bit.

First, we declare a handler to receive `invalid` events. The first thing we do inside that handler is check the source of the event. Recall that the `invalid` event is fired on the form control with a validation error. Therefore, the `srcElement` of the event will be the misbehaving form control.

From the source, we grab the `validity` object. Using this `ValidityState` instance, we can check its individual constraint fields to determine exactly what went wrong. In this case, since we know that our field has a `required` attribute on it, we first check to see if the `valueMissing` constraint has been violated.

If our check succeeds, we can modify the user interface on the page to inform the user that a value needs to be entered for the field in error. Perhaps an alert or an informative error region could be displayed? This is up to you to decide.

Once we've told the user what the error is and how to correct it, we need to decide if we want the browser itself to display its built-in feedback. By default, the browser will do just that. To prevent the browser from showing its own error message, we can call `evt.preventDefault()` to stop the default handling and take care of the matter entirely ourselves.

Once again, the choice here is yours. The HTML5 Forms API provides you with the flexibility to achieve a customized API or to fall back to default browser behavior.

Turning Off Validation

In spite of the power behind the validation API, there are… (ahem) valid reasons why you might want to turn off validation on a control or an entire form. The most common reason is that you might choose to submit the temporary contents of a form to be saved or retrieved for later, even if the contents aren't quite valid yet.

Imagine the case of a user who is entering a complex order entry form, but needs to run an errand midway through the process. Ideally, you might present the user with a "save" button which stores the values of the form by submitting them to the server. However, if the form was only partially completed, validation rules might prevent the content from being submitted. The user would be very displeased if she had to complete or abandon the form due to an unexpected interruption.

To handle this, a form itself can be programmatically set with the attribute `noValidate`, which will cause it to forego any validation logic otherwise present and simply submit the form. Naturally, this attribute can be set either via script or original markup.

A more useful way to turn off validation is to set a `formNoValidate` attribute on a control such as a form submit button. Take the following submit button, set up as a "save" button, for example:

```
<input type="submit" formnovalidate name="save" value="Save current progress">
<input type="submit" name="process" value="Process order">
```

This snippet will create a two normal looking submit buttons. The second will submit the form, as usual. However, the first button is marked with the `noValidate` attribute, causing all validation to be bypassed when it is used. This allows the data to be submitted to the server without checking for correctness. Of course, your server will need to be set up to handle unvalidated data, but best practices dictate that this should be the case at all times.

Building an Application with HTML5 Forms

Now, let's use the tools we've described in this chapter to create a simple signup page which showcases new features in HTML5 Forms. Turning back to our familiar Happy Trails Running Club, we'll create a page for race registration that incorporates new form elements and validation.

As always, the source code for the demo files we show here is available in the code/forms folder. Therefore, we'll spend less attention on the CSS and peripheral markup, and more on the core of the page itself. That being said, let's start with a look at the finished page shown in Figure 7-4, then break it down into sections to tackle one-by-one.

Figure 7-4. Example page with race signup form

This signup page demonstrates many of the elements and APIs we've explored in this chapter, including validation. Although the actual display may look somewhat different on your browser, it should degrade gracefully even if the browser does not support a particular feature.

On to the code!

The header, navigation, and footer have all been seen before on our previous examples. The page now contains a <form> element.

```
<form name="register">
  <p><label for="runnername">Runner:</label>
    <input id="runnername" name="runnername" type="text"
           placeholder="First and last name" required></p>
  <p><label for="phone">Tel #:</label>
    <input id="phone" name="phone" type="tel"
```

```
                placeholder="(xxx) xxx-xxx"></p>
    <p><label for="emailaddress">E-mail:</label>
        <input id="emailaddress" name="emailaddress" type="email"
                placeholder="For confirmation only"></p>
    <p><label for="dob">DOB:</label>
        <input id="dob" name="dob" type="date"
                placeholder="MM/DD/YYYY"></p>
```

In this first section, we see the markup for the four primary inputs: name, phone, email, and birthday. For each, we've set a `<label>` with descriptive text and tied it to the actual control using the `for` attribute. We've also set placeholder text to show a description to the user of just what type of content belongs there.

For the runner name text field, we've made it a required value by setting the `required` attribute. This will cause form validation to kick in with a `valueMissing` constraint if nothing is entered. On the phone input, we've declared it to be of type `tel`. Your browser may or may not display this field differently or provide optimized keyboards.

Similarly, the e-mail field has been marked of type `e-mail`. Any specific handling is up to the browser. Some browsers will throw a `typeMismatch` constraint if they detect that the entered value is not a valid email.

Finally, the date-of-birth field is declared as type `date`. Not many browsers support this yet, but when they do, they will automatically render a date picking control on this input.

```
    <fieldset>
      <legend>T-shirt Size: </legend>
      <p><input id="small" type="radio" name="tshirt" value="small">
         <label for="small">Small</label></p>
      <p><input id="medium" type="radio" name="tshirt" value="medium">
         <label for="medium">Medium</label></p>
      <p><input id="large" type="radio" name="tshirt" value="large">
         <label for="large">Large</label></p>
      <p><label for="style">Shirt style:</label>
         <input id="style" name="style" type="text" list="stylelist" title="Years of
                    participation"></p>
      <datalist id="stylelist">
       <option value="White" label="1st Year">
       <option value="Gray" label="2nd - 4th Year">
       <option value="Navy" label="Veteran (5+ Years)">
      </datalist>
    </fieldset>
```

In our next section, we set out the controls to be used to T-shirt selection. The first few controls are a standard set of radio buttons for selecting a shirt size.

The next section is more interesting. Here, we exercise the `list` attribute and its corresponding `<datalist>` element. In the `<datalist>`, we declare a set of types that should be displayed for this list with distinct values and labels, representing the types of T-shirts available based on veteran status. Although this list is quite simple, the same technique can be used for lengthy lists of dynamic elements.

```
    <fieldset>
      <legend>Expectations:</legend>
      <p>
      <label for="confidence">Confidence:</label>
```

```
            <input id="confidence" name="level" type="range"
                    onchange="setConfidence(this.value)"
                    min="0" max="100" step="5" value="0">
            <span id="confidenceDisplay">0%</span></p>
            <p><label for="notes">Notes:</label>
                <textarea id="notes" name="notes" maxLength="140"></textarea></p>
        </fieldset>
```

In our final section of controls, we create a slider for the user to express his or her confidence in completing the race. For this, we use an input of type `range`. Since our confidence is measured in percentages, we set a `minimum`, a `maximum`, and `step` value on the input. These force a constraint within normal percentage ranges. Additionally, we constrain the movement of the value to 5% step increments, which you will be able to observe if your browser supports a range slider interface control. Although it should not be possible to trigger them through simple control interactions, there are possible validation constraints on this control for `rangeUnderflow`, `rangeOverflow`, and `stepMismatch`.

Because a range control does not show a textual representation of its value by default, we will add one in our application. The `confidenceDisplay` will be manipulated through the `onchange` handler of the range control, but we'll see that in action in just a minute.

Finally, we add a `<textarea>` to contain any extra notes from the registrant. By setting a `maxLength` constraint on the notes control, we allow it to achieve a `tooLong` constraint, perhaps if a lengthy value is pasted into the field.

```
            <p><input type="submit" name="register" value="Register"></p>
        </form>
```

We finish off our control section with a submit button that will send in our form registration. In this default example, the registration is not actually being sent to any server.

There are a few scripts we still need to describe: how we update our confidence slider display, and how we will override the browser's built-in form validation feedback. Although you might find the browser's default handling of form errors to be acceptable, it is always good to know your options.

```
<script type="text/javascript">
    function setConfidence(newVal) {
        document.getElementById("confidenceDisplay").innerHTML = newVal + '%';
    }

    function invalidHandler(evt) {
        // find the label for this form control
        var label = evt.srcElement.parentElement.getElementsByTagName("label")[0];

        // set the label's text color to red
        label.style.color = 'red';

        // stop the event from propagating higher
        evt.stopPropagation();

        // stop the browser's default handling of the validation error
        evt.preventDefault();
    }

    function loadDemo() {
```

```
    // register an event handler on the form to
    // handle all invalid control notifications
    document.register.addEventListener("invalid", invalidHandler, true);
}

window.addEventListener("load", loadDemo, false);
```

```
</script>
```

This code contains a few distinct sections. The first is the `setConfidence()` function. In this function, we handle change events from our confidence range control. Every time the slider value changes, we find the `confidenceDisplay <span>` and update its text accordingly. As you can see, it's very easy to configure.

■ **Note** Why don't `range` elements contain visual displays by default? Perhaps it is so that user interface designers can customize the exact position and appearance of displays. Making the display optional adds a bit of work, but much more flexibility.

The remainder of the code section shows how we override the handling of validation errors. We start by registering event listeners for the special event type `invalid`. In order to capture `invalid` events on all form controls, we register the handler on the form itself, making sure to register for event capture so that events will arrive at our handler.

```
// register an event handler on the form to
// handle all invalid control notifications
document.register.addEventListener("invalid", invalidHandler, true);
```

Now, whenever any of our form elements triggers a validation constraint, our `invalidHandler` will be called. In order to provide more subtle feedback than some of the prominent browsers do by default, we will color the label of the offending form field red. To do so, first we locate the `<label>` by traversing to the parent.

```
// find the label for this form control
var label = evt.srcElement.parentElement.getElementsByTagName("label")[0];
```

```
// set the label's text color to red
label.style.color = 'red';
```

After setting the label to be a lovely red color, we want to stop the browser or any other handler from double handling our invalid event. Using the power of DOM, we call `preventDefault()` to stop any browser default handling of the event, and `stopPropagation()` to keep other handlers from getting access.

```
// stop the event from propagating higher
evt.stopPropagation();
```

```
// stop the browser's default handling of the validation error
evt.preventDefault();
```

And with just a few simple steps, we've provided a validated form with our own special interface validation code!

Practical Extras

Sometimes there are techniques that don't fit into our regular examples, but which nonetheless apply to many types of HTML5 applications. We present to you a short, but common, practical extra here.

The Password is: Validation!

One handy way to use the HTML5 Form validation support for custom validators is to implement the common technique of verifying passwords during a password change. The standard technique is to provide two password fields which must match before the form is submitted successfully. Here, we provide a way to utilize the `setCustomValidation` call to make sure that two password fields are matched before the form submits.

Recall that the `customError` validation constraint gives you a chance to set an error on a form control whenever the standard constraint rules do not apply. Specifically, one good reason to trigger the `customError` constraint is when the validation depends on the concurrent state of multiple controls, such as the two password fields here.

Because the `ValidityState` object is assumed to be live once a reference to it is obtained, it is a good idea to set the custom error on the `ValidityState` whenever the password fields are mismatched and immediately clear the error whenever the fields match again. A good approach for achieving this is to use the onchange event handler for the password fields.

```
<form name="passwordChange">
    <p><label for="password1">New Password:</label>
    <input type="password" id="password1" onchange="checkPasswords()"></p>
    <p><label for="password2">Confirm Password:</label>
    <input type="password" id="password2" onchange="checkPasswords()"></p>
</form>
```

As you can see here, on a trivial form with two password fields, we can register a function to execute every time the value of one of the passwords changes.

```
function checkPasswords() {
  var pass1 = document.getElementById("password1");
  var pass2 = document.getElementById("password2");

  if (pass1.value != pass2.value)
    pass1.setCustomValidity("Your passwords do not match. Please recheck that your
        new password is entered identically in the two fields.");
  else
    pass1.setCustomValidity("");
}
```

Here is one way to handle the password matching. Simply grab the values of the two password fields, and if they do not match, set a custom error. For the sake of a validation routine, it is probably acceptable just to set the error on one of the two password fields. If they do match, set the empty string as the custom error to clear it; this is the specified way for removing a custom error.

Once you've got the error set on the field, you can use the approaches described earlier in this chapter to show feedback to the user and let her change the passwords to match, as expected.

Summary

In this chapter, you have seen how something old—HTML forms—and make it into something new by using new elements, attributes, and APIs available in HTML5. We've seen new controls for advanced input types, with even more to come. We've seen how client validation can be integrated directly into form controls in order to prevent unnecessary server round trips to process bad data. Overall, we've seen ways to reduce the amount of scripting you need to create full-featured applications user interfaces. In the next chapter, we'll investigate how browsers give you the ability to spawn independent execution environments to handle long-running tasks: HTML5 Web Workers.

CHAPTER 8

■ ■ ■

Using the HTML5 Web Workers API

HTML5 Web Workers provide background processing capabilities to web applications and typically run on separate threads so that JavaScript applications using HTML5 Web Workers can take advantage of multicore CPUs. Separating long-running tasks into HTML5 Web Workers also avoids the dreaded slow-script warnings, shown in Figure 8-1, that display when JavaScript loops continue for several seconds.

Figure 8-1. Slow script warning in Firefox

As powerful as Web Workers are, there are also certain things they cannot do. For example, when a script is executing inside a Web Worker it cannot access the web page's `window` object (`window.document`), which means that Web Workers don't have direct access to the web page and the DOM API. Although Web Workers cannot block the browser UI, they can still consume CPU cycles and make the system less responsive.

Let's say you want to create a web application that has to perform some background number crunching, but you do not want those tasks to interfere with the interactivity of the web page itself. Using Web Workers, you can spawn a Web Worker to perform the tasks and add an event listener to listen to messages from the Web Worker as they are sent.

Another use case for Web Workers could be an application that listens for broadcast news messages from a back-end server, posting messages to the main web page as they are received from the back-end server. This Web Worker might use Web Sockets or Server-Sent Events to talk to the back-end server.

In this chapter, we'll explore what you can do with Web Workers. First, we'll discuss how Web Workers work and the level of browser support available at the time of this writing. Then, we'll discuss how you can use the APIs to create new workers and how to communicate between a worker and the context that spawned it. Finally, we'll show you how you can build an application with Web Workers.

Browser Support for HTML5 Web Workers

Browser support for Web Workers is at varying stages and will continue to evolve. As shown in Table 8-1, Web Workers is already supported in many browsers at the time of this writing.

Table 8-1. Opera Supported in version 10.6 and greater

Browser	Details
Chrome	Supported in version 3 and greater
Firefox	Supported in version 3.5 and greater
Internet Explorer	Not supported (yet)
Opera	Supported in version 10.6 and greater
Safari	Supported in version 4 and greater

Using the HTML5 Web Workers API

In this section, we'll explore the use of the Web Workers API in more detail. For the sake of illustration, we've created a simple browser page: `echo.html`. Using Web Workers is fairly straightforward—you create a Web Worker object and pass in a JavaScript file to be executed. Inside the page you set up an event listener to listen to incoming messages and errors that are posted by the Web Worker and if you want to communicate from the page to the Web Worker, you call `postMessage` to pass in the required data. The same is true for the code in the Web Worker JavaScript file—event handlers must be set up to process incoming messages and errors, and communication with the page is handled with a call to `postMessage`.

Checking for Browser Support

Before you call the Web Workers API functions, you will want to make sure there is support in the browser for what you're about to do. This way, you can provide some alternate text, prompting the users of your application to use a more up-to-date browser. Listing 8-1 shows the code you can use to test for browser support.

Listing 8-1. Checking for browser support

```
function loadDemo() {
  if (typeof(Worker) !== "undefined") {
    document.getElementById("support").innerHTML =
            "Excellent! Your browser supports HTML5 Web Workers";
  }
}
```

In this example, you test for browser support in the loadDemo function, which might be called when the page is loaded. A call to typeof(Worker) will return the window's global Worker property, which will be undefined if the browser doesn't support the Web Workers API. In this example, the page is updated to reflect whether there is browser support by updating a previously defined support element on the page with a suitable message, as shown at the top of Figure 8-2.

Figure 8-2. Example of showing whether HTML5 Web Workers is supported

Creating HTML5 Web Workers

Web Workers are initialized with the URL of a JavaScript file, which contains the code the worker will execute. This code sets event listeners and communicates with the script that spawned it. The URL for the JavaScript file can be a relative or absolute URL with the same origin (the same scheme, host, and port) as the main page:

```
worker = new Worker("echoWorker.js");
```

Loading and Executing Additional JavaScript

An application composed of several JavaScript files can contain `<script>` elements that synchronously load JavaScript files as the page loads. However, because Web Workers do not have access to the document object, there is an alternative mechanism for synchronously importing additional JavaScript files from within workers—importScripts:

```
importScripts("helper.js");
```

Importing a JavaScript file simply loads and executes JavaScript into an existing worker. Multiple scripts can be imported by the same call to importScripts. They are executed in the order specified:

```
importScripts("helper.js", "anotherHelper.js");
```

Communicating with HTML5 Web Workers

Once the Web Worker is spawned, you can use the postMessage API to send data to and from Web Workers. This is the same postMessage API that is used for cross-frame and cross-window communication. postMessage can be used to send most JavaScript objects, but not functions or objects with cyclic references.

Let's say that you want to build a simple Web Worker example that allows users to send a message to a worker, which in turn echoes back the message. This example may not be very useful in real life, but it's useful enough to explain the concepts you need to build more complex examples.

Figure 8-3 shows this example web page and its Web Worker in action. The code for this simple page is listed at the end of this section.

Figure 8-3. A simple web page that uses HTML5 Web Workers

To set up proper communication with your Web Worker, code has to be added to the *main page* (the page that calls the Web Worker) as well as the *worker JavaScript file.*

Coding the Main Page

To communicate from the page to the Web Worker, you call `postMessage` to pass in the required data. To listen to incoming messages and errors that are sent by the Web Worker to the page, you set up an event listener.

To set up communication between the main page and the Web Worker, first add the call to `postMessage` to the main page, as follows:

```
document.getElementById("helloButton").onclick = function() {
    worker.postMessage("Here's a message for you");
}
```

In the preceding example, a message is sent to the Web Worker when the user clicks the **Post a Message** button. Next, add an event listener to the page that listens for messages from the Web Worker:

```
worker.addEventListener("message", messageHandler, true);

function messageHandler(e) {
    // process message from worker
}
```

Coding the HTML5 Web Worker JavaScript File

You must now add similar code to theWeb Worker JavaScript file—event handlers must be set up to process incoming messages and errors, and communication with the page is handled with a call to postMessage.

To complete the communication between the page and the Web Worker, first, add the call to postMessage; for example, inside a messageHandler function:

```
function messageHandler(e) {
    postMessage("worker says: " + e.data + " too");
}
```

Next, add an event listener to the Web Worker JavaScript file that handles messages coming from the main page:

```
addEventListener("message", messageHandler, true);
```

In this example, the messageHandler function is called immediately when the message is received so that the message can be echoed back.

Handling Errors

Unhandled errors in an HTML5 Web Worker script fire error events on the Web Worker object. Listening for these error events is especially important when you are debugging scripts that make use of Web Workers. The following shows an example of an error handling function in a Web Worker JavaScript file that logs errors to the console:

```
function errorHandler(e) {
    console.log(e.message, e);
}
```

To handle the errors, you must add an event listener to the main page:

```
worker.addEventListener("error", errorHandler, true);
```

Stopping HTML5 Web Workers

Web Workers don't stop by themselves; but the page that started them can stop them. You may want to reclaim resources when a Web Worker is no longer needed—perhaps when the main page is notified that the Web Worker has finished its tasks. You may also wish to cancel a long-running task in response to user intervention, as follows. Calling **terminate** stops the Web Worker. A terminated Web Worker will no longer respond to messages or perform any additional computations. You cannot restart a worker; instead, you can create a new worker using the same URL.

```
worker.terminate();
```

Using HTML5 Web Workers within HTML5 Web Workers

The Worker API can be used inside Web Worker scripts to create subworkers:

```
var subWorker = new Worker("subWorker.js");
```

LOTS OF WORKERS

Peter says: "If you spawn a Worker that recursively spawns another worker with the same JavaScript source file, you will see some interesting results, to say the least."

Using Timers

Although HTML5 Web Workers cannot access the `window` object, they can make use of the full JavaScript timing API, typically found on the global window:

```
var t = setTimeout(postMessage, 2000, "delayed message");
```

Simple Example Code

For completeness, Listings 9-2 and 9-3 show the code for the simple page and the Web Worker JavaScript file.

Listing 8-2. Simple HTML Page that calls an HTML5 Web Worker

```
<!DOCTYPE html>
<title>Simple HTML5 Web Workers Example</title>

<link rel="stylesheet" href="styles.css">

<h1>Simple HTML5 Web Workers Example</h1>

<p id="support">Your browser does not support HTML5 Web Workers.</p>

<button id="stopButton" >Stop Task</button>
<button id="helloButton" >Post a Message</button>


<script>
    function stopWorker() {
        worker.terminate();
    }

    function messageHandler(e) {
        console.log(e.data);
    }

    function errorHandler(e) {
        console.warn(e.message, e);
    }

    function loadDemo() {
        if (typeof(Worker) !== "undefined") {
            document.getElementById("support").innerHTML =
                "Excellent! Your browser supports HTML5 Web Workers";

            worker = new Worker("echoWorker.js");
            worker.addEventListener("message", messageHandler, true);
            worker.addEventListener("error", errorHandler, true);
```

```
        document.getElementById("helloButton").onclick = function() {
            worker.postMessage("Here's a message for you");
    }

        document.getElementById("stopButton").onclick = stopWorker;
    }
}

window.addEventListener("load", loadDemo, true);


</script>
```

Listing 8-3. Simple HTML5 Web Worker JavaScript file

```
function messageHandler(e) {
    postMessage("worker says: " + e.data + " too");
}

addEventListener("message", messageHandler, true);
```

Building an Application with HTML5 Web Workers

So far, we've focused on using the different Web Worker APIs. Let's see how powerful the Web Workers API can really be by building an application: a web page with an image-blurring filter, parallelized to run on multiple Web Workers. Figure 8-4 shows what this application looks like in action.

Figure 8-4. HTML5 Web Worker–based web page with image-blurring filter

This application sends image data from a canvas to several Web Workers (you can specify how many). The Web Workers then process the image with a simple box-blur filter. This may take several seconds, depending on the size of the image and the computational resources available (even machines with fast CPUs may have load from other processes, causing JavaScript execution to take more wall-clock time to complete).

However, because the heavy lifting takes place in Web Workers, there is no danger of slow-script warnings and, therefore, no need to manually partition the task into scheduled slices—something you would have to consider if you could not use Web Workers.

Coding the blur.js Helper Script

Inside the `blur.js` application page, we can use a straightforward implementation of a blur filter that loops until it has completely processed its input, as shown in Listing 8-4.

Listing 8-4. A JavaScript box-blur implementation in the file blur.js

```javascript
function inRange(i, width, height) {
    return ((i>=0) && (i < width*height*4));
}

function averageNeighbors(imageData, width, height, i) {
    var v = imageData[i];

    // cardinal directions
    var north = inRange(i-width*4, width, height) ? imageData[i-width*4] : v;
    var south = inRange(i+width*4, width, height) ? imageData[i+width*4] : v;
    var west = inRange(i-4, width, height) ? imageData[i-4] : v;
    var east = inRange(i+4, width, height) ? imageData[i+4] : v;

    // diagonal neighbors
    var ne = inRange(i-width*4+4, width, height) ? imageData[i-width*4+4] : v;
    var nw = inRange(i-width*4-4, width, height) ? imageData[i-width*4-4] : v;
    var se = inRange(i+width*4+4, width, height) ? imageData[i+width*4+4] : v;
    var sw = inRange(i+width*4-4, width, height) ? imageData[i+width*4-4] : v;

    // average
    var newVal = Math.floor((north + south + east + west + se + sw + ne + nw + v)/9);

    if (isNaN(newVal)) {
        sendStatus("bad value " + i + " for height " + height);
        throw new Error("NaN");
    }
    return newVal;
}

function boxBlur(imageData, width, height) {
    var data = [];
    var val = 0;
    for (var i=0; i<width*height*4; i++) {
        val = averageNeighbors(imageData, width, height, i);
        data[i] = val;
    }

    return data;
}
```

In brief, this algorithm blurs an image by averaging nearby pixel values. For a large image with millions of pixels, this takes a substantial amount of time. It is very undesirable to run a loop such as this in the UI thread. Even if a slow-script warning did not appear, the page UI would be unresponsive until the loop terminated. For this reason, it makes a good example of background computation in Web Workers.

Coding the blur.html Application Page

Listing 8-5 shows the code for the HTML page that calls the Web Worker. The HTML for this example is kept simple for reasons of clarity. The purpose here is not to build a beautiful interface, but to provide a simple skeleton that can control the Web Workers and demonstrate them in action. In this application, a `canvas` element that displays the input image is injected into the page. We have buttons to start blurring the image, stop blurring, reset the image, and specify the number of workers to spawn.

Listing 8-5. Code for the page blur.html

```html
<!DOCTYPE html>
<title>HTML5 Web Workers</title>
<link rel="stylesheet" href = "styles.css">

<h1>HTML5 Web Workers</h1>

<p id="status">Your browser does not support HTML5 Web Workers.</p>


<button id="startBlurButton" disabled>Blur</button>
<button id="stopButton" disabled>Stop Workers</button>
<button onclick="document.location = document.location;">Reload</button>

<label for="workerCount">Number of Workers</label>
<select id="workerCount">
    <option>1</option>
    <option selected>2</option>
    <option>4</option>
    <option>8</option>
    <option>16</option>
</select>

<div id="imageContainer"></div>
<div id="logOutput"></div>
```

Next, let's add the code to create workers to the file `blur.html`. We instantiate a `worker` object, passing in a URL of a JavaScript file. Each instantiated worker will run the same code but be responsible for processing different parts of the input image:

```javascript
function initWorker(src) {
    var worker = new Worker(src);
    worker.addEventListener("message", messageHandler, true);
    worker.addEventListener("error", errorHandler, true);
    return worker;
}
```

Let's add the error handling code to the file `blur.html`, as follows. In the event of an error in the worker, the page will be able to display an error message instead of continuing unaware. Our example shouldn't encounter any trouble, but listening for error events is generally a good practice and is invaluable for debugging.

```
function errorHandler(e) {
    log("error: " + e.message);
}
```

Coding the blurWorker.js Web Worker Script

Next, we add the code that our workers use to communicate with the page to the file `blurWorker.js` (see Listing 8-6). As the Web Workers finish blocks of computation, they can use `postMessage` to inform the page that they have made progress. We will use this information to update the image displayed on the main page. After creation, our Web Workers wait for a message containing image data and the instruction to commence blurring. This message is a JavaScript object containing the type of message and the image data represented as an array of Numbers.

Listing 8-6. Sending and handling image data in the file blurWorker.js

```
function sendStatus(statusText) {
    postMessage({"type" : "status",
                 "statusText" : statusText}
                );
}

function messageHandler(e) {
    var messageType = e.data.type;
    switch (messageType) {
        case ("blur"):
            sendStatus("Worker started blur on data in range: " +
                            e.data.startX + "-" + (e.data.startX+e.data.width));
            var imageData = e.data.imageData;
            imageData = boxBlur(imageData, e.data.width, e.data.height, e.data.startX);

            postMessage({"type" : "progress",
                         "imageData" : imageData,
                         "width" : e.data.width,
                         "height" : e.data.height,
                         "startX" : e.data.startX
                        });
            sendStatus("Finished blur on data in range: " +
                            e.data.startX + "-" + (e.data.width+e.data.startX));
            break;
        default:
            sendStatus("Worker got message: " + e.data);
    }
}
addEventListener("message", messageHandler, true);
```

Communicating with the Web Workers

In the file `blur.html`, we can use our workers by sending them some data and arguments that represent a blur task. This is done by using `postMessage` to send a JavaScript object containing the Array of RGBA image data, the dimensions of the source image, and the range of pixels for which the worker is responsible. Each worker processes a different section of the image based on the message it receives:

```
function sendBlurTask(worker, i, chunkWidth) {
        var chunkHeight = image.height;
        var chunkStartX = i * chunkWidth;
        var chunkStartY = 0;
        var data = ctx.getImageData(chunkStartX, chunkStartY,
                                    chunkWidth, chunkHeight).data;

        worker.postMessage({'type' : 'blur',
                            'imageData' : data,
                            'width' : chunkWidth,
                            'height' : chunkHeight,
                            'startX' : chunkStartX});
}
```

CANVAS IMAGE DATA

Frank says: "`postMessage` is specified to allow efficient serialization of `imageData` objects for use with the canvas API. Some browsers that include the Worker and `postMessage` APIs may not support the extended serialization capabilities of `postMessage`. Firefox 3.5, for instance, cannot send `imageData` objects with `postMessage`, but future versions of Firefox may be able to do so.

Because of this, our image processing example presented in this chapter sends `imageData.data` (which serializes like a JavaScript Array) instead of sending the `imageData` object itself. As the Web Workers compute their tasks, they communicate their status and results back to the page. Listing 8-6 shows how data is sent from the worker(s) to the page after it has been processed by the blur filter. Again, the message contains a JavaScript object with fields for image data and coordinates marking the boundaries of the processed section."

On the HTML page side, a message handler consumes this data and uses it to update the canvas with the new pixel values. As processed image data comes in, the result is immediately visible. We now have a sample application that can process images while potentially taking advantage of multiple CPU cores. Moreover, we didn't lock up the UI and make it unresponsive while the Web Workers were active. Figure 8-5 shows the application in action.

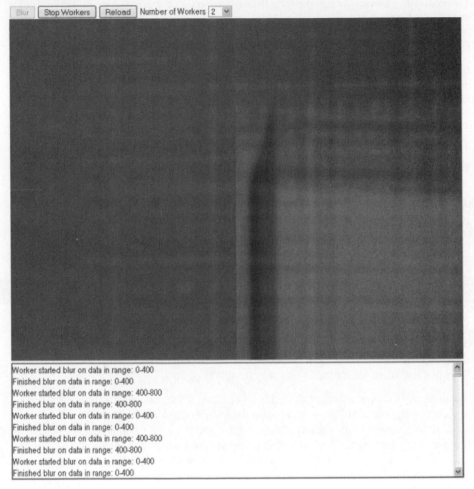

Figure 8-5. The blur application in action

The Application in Action

To see this example in action, the page blur.html has to be served up by a web server (for example, Apache or Python's SimpleHTTPServer). To following steps show how you can use Python SimpleHTTPServer to run the application:

1. Install Python.

2. Navigate to the directory that contains the example file (blur.html).

3. Start Python as follows:

   ```
   python -m SimpleHTTPServer 9999
   ```

4. Open a browser and navigate to http://localhost:9999/blur.html. You should now see the page shown in Figure 8-5.

Example Code

For completeness, Listings 9-7, 9-8, and 9-9 contain the full code for the example application.

Listing 8-7. Content of the file blur.html

```html
<!DOCTYPE html>
<title>HTML5 Web Workers</title>
<link rel="stylesheet" href = "styles.css">

<h1>HTML5 Web Workers</h1>

<p id="status">Your browser does not support HTML5 Web Workers.</p>


<button id="startBlurButton" disabled>Blur</button>
<button id="stopButton" disabled>Stop Workers</button>
<button onclick="document.location = document.location;">Reload</button>

<label for="workerCount">Number of Workers</label>
<select id="workerCount">
    <option>1</option>
    <option selected>2</option>
    <option>4</option>
    <option>8</option>
    <option>16</option>
</select>

<div id="imageContainer"></div>
<div id="logOutput"></div>
<script>
```

```
var imageURL = "example2.png";
var image;
var ctx;
var workers = [];

function log(s) {
    var logOutput = document.getElementById("logOutput");
    logOutput.innerHTML = s + "<br>" + logOutput.innerHTML;
}

function setRunningState(p) {
    // while running, the stop button is enabled and the start button is not
    document.getElementById("startBlurButton").disabled = p;
    document.getElementById("stopButton").disabled = !p;
}

function initWorker(src) {
    var worker = new Worker(src);
    worker.addEventListener("message", messageHandler, true);
    worker.addEventListener("error", errorHandler, true);
    return worker;
}

function startBlur() {
    var workerCount = parseInt(document.getElementById("workerCount").value);
    var width = image.width/workerCount;

    for (var i=0; i<workerCount; i++) {
        var worker = initWorker("blurWorker.js");
        worker.index = i;
        worker.width = width;
        workers[i] = worker;

        sendBlurTask(worker, i, width);
    }
    setRunningState(true);
}

function sendBlurTask(worker, i, chunkWidth) {
        var chunkHeight = image.height;
        var chunkStartX = i * chunkWidth;
        var chunkStartY = 0;
        var data = ctx.getImageData(chunkStartX, chunkStartY,
                                    chunkWidth, chunkHeight).data;

        worker.postMessage({'type' : 'blur',
                            'imageData' : data,
                            'width' : chunkWidth,
                            'height' : chunkHeight,
                            'startX' : chunkStartX});
}
```

```
function stopBlur() {
    for (var i=0; i<workers.length; i++) {
        workers[i].terminate();
    }
    setRunningState(false);
}

function messageHandler(e) {
    var messageType = e.data.type;
    switch (messageType) {
        case ("status"):
            log(e.data.statusText);
            break;
        case ("progress"):
            var imageData = ctx.createImageData(e.data.width, e.data.height);

            for (var i = 0; i<imageData.data.length; i++) {
                var val = e.data.imageData[i];
                if (val === null || val > 255 || val < 0) {
                    log("illegal value: " + val + " at " + i);
                    return;
                }

                imageData.data[i] = val;
            }
            ctx.putImageData(imageData, e.data.startX, 0);

            // blur the same tile again
            sendBlurTask(e.target, e.target.index, e.target.width);
            break;
        default:
            break;
    }
}

function errorHandler(e) {
    log("error: " + e.message);
}

function loadImageData(url) {

    var canvas = document.createElement('canvas');
    ctx = canvas.getContext('2d');
    image = new Image();
    image.src = url;

    document.getElementById("imageContainer").appendChild(canvas);

    image.onload = function(){
        canvas.width = image.width;
        canvas.height = image.height;
        ctx.drawImage(image, 0, 0);
```

```
            window.imgdata = ctx.getImageData(0, 0, image.width, image.height);
            n = ctx.createImageData(image.width, image.height);
            setRunningState(false);
            log("Image loaded: " + image.width + "x" + image.height + " pixels");
        };
    }

function loadDemo() {
        log("Loading image data");

        if (typeof(Worker) !== "undefined") {
            document.getElementById("status").innerHTML = "Your browser supports HTML5 Web
Workers";

            document.getElementById("stopButton").onclick = stopBlur;
            document.getElementById("startBlurButton").onclick = startBlur;

            loadImageData(imageURL);

            document.getElementById("startBlurButton").disabled = true;
            document.getElementById("stopButton").disabled = true;
        }

    }

window.addEventListener("load", loadDemo, true);
</script>
```

Listing 8-8. Content of the file blurWorker.js

```
importScripts("blur.js");

function sendStatus(statusText) {
    postMessage({"type" : "status",
                "statusText" : statusText}
            );
}

function messageHandler(e) {
    var messageType = e.data.type;
    switch (messageType) {
        case ("blur"):
            sendStatus("Worker started blur on data in range: " +
                        e.data.startX + "-" + (e.data.startX+e.data.width));
            var imageData = e.data.imageData;
            imageData = boxBlur(imageData, e.data.width, e.data.height, e.data.startX);

            postMessage({"type" : "progress",
                        "imageData" : imageData,
```

```
                              "width" : e.data.width,
                              "height" : e.data.height,
                              "startX" : e.data.startX
                          });
                sendStatus("Finished blur on data in range: " +
                          e.data.startX + "-" + (e.data.width+e.data.startX));
                break;
            default:
                sendStatus("Worker got message: " + e.data);
        }
    }
}

addEventListener("message", messageHandler, true);
```

Listing 8-9. Content of the file blur.js

```
function inRange(i, width, height) {
    return ((i>=0) && (i < width*height*4));
}

function averageNeighbors(imageData, width, height, i) {
    var v = imageData[i];

    // cardinal directions
    var north = inRange(i-width*4, width, height) ? imageData[i-width*4] : v;
    var south = inRange(i+width*4, width, height) ? imageData[i+width*4] : v;
    var west = inRange(i-4, width, height) ? imageData[i-4] : v;
    var east = inRange(i+4, width, height) ? imageData[i+4] : v;

    // diagonal neighbors
    var ne = inRange(i-width*4+4, width, height) ? imageData[i-width*4+4] : v;
    var nw = inRange(i-width*4-4, width, height) ? imageData[i-width*4-4] : v;
    var se = inRange(i+width*4+4, width, height) ? imageData[i+width*4+4] : v;
    var sw = inRange(i+width*4-4, width, height) ? imageData[i+width*4-4] : v;

    // average
    var newVal = Math.floor((north + south + east + west + se + sw + ne + nw + v)/9);

    if (isNaN(newVal)) {
        sendStatus("bad value " + i + " for height " + height);
        throw new Error("NaN");
    }
    return newVal;
}

function boxBlur(imageData, width, height) {
    var data = [];
    var val = 0;
```

```
    for (var i=0; i<width*height*4; i++) {
        val = averageNeighbors(imageData, width, height, i);
        data[i] = val;
    }

    return data;
}
```

Summary

In this chapter, you have seen how Web Workers can be used to create web applications with background processing. This chapter showed you how Web Workers work and the level of browser support available at the time of this writing. We discussed how you can use the APIs to create new workers and how you communicate between a worker and the context that spawned it. Finally, we showed you how you can build an application with Web Workers. In the next chapter, we'll demonstrate more ways that HTML5 lets you keep local copies of data and reduce the amount of network overhead in your applications.

CHAPTER 9

■ ■ ■

Using the HTML5 Web Storage API

In this chapter, we will explore what you can do with HTML5 Web Storage—sometimes referred to as DOMStorage—an API that makes it easy to persist data across web requests. Before the Web Storage API, remote web servers needed to store any data that persisted by sending it back and forth from client to server. With the advent of the Web Storage API, developers can now store data directly on the client side in the browser for repeated access across requests or to be retrieved long after you completely close the browser, thus reducing network traffic.

In this chapter, we'll first look at how Web Storage differs from cookies and then explore how you can store and retrieve data. Next, we will look at the differences between `localStorage` and `sessionStorage`, the attributes and functions that the storage interface provides, and how you can handle Web Storage events. We wrap up with a look at Web SQL Database API and a few practical extras.

Overview of HTML5 Web Storage

To explain the Web Storage API, it is best to review its predecessor, the intriguingly named cookie. Browser cookies—named after an age-old programming technique for passing small data values between programs, the magic cookie—are a built-in way of sending text values back and forth from server to client. Servers can use the values they put into these cookies to track user information across web pages. Cookie values are transmitted back and forth every time a user visits a domain. For example, cookies can store a session identifier that allows a web server to know which shopping cart belongs to a user by storing a unique ID in a browser cookie that matches the server's own shopping cart database. Then, as a user moves from page to page, the shopping cart can be updated consistently. Another use for cookies is to store local values into an application so that these values can be used on subsequent page loads.

Cookie values can also be used for operations that are slightly less desirable to users, such as tracking which pages a user visits for the sake of targeted advertising. As such, some users have demanded browsers include the functionality to allow them to block or remove cookies either all the time or for specific sites.

Love them or hate them, cookies have been supported by browsers since the earliest days of the Netscape browser, back in the mid-1990s. Cookies are also one of the few features that have been consistently supported across browser vendors since the early days of the Web. Cookies allow data to be tracked across multiple requests, as long as that data is carefully coordinated between the server and the browser code. Despite their ubiquity, cookies have some well-known drawbacks:

- Cookies are extremely limited in size. Generally, only about 4KB of data can be set in a cookie, meaning they are unacceptable for large values such as documents or mail.

- Cookies are transmitted back and forth from server to browser on every request scoped to that cookie. Not only does this mean that cookie data is visible on the network, making them a security risk when not encrypted, but also that any data persisted as cookies will be consuming network bandwidth every time a URL is loaded. Now, the relatively small size of cookies makes more sense.

In many cases, the same results could be achieved without involving a network or remote server. This is where the HTML5 Web Storage API comes in. By using this simple API, developers can store values in easily retrievable JavaScript objects that persist across page loads. By using either `sessionStorage` or `localStorage`, developers can choose to let those values survive either across page loads in a single window or tab or across browser restarts, respectively. Stored data is not transmitted across the network, and is easily accessed on return visits to a page. Furthermore, larger values can be persisted using the Web Storage API values as high as a few megabytes. This makes Web Storage suitable for document and file data that would quickly blow out the size limit of a cookie.

Browser Support for HTML5 Web Storage

Web Storage is one of the most widely adopted features of HTML5. In fact, all currently shipping browser versions support Web Storage in some capacity, and together they constitute a majority of browsers currently deployed. Table 9-1 shows that Web Storage is already supported in many browsers.

Table 9-1. Browser Support for HTML5 Web Storage

Browser	Details
Chrome	Supported in version 3.0 and greater
Firefox	Supported in version 3.0 and greater
Internet Explorer	Supported in version 8.0 and greater
Opera	Supported in version 10.5 and greater
Safari	Supported in version 4.0 and greater

HTML5 Web Storage is one of the safest APIs to use in your web applications today because of its widespread support. As usual, though, it is a good idea to first test if Web Storage is supported, before you use it. The section "Checking for Browser Support" later in this chapter will show you how you can programmatically check if Web Storage is supported.

Using the HTML5 Web Storage API

The Web Storage API is surprisingly simple to use. We'll start by covering simple storage and retrieval of values and then move on to the differences between **sessionStorage** and **localStorage**. Finally, we'll look at the more advanced aspects of the API, such as event notification when values change.

Checking for Browser Support

The storage database for a given domain is accessed directly from the **window** object. Therefore, determining if a user's browser supports the Web Storage API is as easy as checking for the existence of **window.sessionStorage** or **window.localStorage**. Listing 9-1 shows a routine that checks for storage support and displays a message about the browser's support for the Web Storage API. This routine is part of the **browser-test.html** file and located in the **code/storage** folder. Instead of this code, you can also use Modernizr, which handles some cases that may result in a false positive, such as the lack of storage support in Chrome's incognito mode.

Listing 9-1. Checking for Web Storage Support

```
function checkStorageSupport() {

  //sessionStorage
  if (window.sessionStorage) {
    alert('This browser supports sessionStorage');
  } else {
    alert('This browser does NOT support sessionStorage');
  }

  //localStorage
  if (window.localStorage) {
    alert('This browser supports localStorage');
  } else {
    alert('This browser does NOT support localStorage');
  }
}
```

Figure 9-1 shows this check for storage support in action.

Figure 9-1. Checking for browser support

Many browsers do not support **sessionStorage** for files accessed directly from the file system. Make sure you serve up the pages from a web server when you run the examples in this chapter. For example, you can start Python's simple HTTP server in the **code/storage** directory as follows:

```
python -m SimpleHTTPServer 9999
```

After that, you can access the files at **http://localhost:9999/**. For example, **http://localhost:9999/browser-test.html**.

■ **Note** As with many APIs, it is possible that a given browser supports only some of the standard. However, because the Web Storage API is quite small, consistent implementation is already widespread. Consider, also, that users may choose to turn off Web Storage in their browsers for security reasons even if the browser itself supports the API.

Setting and Retrieving Values

For now, we'll focus on the session storage capability as you learn to set and retrieve simple values in a page. Setting a value can easily be done in a single statement, which we'll initially write using the long-hand notation:

```
window.sessionStorage.setItem('myFirstKey', 'myFirstValue');
```

There are three important points to notice from this storage access statement:

- The object implementing the Web Storage API is attached to the window, so `window.sessionStorage` contains the functions you need to call.

- The function we are calling is `setItem`, which takes a key string and a value string. Although the formal Web Storage API supports passing in nonstring values, current browsers are limited in the value types they support.

- This particular call will set into the session storage the string `myFirstValue`, which can later be retrieved by the key `myFirstKey`.

To retrieve the value, the long-hand notation involves making a call to the `getItem` function. For example, if we augmented our previous example with the following statement

```
alert(window.sessionStorage.getItem('myFirstKey'));
```

the browser raises a JavaScript alert displaying the text `myFirstValue`. As you can see, setting and retrieving values from the Web Storage API is very straightforward.

However, there is an even simpler way to access the storage objects in your code. You are also able to use expando-properties to set values in storage. Using this approach, the `setItem` and `getItem` calls can be avoided entirely by simply setting and retrieving values corresponding to the key-value pair directly on the `sessionStorage` object. Using this approach, our value set call can be rewritten as follows:

```
window.sessionStorage.myFirstKey = 'myFirstValue';
```

Similarly, the value retrieval call can be rewritten like so:

```
alert(window.sessionStorage.myFirstKey);
```

That's it for the basics. You now have all the knowledge you need to use session storage in your application. However, you might be wondering what's so special about this `sessionStorage` object. After all, JavaScript allows you to set and get properties on nearly any object. The difference is in the scope. What you may not have realized is that our example set and get calls do not need to occur in the same web page. As long as pages are served from the same origin—the combination of scheme, host, and port—then values set on `sessionStorage` can be retrieved from other pages using the same keys. This also applies to subsequent loads of the same page. As a developer, you are probably used to the idea that changes made in script will disappear whenever a page is reloaded. That is no longer true for values that are set in the Web Storage API; they will continue to exist across page loads.

Plugging Data Leaks

How long do the values persist? For objects set into `sessionStorage`, they will persist as long as the browser window (or tab) is not closed. As soon as a user closes the window—or browser, for that matter—the `sessionStorage` values are cleared out. It is useful to consider a `sessionStorage` value to be somewhat like a sticky note reminder. Values put into `sessionStorage` won't last long, and you should not put anything truly valuable into them, as the values are not guaranteed to be around whenever you are looking for them.

Why, then, would you choose to use the session storage area in your web application? Session storage is perfect for short-lived processes that would normally be represented in wizards or dialogs. If you have data to store over the course of a few pages, that you would not be keen to have resurface the next time a user visits your application, feel free to store them in the session storage area. In the past, these types of values might be submitted by forms and cookies and transmitted back and forth on every page load. Using storage eliminates that overhead.

The `sessionStorage` API has another very specific use that solves a problem that has plagued many web-applications: scoping of values. Take, for example, a shopping application that lets you purchase airline tickets. In such an application, preference data such as the ideal departure date and return date could be sent back and forth from browser to server using cookies. This allows the server to remember previous choices as the user moves through the application, picking seats and a choice of meals.

However, it is very common for users to open multiple windows as they shop for travel deals, comparing flights from different vendors for the same departure time. This causes problems in a cookie system, because if a user switches back and forth between browser windows while comparing prices and availability, they are likely to set cookie values in one window that will be unexpectedly applied to another window served from the same URL on its next operation. This is sometimes referred to as leaking data and is caused by the fact that cookies are shared based on the origin where they are stored. Figure 9-2 shows how this can play out.

Figure 9-2. Data leakage while using a travel site to compare prices

Using `sessionStorage`, on the other hand, allows temporary values like a departure date to be saved across pages that access the application but not leak into other windows where the user is also browsing for flights. Therefore, those preferences will be isolated to each window where the corresponding flights are booked.

Local Versus Session Storage

Sometimes, an application needs values that persist beyond the life of a single tab or window or need to be shared across multiple views. In these cases, it is more appropriate to use a different HTML5 Web Storage implementation: `localStorage`. The good news is that you already know how to use `localStorage`. The only programmatic difference between `sessionStorage` and `localStorage` is the name by which each is accessed—through the `sessionStorage` and `localStorage` objects, respectively. The primary behavioral differences are how long the values persist and how they are shared. Table 9-2 shows the differences between the two types of storage.

Table 9-2. Differences Between sessionStorage and localStorage

sessionStorage	localStorage
Values persist only as long as the window or tab in which they were stored.	Values persist beyond window and browser lifetimes.
Values are only visible within the window or tab that created them.	Values are shared across every window or tab running at the same origin.

Other Web Storage API Attributes and Functions

The HTML5 Web Storage API is one of the simplest in the HTML5 set. We have already looked at both explicit and implicit ways to set and retrieve data from the session and local storage areas. Let's complete our survey of the API by looking at the full set of available attributes and function calls.

The `sessionStorage` and `localStorage` objects can be retrieved from the `window` object of the document in which they are being used. Other than their names and the duration of their values, they are identical in functionality. Both implement the `Storage` interface, which is shown in Listing 9-2.

Listing 9-2. The Storage Interface

```
interface Storage {
  readonly attribute unsigned long length;
  getter DOMString key(in unsigned long index);
  getter any getItem(in DOMString key);
  setter creator void setItem(in DOMString key, in any data);
  deleter void removeItem(in DOMString key);
  void clear();
};
```

Let's look at the attributes and functions here in more detail.

- The **length** attribute specifies how many key-value pairs are currently stored in the storage object. Remember that storage objects are specific to their origin, so that implies that the items (and length) of the storage object only reflect the items stored for the current origin.

- The **key(index)** function allows retrieval of a given key. Generally, this is most useful when you wish to iterate across all the keys in a particular storage object. Keys are zero-based, meaning that the first key is at index (0) and the last key is at index (length – 1). Once a key is retrieved, it can be used to fetch its corresponding value. Keys will retain their indices over the life of a given storage object unless a key or one of its predecessors is removed.

- As you've already seen, **getItem(key)** function is one way to retrieve the value based on a given key. The other is to reference the key as an array index to the storage object. In both cases, the value **null** will be returned if the key does not exist in storage.

- Similarly, **setItem(key, value)** function will put a value into storage under the specified key name, or replace an existing value if one already exists under that key name. Note that it is possible to receive an error when setting an item value; if the user has storage turned off for that site, or if the storage is already filled to its maximum amount, a **QUOTA_EXCEEDED_ERR** error will be thrown during the attempt. Make sure to handle such an error should your application depend on proper storage behavior.

Figure 9-3. Quota Exceeded Error in Chrome

- The `removeItem(key)` function does exactly as you might expect. If a value is currently in storage under the specified key, this call will remove it. If no item was stored under that key, no action is taken.

■ **Note** Unlike some collection and data frameworks, removing an item does not return the old value as a result of the call to remove it. Make sure you've stored any copy you need independent of the removal.

- Finally, the `clear()` function removes all values from the storage list. It is safe to call this on an empty storage object; as such, a call will simply do nothing.

DISK SPACE QUOTA

Peter says: "The specification recommends that browsers allow five megabytes per origin. Browsers should prompt the user when the quota is reached in order to grant more space and may also provide ways for users to see how much space each origin is using.

In reality, the behavior is still a bit inconsistent. Some browsers silently allow a larger quota or prompt for a space increase, while others simply throw the QUOTA_EXCEEDED_ERR error shown in Figure 9-3. The test file `testQuota.html` used in this example is located in the `code/storage` directory."

Communicating Web Storage Updates

Sometimes, things get a little more complicated, and storage needs to be accessed by more than one page, browser tab, or worker. Perhaps your application needs to trigger many operations in succession whenever a storage value is changed. For just these cases, the HTML5 Web Storage API includes an event mechanism to allow notifications of data updates to be communicated to interested listeners. Web Storage events are fired on the window object for every window of the same origin as the storage operation, regardless of whether or not the listening window is doing any storage operations itself.

■ **Note** Web Storage events can be used to communicate between windows on the same origin. This will be explored a bit more thoroughly in the "Practical Extras" section.

To register to receive the storage events of a window's origin, simply register an event listener, for example:

```
window.addEventListener("storage", displayStorageEvent, true);
```

As you can see, the name **storage** is used to indicate interest in storage events. Any time a **Storage** event—either **sessionStorage** or **localStorage**—for that origin is raised any registered event listener will receive the storage event as the specified event handler. The storage event itself takes the form shown in Listing 9-3.

Listing 9-3. The StorageEvent Interface

```
interface StorageEvent : Event {
  readonly attribute DOMString key;
  readonly attribute any oldValue;
  readonly attribute any newValue;
  readonly attribute DOMString url;
  readonly attribute Storage storageArea;
};
```

The **StorageEvent** object will be the first object passed to the event handler, and it contains all the information necessary to understand the nature of the storage change.

- The **key** attribute contains the key value that was updated or removed in the storage.

- The **oldValue** contains the previous value corresponding to the key before it was updated, and the **newValue** contains the value after the change. If the value was newly added, the **oldValue** will be null, and if the value has been removed, the **newValue** will be null.

- The **url** will point to the origin where the **storage** event occurred.

- Finally, the **storageArea** provides a convenient reference to the **sessionStorage** or **localStorage** where the value was changed. This gives the handler an easy way to query the storage for current values or make changes based on other storage changes.

Listing 9-4 shows a simple event handler, which will raise an alert dialog with the contents of any storage event fired on the page's origin.

Listing 9-4. Event Handler that Displays Content of a Storage Event

```
// display the contents of a storage event
function displayStorageEvent(e) {
  var logged = "key:" + e.key + ", newValue:" + e.newValue + ", oldValue:" +
               e.oldValue +", url:" + e.url + ", storageArea:" + e.storageArea;

  alert(logged);
}

// add a storage event listener for this origin
window.addEventListener("storage", displayStorageEvent, true);
```

Exploring Web Storage

Since HTML5 Web Storage is very similar in function to cookies, it is not too surprising that the most advanced browsers are treating them in a very similar manner. Values that are stored into `localStorage` or `sessionStorage` can be browsed similar to cookies in the latest browsers, as shown in Figure 9-4.

Figure 9-4. Storage values in Google Chrome's Storage Panel

This interface also grants users the ability to remove storage values as desired and easily see what values a given web site is recording while they visit the pages. Not surprisingly, the Safari browser from Apple has a similar, unified display for cookies and storage, as it is based on the same underlying WebKit rendering engine as Chrome is. Figure 9-5 shows the Safari Storage panel.

Figure 9-5. Storage values in Safari's Storage panel

The Opera browsers goes one step further, by allowing users to not only browse and delete storage values but also create them as shown in Figure 9-6.

Figure 9-6. Storage values in Opera's Storage panel

As Web Storage becomes more widely implemented by the various browser vendors, expect both the capacity and tooling available to users and developers to expand rapidly.

Building an Application with HTML5 Web Storage

Now, let's put together what you've learned by integrating storage into a web application. As applications grow more complex, it becomes increasingly important to manage as much data as possible without server interaction. Keeping data local to the client reduces network traffic and increases responsiveness by fetching data from a local machine instead of a remote location.

One common problem developers grapple with is how to manage data as users move from page to page within an application. Traditionally, web applications achieve this by storing data on a server and moving it back and forth while the user navigates pages. Alternatively, the application may attempt to keep the user in a single page and update everything dynamically. However, users are prone to wander, and getting data back into the display quickly when a user returns to your application's page is a great way to enhance the user experience.

In our sample application, we'll show how to store temporary application data locally while the user moves from page to page on a web site and quickly load it from storage on each page. To accomplish this, we'll build on the examples of previous chapters. In Chapter 4, we showed how easy it is to gather a user's current location. Then, in Chapter 6, we demonstrated how to take location data and send it to a remote server so that it can be viewed by any number of interested users. Here, we will go one step further: we will listen for broadcasted location data delivered via a WebSocket and store it in local storage so that it is immediately available as users move from page to page.

Imagine that our running club has live location information from its race participants being broadcast from their mobile devices and shared via a WebSocket server. It would be simple for a web application to display the current position of every racer live and in real time, as the racers upload new position information during the race. And a smart web site would cache those race positions to display them quickly as a user navigated among the pages of the site. That's exactly what we're going to build.

In order to achieve this, we'll need to introduce a demonstration web site that can save and restore our racer data. We've created a three-page example running race site and placed it in our online resources in the folder **code/storage**, but you can use any site of your choosing for your own demonstration. The key here is merely that you have multiple web pages that are easily traversed by a user. We will insert a bit of dynamic content into those pages to represent a live leader board, or a list of race participants and their current distance from the finish line. Figure 9-7 shows the three pages that make up the race site.

Figure 9-7. The example race website

Each of our web pages will contain a common section to display the leader board data. Each entry in the leader board will show the name of one of our racers and his or her current distance from the finish line. When any of our pages is loaded, it will make a WebSocket connection to a race broadcast server and listen for messages indicating the position of a racer. The racers, in turn, will be sending their current position to the same broadcast server, causing the position data to stream down to the page in real time.

All of this has been covered in previous chapters related to Geolocation and WebSockets. In fact, much of the demonstration code here is shared with the examples from earlier in this book. However, there is one key difference in this example: when the data arrives in the page, we will store it in the session storage area for later retrieval. Then, whenever a user navigates to a new page, the stored data will be retrieved and displayed before making a new WebSocket connection. In this way, the temporary data is transferred from page to page without using any cookies or web server communication.

Just as we did in the WebSockets chapter, we'll send our racer location messages across the web in a simple format that is easy to read and parse. This format is a **String** that uses the semicolon character (**;**) as a delimiter separating the chunks of data: name, latitude, and longitude. For example, a racer named Racer X who is at latitude 37.20 and longitude –121.53 would be identified with the following string:

```
;Racer X;37.20;-121.53
```

Now, let's dig into the code itself. Each of our pages will contain identical JavaScript code to connect to the WebSocket server, process and display leader board messages, and save and restore the leader board using **sessionStorage**. As such, this code would be a prime candidate to include in a JavaScript library in a real application.

First, we'll establish a few utility methods that you've seen before. To calculate the distance of any particular racer from the finish line, we need routines to calculate distance between two geolocation positions as shown in Listing 9-5.

Listing 9-5. Distance Calculation Routine

```
// functions for determining the distance between two
// latitude and longitude positions
function toRadians(num) {
  return num * Math.PI / 180;
}
```

```
function distance(latitude1, longitude1, latitude2, longitude2) {
  // R is the radius of the earth in kilometers
  var R = 6371;

  var deltaLatitude = toRadians((latitude2-latitude1));
  var deltaLongitude = toRadians((longitude2-longitude1));
  latitude1 = toRadians(latitude1), latitude2 = toRadians(latitude2);

  var a = Math.sin(deltaLatitude/2) *
          Math.sin(deltaLatitude/2) +
          Math.cos(latitude1) *
          Math.cos(latitude2) *
          Math.sin(deltaLongitude/2) *
          Math.sin(deltaLongitude/2);

  var c = 2 * Math.atan2(Math.sqrt(a),
                         Math.sqrt(1-a));
  var d = R * c;
  return d;
}

// latitude and longitude for the finish line in the Lake Tahoe race
var finishLat = 39.17222;
var finishLong = -120.13778;
```

In this familiar set of functions—used earlier in Chapter 6—we calculate the distance between two points with a **distance** function. The details are not of particular importance, nor are they the most accurate representation of distance along a racetrack, but they'll do for our example.

In the final lines, we establish a latitude and longitude for the finish line location of the race. As you'll see, we will compare these coordinates with incoming racer positions to determine the racers' distance from the finish line, and thus, their ranks in the race.

Now, let's look at a tiny snippet of the HTML markup used to display the page.

```
<h2>Live T216 Leaderboard</h2>
<p id="leaderboardStatus">Leaderboard: Connecting...</p>
<div id="leaderboard"></div>
```

Although most of the page HTML is irrelevant to our demonstration, in these few lines, we declare some named elements with the IDs **leaderboardStatus** and **leaderboard**. The **leaderboardStatus** is where we will display the connection information for our WebSocket. And the leaderboard itself is where we will insert **div** elements to indicate the position information we are receiving from our WebSocket messages, using the utility function shown in Listing 9-6.

Listing 9-6. Position Information Utility Function

```
// display the name and distance in the page
function displayRacerLocation(name, distance) {
    // locate the HTML element for this ID
    // if one doesn't exist, create it
    var incomingRow = document.getElementById(name);
    if (!incomingRow) {
```

```
        incomingRow = document.createElement('div');
        incomingRow.setAttribute('id', name);
        incomingRow.userText = name;

        document.getElementById("leaderboard").appendChild(incomingRow);
    }

    incomingRow.innerHTML = incomingRow.userText + " is " +
                        Math.round(distance*10000)/10000 + " km from the finish line";
}
```

This utility is a simple display routine, which takes the racer's name and distance from the finish line. Figure 9-8 shows what the leader board section looks like on the **index.html** page.

Figure 9-8. The race leader board

The name is used for two purposes; not only is it placed into the status message for that racer but it is also used to reference the unique **div** element where that racer's status is stored. If a **div** for our racer already exists, we will find it when we look it up using the standard **document.getElementById()** routine. If a **div** does not already exist in the page for that racer, we will create one and insert it into the **leaderboard** area. Either way, we update the **div** element corresponding to that racer with the latest distance from the finish line, which will immediately update it in the display of the page. If you have already read Chapter 6, this will be familiar to you from the example application we created there.

Our next function is the message processor that will be called whenever data is returned from the broadcasting race WebSocket server, as shown in Listing 9-7.

Listing 9-7. WebSocket Message Processing Function

```
// callback when new position data is retrieved from the websocket
function dataReturned(locationData) {
    // break the data into ID, latitude, and longitude
    var allData = locationData.split(";");
    var incomingId   = allData[1];
    var incomingLat  = allData[2];
    var incomingLong = allData[3];
```

```
        // update the row text with the new values
        var currentDistance = distance(incomingLat, incomingLong, finishLat, finishLong);

        // store the incoming user name and distance in storage
        window.sessionStorage[incomingId] = currentDistance;

        // display the new user data in the page
        displayRacerLocation(incomingId, currentDistance);
    }
```

This function takes a string in the format described previously, a semicolon-separated message containing the name, latitude, and longitude of a racer. Our first step is to split it into its component parts using the JavaScript **split()** routine to produce the **incomingId**, **incomingLat**, and **incomingLong**, respectively.

Next, it passes the racer's latitude and longitude, as well as the latitude and longitude of the finish line, to the **distance** utility method we defined earlier, storing the resulting distance in the **currentDistance** variable.

Now that we actually have some data worth storing, we can look at the call which exercises HTML5 Web Storage.

```
        // store the incoming user name and distance in storage
        window.sessionStorage[incomingId] = currentDistance;
```

In this line, we use the **sessionStorage** object on the window to store the current distance of the racer from the finish line as a value under the name and ID of the racer. In other words, we will set a value on the session storage with the key being the racer's name and the value being that racer's distance from the finish. As you will see momentarily, this data will be retrieved from storage as the user navigates from page to page on the web site. At the end of the function, we call the **displayLocation()** routine we previously defined to make sure that this most recent location update is displayed visually in the current page.

Now, on to our final function in our storage example—the load routine shown in Listing 9-8 that fires whenever visitors access the web page.

Listing 9-8. Initial Page Load Routine

```
// when the page loads, make a socket connection to the race broadcast server
function loadDemo() {
    // make sure the browser supports sessionStorage
    if (typeof(window.sessionStorage) === "undefined") {
        document.getElementById("leaderboardStatus").innerHTML = "Your browser does↵
                not support HTML5 Web Storage";
        return;
    }

    var storage = window.sessionStorage;

    // for each key in the storage database, display a new racer
    // location in the page
    for (var i=0; i < storage.length; i++) {
        var currRacer = storage.key(i);
        displayRacerLocation(currRacer, storage[currRacer]);
    }
```

```
// test to make sure that Web Sockets are supported
if (window.WebSocket) {

    // the location where our broadcast WebSocket server is located
    url = "ws://websockets.org:7999/broadcast";
    socket = new WebSocket(url);
    socket.onopen = function() {
        document.getElementById("leaderboardStatus").innerHTML = "Leaderboard:

                Connected!";
    }
    socket.onmessage = function(e) {
        dataReturned(e.data);
    }
}
}
```

This is a longer function than the others, and there is a lot going on. Let's take it step by step. First, as shown in Listing 9-9, we do a basic error check to make sure that the browser viewing the page supports **sessionStorage** by checking for its presence on the window object. If **sessionStorage** is not accessible, we simply update the **leaderboardStatus** area to indicate as much, and the return out of the loading routine. We won't be attempting to work around lack of browser storage in this example.

Listing 9-9. Checking for Browser Support

```
// make sure the browser supports sessionStorage
if (typeof(window.sessionStorage) === "undefined") {
    document.getElementById("leaderboardStatus").innerHTML = "Your browser does
            not support HTML5 Web Storage";
    return;
}
```

___

■ **Note** It is possible to rework this demonstration to simply forgo any persistence of data between page navigations and start each page load with a clean leader board if storage is not supported. However, our goal here is to show how storage optimizes the experience for both the user and the network.

___

The next thing we do on page load is to use the storage to retrieve any racer distance results that have already been served to this or other pages of our website. Recall that we are running an identical block of script code on every one of our site pages, so that the leader board follows the users as they browses around various locations. As such, the leader board may already have stored values into storage from other pages that will be retrieved and displayed here directly on load as shown in Listing 9-10. The previously saved values will follow the user during navigation, as long as the user does not close the window, tab, or browser, thus clearing out the session storage.

Listing 9-10. Displaying Stored Racer Data

```
var storage = window.sessionStorage;

// for each key in the storage database, display a new racer
// location in the page
for (var i=0; i < storage.length; i++) {
    var currRacer = storage.key(i);
    displayRacerLocation(currRacer, storage[currRacer]);
}
```

This is an important section of code. Here, we query the session for its length—in other words, the number of keys the storage contains. Then, we grab each key using **storage.key()** and store it into the **currRacer** variable, later using that variable to reference the key's corresponding value with **storage[currRacer]**. Together, the key and its value represent a racer and that racer's distance, which were stored on a visit to a previous page.

Once we have a previously stored racer name and distance, we display them using the **displayRacerLocation()** function. This all happens very quickly on page load, causing the page to instantaneously fill its leader board with previously transmitted values.

■ **Note** Our sample application relies on being the only application that stores values into the session storage area. If your application needs to share the storage object with other data, you will need to use a more nuanced key strategy than simply storing the keys at root level. We'll look at another storage strategy in the "Practical Extras" section.

Our last piece of load behavior is to hook up the page to the racer broadcast server using a simple WebSocket, as shown in Listing 9-11.

Listing 9-11. Connecting to the WebSocket Broadcast Service

```
// test to make sure that WebSocket is supported
if (window.WebSocket) {

    // the location where our broadcast WebSocket server is located
    url = "ws://websockets.org:7999/broadcast";
    socket = new WebSocket(url);
    socket.onopen = function() {
        document.getElementById("leaderboardStatus").innerHTML = "Leaderboard:↵
                Connected!";
    }
    socket.onmessage = function(e) {
        dataReturned(e.data);
    }
}
```

As we did before in our WebSocket chapter, we first check to make sure that the browser supports WebSocket by checking for the existence of the `window.WebSocket` object. Once we have verified that it exists, we connect to the URL where our WebSocket server is running. This server broadcasts racer location messages of the semicolon-separated format listed previously, and whenever we receive one of those messages via the `socket.onmessage` callback, we call our previously discussed `dataReturned()` function to process and display it. We also use the `socket.onopen` callback to update our `leaderboardStatus` area with a simple diagnostic message to indicate that the socket opened successfully.

That's it for our `load` routine. The final block of code we declare in our script block is the registration function, which requests that the `loadDemo()` function is called whenever page load is complete:

```
// add listeners on page load and unload
window.addEventListener("load", loadDemo, true);
```

As you have seen many times before, this event listener requests that our `loadDemo()` function will be called when the window has completed loading.

But how do we get racer data transmitted from the trails to the broadcast WebSocket server and into our pages? Well, we could actually use the tracker example previously declared in the WebSocket chapter by simply pointing its connect URL to the broadcast server listed previously. After all, the data string formats were chosen to be the same. However, we have also created a very simple racer broadcast source page, shown in Listing 9-12, which serves a similar purpose. This page would theoretically be run on the mobile devices of the race participants. Although it does not include any HTML5 Web Storage code itself, it is a convenient way to transmit the properly formatted data when run in a browser with both WebSocket and Geolocation support. The file `racerBroadcast.html` is available from the web site sample area provided for this book.

Listing 9-12. Contents of the File racerBroadcast.html

```
<!DOCTYPE html>

<html>

<head>
<title>Racer Broadcast</title>
<link rel="stylesheet" href="styles.css">
</head>

<body onload="loadDemo()">

<h1>Racer Broadcast</h1>

Racer name: <input type="text" id="racerName" value="Racer X"/>
<button onclick="startSendingLocation()">Start</button>

<div><strong>Geolocation</strong>: <p id="geoStatus">HTML5 Geolocation not↵
 started.</p></div>
<div><strong>WebSocket</strong>: <p id="socketStatus">HTML5 Web Sockets are↵
 <strong>not</strong> supported in your browser.</p></div>

<script type="text/javascript">
```

```
// reference to the Web Socket
var socket;

var lastLocation;

function updateSocketStatus(message) {
    document.getElementById("socketStatus").innerHTML = message;
}

function updateGeolocationStatus(message) {
    document.getElementById("geoStatus").innerHTML = message;
}

function handleLocationError(error) {
    switch(error.code)
    {
    case 0:
      updateGeolocationStatus("There was an error while retrieving your location: " +
                             error.message);
      break;
    case 1:
      updateGeolocationStatus("The user prevented this page from retrieving a
                             location.");
      break;
    case 2:
      updateGeolocationStatus("The browser was unable to determine your location: " +
                             error.message);
      break;
    case 3:
      updateGeolocationStatus("The browser timed out before retrieving the location.");
      break;
    }
}

function loadDemo() {
    // test to make sure that Web Sockets are supported
    if (window.WebSocket) {

        // the location where our broadcast WebSocket server is located
        url = "ws://websockets.org:7999/broadcast";
        socket = new WebSocket(url);
        socket.onopen = function() {
            updateSocketStatus("Connected to WebSocket race broadcast server");
        }
    }
}

function updateLocation(position) {
    var latitude = position.coords.latitude;
    var longitude = position.coords.longitude;
    var timestamp = position.timestamp;
```

```
        updateGeolocationStatus("Location updated at " + timestamp);

        // Schedule a message to send my location via WebSocket
        var toSend =     ";" + document.getElementById("racerName").value
                        + ";" + latitude + ";" + longitude;
        setTimeout("sendMyLocation('" + toSend + "')", 1000);
    }

    function sendMyLocation(newLocation) {
        if (socket) {
            socket.send(newLocation);
            updateSocketStatus("Sent: " + newLocation);
        }
    }

    function startSendingLocation() {
        var geolocation;
        if(navigator.geolocation) {
            geolocation = navigator.geolocation;
            updateGeolocationStatus("HTML5 Geolocation is supported in your browser.");
        }
        else {
            geolocation = google.gears.factory.create('beta.geolocation');
            updateGeolocationStatus("Geolocation is supported via Google Gears");
        }

        // register for position updates using the Geolocation API
        geolocation.watchPosition(updateLocation,
                                  handleLocationError,
                                  {maximumAge:20000});
    }
</script>
</body>
</html>
```

We won't spend too much space covering this file in detail, as it is nearly identical to the tracker example in Chapter 6. The primary difference is that this file contains a text field for entering the racer's name:

```
Racer name: <input type="text" id="racerName" value="Racer X"/>
```

The racer's name is now sent to the broadcast server as part of the data string:

```
var toSend =     ";" + document.getElementById("racerName").value
                + ";" + latitude + ";" + longitude;
```

To try it out for yourself, open two windows in a browser that supports HTML5 Web Storage, Geolocation, and WebSocket, such as Google Chrome. In the first, load the running club's index.html page. You will see it connect to the race broadcast site using WebSocket and then await any racer data notifications. In the second window, open the `racerBroadcast.html` file. After this page, too, has connected to the WebSocket broadcast site, enter a name for your racer, and click the Start button. You'll see that the racer broadcast has transmitted the location of your favorite racer, and it should show up in the leader board in your other browser window. Figure 9-9 shows what this looks like.

Figure 9-9. Race page and racerBroadcast.html side by side

Now, navigate to other racing club pages using the Signup and About the Race links on the left side of the page. Because all of these pages have been configured to load our script, they will immediately load and populate the leader board with the previous racer data, which was delivered while browsing other pages. Send more racer status notifications (from the broadcast page), and you'll see them propagate through the club site pages as you navigate, as well.

Now that we've finished our code, let's review what we've built. We've created a simple function block, suitable for inclusion in a shared JavaScript library, which connects to a WebSocket broadcast server and listens for racer updates. When an update is received, the script displays the position in the page *and* stores it using HTML5 `sessionStorage`. When the page is loaded, it checks for any previously stored racer position values, thus maintaining the state as the user navigates the site. What are some of the benefits we gain from this approach?

- *Reduced network traffic:* Race information is stored locally in the browser. Once it arrives, it sticks around for every page load, rather than using cookies or server requests to fetch it again.

- *Immediate display of values:* The browser pages themselves can be cached rather than loaded from the network, because the dynamic parts of the page—the current leaderboard status—are local data. This data is rapidly displayed without any network load time.

- *Transient storage*: The race data isn't very useful after the race has completed. Consequently, we store it in session storage area, meaning it is discarded when the window or tab is shut down, and it no longer consumes any space.

A WORD ABOUT BULLETPROOFING

Brian says: "We've accomplished a lot in this example using only a few lines of script code. But don't be lulled into thinking everything is this easy in a real, publicly accessible website. We took some shortcuts that simply are not acceptable for a production application.

For example, our message format does not support similarly named racers and would best be replaced by a unique identifier representing each racer. Our distance calculation is "as the crow flies" and not truly indicative of progress in an off-road race. Standard disclaimers apply—more localization, more error checking, and more attention to detail will make your site work for all participants."

This same technique we demonstrated in this example can be applied to any number of data types: chat, e-mail, and sports scores are other examples that can be cached and displayed from page to page using local or session storage just as we've shown here. If your application sends user-specific data back and forth from browser to server at regular intervals, consider using HTML5 Web Storage to streamline your flow.

The Future of Browser Database Storage

The key-value Storage API is great for persisting data, but what about indexed storage that can be queried? HTML5 applications will have access to indexed databases as well. The exact details of the database APIs are still solidifying, and there are multiple proposals. One of the proposals, Web SQL Database, has been implemented in Safari, Chrome, and Opera. Table 9-3 shows the browser support for Web SQL Database.

Table 9-3. Browser Support for HTML5 Web SQL Database

Browser	Details
Chrome	Supported in version 3.0 and greater
Firefox	Not supported
Internet Explorer	Not supported
Opera	Supported in version 10.5 and greater
Safari	Supported in version 3.2 and greater

Web SQL Database allows applications access to SQLite through an asynchronous JavaScript interface. Although it will not be part of the common Web platform nor the eventual recommended database API for HTML5 applications, the SQL API can be useful when targeting a specific platform such as mobile Safari. In any case, this API shows off the power of databases in the browser. Just like the other storage APIs, the browser can limit the amount of storage available to each origin and clear out the data when user data is cleared.

THE FATE OF WEB SQL DATABASE

Frank says: "Even though Web SQL DB is already in Safari, Chrome, and Opera, it will not be implemented in Firefox and it is listed as 'stalled' on the WHATWG wiki. The specification defines an API for executing SQL statements given as strings and defers to SQLite for the SQL dialect. Since it is undesirable for a standard to require a specific implementation of SQL, Web SQL Database has been surpassed by a newer specification, Indexed Database (formerly WebSimpleDB), which is simpler and not tied to a specific SQL database version. Browser implementations of Indexed Database are currently in progress."

Because Web SQL Database is already implemented in the wild, we are including a basic example but omiting the complete details of the API. This example demonstrates the basic use of the Web SQL Database API. It opens a database called **mydb**, creates a **racers** table if a table by that name does not already exist, and populates the table with a list of predefined names. Figure 9-10 shows this database with racers table in Safari's Web Inspector.

Figure 9-10. Database with racers table in Safari's Web Inspector

To begin, we open a database by name. The **window.openDatabase()** function returns a **Database** object through which database interaction takes place. The **openDatabase()** function takes a name as well as an optional version and description. With an open database, application code can now start transactions. SQL statements are executed in the context of a transaction using the **transaction.executeSql()** function. This simple example uses **executeSql()** to create a table, insert racer names into the table, and later query the database to create an HTML table. Figure 9-11 shows the output HTML file with the list of names retrieved from the table.

Web SQL Database

Id	Name
1	Peter Lubbers
2	Brian Albers
3	Frank Salim

Figure 9-11. sql.html displaying the results of SELECT * FROM racers

Database operations can take some time to complete. Instead of blocking script execution until a result set is available, queries run in the background. When the results are available, a function given as the third argument to **executeSQL()** is called back with the transaction and the result set as arguments.

Listing 9-13 shows the complete code for the file **sql.html**; the sample code shown is also located in the **code/storage** folder.

Listing 9-13. Using the Web SQL Database API

```
<!DOCTYPE html>
<title>Web SQL Database</title>
<script>

    // open a database by name
    var db = openDatabase('db', '1.0', 'my first database', 2 * 1024 * 1024);

    function log(id, name) {
        var row = document.createElement("tr");
        var idCell = document.createElement("td");
        var nameCell = document.createElement("td");
        idCell.textContent = id;
        nameCell.textContent = name;
        row.appendChild(idCell);
        row.appendChild(nameCell);

        document.getElementById("racers").appendChild(row);
    }

    function doQuery() {
        db.transaction(function (tx) {
                tx.executeSql('SELECT * from racers', [], function(tx, result) {
                    // log SQL result set
                    for (var i=0; i<result.rows.length; i++) {
                        var item = result.rows.item(i);
                        log(item.id, item.name);
                    }
```

```
                         });
                    });
            }

    function initDatabase() {
        var names = ["Peter Lubbers", "Brian Albers", "Frank Salim"];

        db.transaction(function (tx) {
                tx.executeSql('CREATE TABLE IF NOT EXISTS racers (id integer primary key↵
autoincrement, name)');

                for (var i=0; i<names.length; i++) {
                    tx.executeSql('INSERT INTO racers (name) VALUES (?)', [names[i]]);
                }

                doQuery();
            });
    }

    initDatabase();

</script>

<h1>Web SQL Database</h1>

<table id="racers" border="1" cellspacing="0" style="width:100%">
    <th>Id</th>
    <th>Name</th>
</table>
```

Practical Extras

Sometimes, there are techniques that don't fit into our regular examples but nonetheless apply to many types of HTML5 applications. We present to you some short, but common, practical extras here.

JSON Object Storage

Although the specification for HTML5 Web Storage allows for objects of any type to be stored as key-value pairs, in current implementations, some browsers limit values to be text string data types. There is a practical workaround, however, due to the fact that modern versions of browsers contain built-in support for JavaScript Object Notation (JSON).

JSON is a standard for data-interchange that can represent objects as strings and vice-versa. JSON has been used for over a decade to transmit objects from browser clients to servers over HTTP. Now, we can use it to serialize complex objects in and out of Web Storage in order to persist complex data types. Consider the script block in Listing 9-14.

Listing 9-14. JSON Object Storage

```
<script>

  var data;

  function loadData() {
    data = JSON.parse(sessionStorage["myStorageKey"])
  }

  function saveData() {
    sessionStorage["myStorageKey"] = JSON.stringify(data);
  }

  window.addEventListener("load", loadData, true);
  window.addEventListener("unload", saveData, true);

</script>
```

As you can see, the script contains event listeners to register handlers for load and unload events in the browser window. In this case, the handlers call the `loadData()` and `saveData()` functions, respectively.

In the `loadData()` function, the session storage area is queried for the value of a storage key, and that key is passed to the `JSON.parse()` function. The `JSON.parse()` routine will take a previously saved string representation of an object and reconstitute it into a copy of the original. This routine is called every time the page loads.

Similarly, the `saveData()` function takes a data value and calls `JSON.stringify()` on it to turn it into a string representation of the object. That string is, in turn, stored back into storage. By registering the `saveData()` function on the `unload` browser event, we ensure that it is called every time the user navigates away or shuts down the browser or window.

The practical result of these two functions is that any object we wish to track in storage, no matter if it is a complex object type, can be stored and reloaded as users navigate in and out of the application. This allows developers to extend the techniques we have already shown to nontext data.

A Window into Sharing

As alluded to in an earlier section, the ability for HTML5 Web Storage events to fire in any window browsing the same origin has some powerful implications. It means that storage can be used to send messages from window to window, even if they are not all using the storage object itself. This, in turn implies that we can now share data across windows that have the same origin.

Let's see how this works using some code samples. To listen to cross-window messages, a simple script needs only to register a handler for storage events. Let's assume that a page running at `http://www.example.com/storageLog.html` contains the code shown in Listing 9-15 (the sample file `storageLog.html` for this example is also located in the `code/storage` folder):

Listing 9-15. Cross-Window Communication Using Storage

```
// display records of new storage events
function displayStorageEvent(e) {
  var incomingRow = document.createElement('div');
  document.getElementById("container").appendChild(incomingRow);

  var logged = "key:" + e.key + ", newValue:" + e.newValue + ", oldValue:" +
               e.oldValue + ", url:" + e.url + ", storageArea:" + e.storageArea;
               incomingRow.innerHTML = logged;
}

// add listeners on storage events
window.addEventListener("storage", displayStorageEvent, true);
```

After registering an event listener for the **storage** event type, this window will receive notification of storage changes in any pages. For example, if a browser window viewing **http://www.example.com/browser-test.html** that is currently browsing the same origin sets or changes a new storage value, the **storageLog.html** page will receive a notification. Therefore, to send a message to a receiving window, the sending window need only modify a storage object, and its old and new values will be sent as part of the notification. For example, if a storage value is updated using **localStorage.setItem()**, then the **displayStorageEvent()** handler in the **storageLog.html** page hosted at the same origin will receive an event. By carefully coordinating event names and values, the two pages can now communicate, a feat which has been difficult to accomplish before. Figure 9-12 shows the **storageLog.html** page in action, simply logging storage events it receives.

Figure 9-12. The storageLog.html page logging storage eventsSummary

Summary

In this chapter, we showed how HTML5 Web Storage can be used as an alternative to browser cookies for keeping local copies of data across windows, tabs, and (with `localStorage`) even across browser restarts. You've seen that data can be appropriately segregated between windows by using `sessionStorage`, and shared—even across windows—by using storage events. In our full-fledged example, we showed a practical way to use storage to track data from page to page as users navigate a website, which could just as easily be applied to other data types. We even demonstrated how nontext data types can be stored when a page loads or unloads to save and restore the state of a page across visits.

In the next chapter, we'll show you how HTML5 lets you create offline applications.

CHAPTER 10

■ ■ ■

Creating HTML5 Offline Web Applications

In this chapter, we will explore what you can do with offline HTML5 applications. HTML5 applications do not necessarily require constant access to the network, and loading cached resources can now be more flexibly controlled by developers.

Overview of HTML5 Offline Web Applications

The first, and most obvious, reason to use the application cache is offline support. In the age of universal connectivity, offline applications are still desirable. What do you do when you do not have a network connection? Before you say the days of intermittent connectivity are over, consider the following:

- Do all of the flights you take have onboard Wi-Fi?

- Do you have perfect signal coverage on your mobile Internet device (when was the last time you saw zero bars)?

- Can you count on having an Internet connection when you give presentations?

As more application move to the Web, it is tempting to assume 24/7 uninterrupted connectivity for all users, but the reality of the Internet is that interruptions happen and, in situations like air travel, can happen predictably for several hours at a time.

Intermittent connectivity has been the Achilles' heel of network computing systems. If your applications depend on communication with remote hosts, and those hosts are unreachable, you're out of luck. However, when you do have an Internet connection, web applications can always be up-to-date, because the code loads from a remote location on each use.

If your applications require only occasional communication, they can still be useful as long as the application resources are stored locally. With the advent of browser-only devices, web applications that continue to function without continuous connectivity will only grow more important. Desktop applications that do not require continuous connectivity have historically held that advantage over web applications.

HTML5 exposes control over application caching to get the best of both worlds: applications built with web technology that run in the browser and update when they are online but can also be used offline. However, this new offline application feature must be used explicitly, because current web servers do not provide any default caching behavior for offline applications.

The HTML5 offline application cache makes it possible to augment an application to run without a network connection. You do not need a connection to the Internet just to draft an e-mail. HTML5 introduces the offline application cache that allows a Web application to run without network connectivity.

An application developer can specify specific additional resources comprising an HTML5 application (HTML, CSS, JavaScript, and images) to make an application available for offline use. There are many use cases for this, for example:

- Read and compose e-mail

- Edit documents

- Edit and display presentations

- Create to-do lists

Using offline storage can avoid the normal network requests needed to load an application. If the cache manifest is up to date, the browser knows it does not need to check if the other resources are also up to date, and most of the application can load very quickly out of the local application cache. Additionally, loading resources out of a cache (instead of making multiple HTTP requests to see if resources have been updated) saves bandwidth, which can be especially important for mobile web applications. Currently, slower loading is one way that web applications suffer in comparison with desktop applications. Caching can offset that.

The application cache gives developers explicit control over caching. The *cache manifest* file allows you to group related resources into a logical application. This is a powerful concept that can give web applications some of the characteristics of desktop applications. You can use this additional power in new, creative ways.

Resources identified in the cache manifest file create what is known as an *application cache*, which is the place where browsers store the resources persistently, typically on disk. Some browsers give users a way to view the data in the application cache. For example, the about:cache page in the latest version of Firefox shows you details about the application cache and a way to view individual files in the cache, as shown in Figure 10-1.

Figure 10-1. Viewing the offline cache in Firefox

Browser Support for HTML5 Offline Web Applications

Table 10-1 shows the browser support for HTML5 offline web applications at the time of this writing. As you can see, HTML5 offline web applications are already supported in many browsers.

Table 10-1. Browser Support for HTML5 Offline Application Cache

Browser	Details
Chrome	Supported in version 4.0 and greater
Firefox	Supported in version 3.5 and greater
Internet Explorer	Not supported
Opera	Supported in version 10.6 and greater
Safari	Supported in version 4.0 and greater

Due to the varying levels of support, it is a good idea to first test if HTML5 offline web applications are supported before you use these elements.

Using the HTML5 Offline Web Application API

In this section, we will explore the specifics of how you can use the Offline Web Applications API.

Checking for Browser Support

Before you try to use the Offline Web Applications API, it is a good idea to check for browser support. Listing 10-1 shows how you can do that.

Listing 10-1. Checking Browser Support for the Offline Web Applications API

```
if(window.applicationCache) {
  // this browser supports offline applications
}
```

Creating a Simple Offline Application

Let's say that you want to create a one-page application that consists of an HTML document, a style sheet, and a JavaScript file. To add offline support to your HTML5 application, you include a `manifest` attribute on the `html` element as shown in the Listing 10-2.

Listing 10-2. The manifest Attribute on the HTML Element

```
<!DOCTYPE html>
<html manifest="application.manifest">
  .
  .
  .
</html>
```

Alongside the HTML document, provide a manifest file specifying which resources to cache. Listing 10-3 shows the contents of an example cache manifest file.

Listing 10-3. Contents of an Example Cache Manifest File

```
CACHE MANIFEST
example.html
example.js
example.css
example.gif
```

Going Offline

To make applications aware of intermittent connectivity, there are additional events exposed by HTML5 browsers. Your applications may have different modes for online and offline behavior. Some additions to the window.navigator object make that easier. First, navigator.onLine is a Boolean property that indicates whether the browser believes it is online. Of course, a true value of onLine is not a definite assurance that the servers that your web application must communicate with are reachable from the user's machine. On the other hand, a false value means the browser will not even attempt to connect out over the network. Listing 10-4 shows how you can check to see if your page is online or offline. This even works in Internet Explorer.

Listing 10-4. Checking Online Status

```
// When the page loads, set the status to online or offline
function loadDemo() {
  if (navigator.onLine) {
    log("Online");
  } else {
    log("Offline");
  }
}

// Now add event listeners to notify a change in online status
window.addEventListener("online", function(e) {
  log("Online");
}, true);

window.addEventListener("offline", function(e) {
  log("Offline");
}, true);
```

Manifest Files

Offline applications consist of a manifest listing one or more resources that browser will cache for offline use. Manifest files have the MIME type text/cache-manifest. The SimpleHTTPServer module in the Python standard library will serve files with the .manifest extension with the header Content-type: text/cache-manifest. To configure settings, open the file PYTHON_HOME/Lib/mimetypes.py, and add the following line:

```
'.manifest'    : 'text/cache-manifest manifest',
```

Other web servers may require additional configuration. For example, for Apache HTTP Server, you can update the mime.types file in the conf folder by adding the following line:

```
text/cache-manifest manifest
```

The manifest syntax is simple line separated text beginning with CACHE MANIFEST. Lines can end in CR, LF, or CRLF—the format is flexible—but the text must be UTF-8 encoded, which is the typical output for most text editors.

Listing 10-5. Example Manifest File with All Possible Sections

```
#comments begin with the hash symbol
CACHE MANIFEST
# files to cache
about.html
html5.css
index.html
happy-trails-rc.gif
lake-tahoe.JPG

#do not cache signup page
NETWORK
signup.html

FALLBACK
signup.html     offline.html
/app/ajax/      default.html
```

Let's look at the different sections.

If no heading is specified, `CACHE MANIFEST` is the default section. The following simple manifest specifies that two files are to be cached:

```
CACHE MANIFEST
application.js
style.css
```

By listing a file in the `CACHE MANIFEST` section, you instruct the browser to serve the file from the application cache, even if the application is online. It is unnecessary to specify the application's main HTML resource. The HTML document that initially pointed to the manifest file is implicitly included. However, if you want to cache multiple HTML documents or if you would like multiple HTML documents to act as possible entry points for the cacheable application, they should all be listed in the cache manifest file.

`FALLBACK` entries allow you to give alternate paths to replace resources that cannot be fetched. The manifest in Listing 10-5 would cause requests to `/app/ajax/` or subpaths beginning with `/app/ajax/` to fall back to `default.html` when `/app/ajax/*` is unreachable.

`NETWORK` denotes resources that are always fetched using the network—even if a cached resource matches the request path.

The applicationCache API

The applicationCache API is an interface for working with the application cache. A new `window.applicationCache` object fires several events related to the state of the cache. The object has a numerical property, `window.applicationCache.status`, which indicates the state of the cache. The six states a cache can have are shown in Table 10-2.

Table 10-2. The Six Cache States

Numerical Property	Cache Status
0	UNCACHED
1	IDLE
2	CHECKING
3	DOWNLOADING
4	UPDATEREADY
5	OBSOLETE

Most pages on the Web today do not specify cache manifests and are uncached. Idle is the typical state for an application with a cache manifest. An application in the idle state has all its resources stored by the browser with no updates in progress. A cache enters the obsolete state if there was at one point a valid cache but the manifest is now missing. There are events (and callback attributes) in the API that correspond to some of these states. For instance, when the cache enters the idle state after an update, the cached event fires. At that time, an application might notify the user that they can disconnect from the network and still expect the application to be available in offline mode. Table 10-3 shows some common events and their associated caches states.

Table 10-3. Common Events and Their Cache States

Event	Associated Cache State
onchecking	CHECKING
ondownloading	DOWNLOADING
onupdateready	UPDATEREADY
onobsolete	OBSOLETE
oncached	IDLE

Additionally, there are events indicating update progress, when no update is available, or when an error has occurred:

- onerror
- onnoupdate
- onprogress

`window.applicationCache` has an `update()` method. Calling `update()` requests that the browser update the cache. This includes checking for a new version of the manifest file and downloading new resources if necessary. If there is no cache or if the cache is obsolete, an error will be thrown.

Building an Application with HTML5 Offline Web Applications

In this example application, we will track a runner's location while out on the trail (with intermittent or no connectivity). For example, Peter goes running, and he will have his new HTML5 Geolocation–enabled phone and HTML5 web browser with him, but there is not always a great signal out in the woods around his house. He wants to use this application to track and record his location even when he cannot use the Internet.

When offline, the Geolocation API should continue to work on devices with hardware geolocation (such as GPS) but obviously not on devices that use IP geolocation. IP geolocation requires network connectivity to map the client's IP address to coordinates. In addition, offline applications can always access persistent storage on the local machine through APIs such as local storage or Web SQL Database. Figure 10-2 shows the application in action.

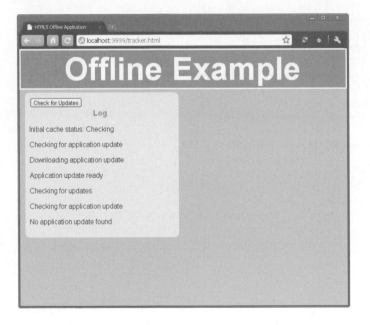

Figure 10-2. The application in action

To run this application, you will need a web server serving these static resources. Remember that the manifest file must be served with the content type `text/cache-manifest`. If your browser supports the application cache, but the file is served with the incorrect content type, you will probably see a cache error.

To run this application with complete functionality, you will need a server that can receive geolocation data. The server-side complement to this example would presumably store, analyze, and make available this data. It may or may not be served from the same origin as the static application.

Figure 10-3 shows the example application running in offline mode in Firefox. The example files for this application are located at the book web site in the 'Offline' section.

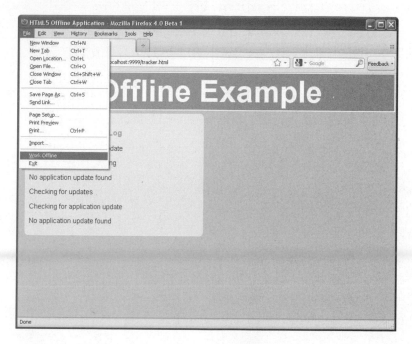

Figure 10-3. The application in action in offline mode

Creating a Manifest File for the Application Resources

First, create the `tracker.manifest` file as follows. This will list the files that are part of this application:

```
CACHE MANIFEST
# JavaScript
./offline.js
#./tracker.js
./log.js

# stylesheets
./html5.css

# images
```

Creating the HTML Structure and CSS of the UI

This is the basic UI structure of the example. Both `tracker.html` and `html5.css` will be cached, so the application will be served from the application cache.

```
<!DOCTYPE html>
<html lang="en" manifest="tracker.manifest">
<head>
    <title>HTML5 Offline Application</title>
    <script src="log.js"></script>
    <script src="offline.js"></script>
    <script src="tracker.js"></script>
    <link rel="stylesheet" href="html5.css">
</head>

<body>
    <header>
      <h1>Offline Example</h1>
    </header>

    <section>
      <article>
        <button id="installButton">Check for Updates</button>
        <h3>Log</h3>
        <div id="info">
        </div>
      </article>
    </section>
</body>
</html>
```

There are a couple of things to note in this HTML that pertain to this application's offline capabilities. The first is the `manifest` attribute on the HTML element. Most of the HTML examples in this book omit the `<html>` element because it is optional in HTML5. However, the ability to cache offline depends on specifying the manifest file.

The second thing to note is the button. That will give the user control over installing this application for offline use.

Creating the Offline JavaScript

For this example, the JavaScript is contained in multiple `.js` files included with `<script>` tags. These scripts are cached along with the HTML and CSS.

```
<offline.js>
/*
 * log each of the events fired by window.applicationCache
 */
```

```
window.applicationCache.onchecking = function(e) {
    log("Checking for application update");
}

window.applicationCache.onnoupdate = function(e) {
    log("No application update found");
}

window.applicationCache.onupdateready = function(e) {
    log("Application update ready");
}

window.applicationCache.onobsolete = function(e) {
    log("Application obsolete");
}

window.applicationCache.ondownloading = function(e) {
    log("Downloading application update");
}

window.applicationCache.oncached = function(e) {
    log("Application cached");
}

window.applicationCache.onerror = function(e) {
    log("Application cache error");
}

window.addEventListener("online", function(e) {
    log("Online");
}, true);

window.addEventListener("offline", function(e) {
    log("Offline");
}, true);


/*
 * Convert applicationCache status codes into messages
 */
showCacheStatus = function(n) {
    statusMessages = ["Uncached","Idle","Checking","Downloading","Update Ready","Obsolete"];
    return statusMessages[n];
}

install = function() {
    log("Checking for updates");
    try {
        window.applicationCache.update();
```

```
        } catch (e) {
            applicationCache.onerror();
        }
    }

    onload = function(e) {
        // Check for required browser features
        if (!window.applicationCache) {
            log("HTML5 Offline Applications are not supported in your browser.");
            return;
        }

        if (!navigator.geolocation) {
            log("HTML5 Geolocation is not supported in your browser.");
            return;
        }

        if (!window.localStorage) {
            log("HTML5 Local Storage not supported in your browser.");
            return;
        }

        log("Initial cache status: " + showCacheStatus(window.applicationCache.status));
        document.getElementById("installButton").onclick = checkFor;
    }

    <log.js>
    log = function() {
        var p = document.createElement("p");
        var message = Array.prototype.join.call(arguments, " ");
        p.innerHTML = message;
        document.getElementById("info").appendChild(p);
    }
```

Check for ApplicationCache Support

In addition to the offline application cache, this example uses geolocation and local storage. We ensure that the browser supports all of these features when the page loads.

```
    onload = function(e) {
        // Check for required browser features
        if (!window.applicationCache) {
            log("HTML5 Offline Applications are not supported in your browser.");
            return;
        }

        if (!navigator.geolocation) {
            log("HTML5 Geolocation is not supported in your browser.");
            return;
        }
```

```
    if (!window.localStorage) {
        log("HTML5 Local Storage not supported in your browser.");
        return;
    }

    if (!window.WebSocket) {
        log("HTML5 WebSocket is not supported in your browser.");
        return;
    }

    log("Initial cache status: " + showCacheStatus(window.applicationCache.status));
    document.getElementById("installButton").onclick = install;
}
```

Adding the Update Button Handler

Next, add an update handler that updates the application cache as follows:

```
install = function() {
    log("Checking for updates");
    try {
        window.applicationCache.update();
    } catch (e) {
        applicationCache.onerror();
    }
}
```

Clicking this button will explicitly start the cache check that will cause all cache resources to be downloaded if necessary. When available updates have completely downloaded, a message is logged in the UI. At this point, the user knows that the application has successfully installed and can be run in offline mode.

Add Geolocation Tracking Code

This code is based on the geolocation code from Chapter 4. It is contained in the `tracker.js` JavaScript file.

```
/*
 * Track and report the current location
 */
var handlePositionUpdate = function(e) {
    var latitude = e.coords.latitude;
    var longitude = e.coords.longitude;
    log("Position update:", latitude, longitude);
    if(navigator.onLine) {
        uploadLocations(latitude, longitude);
    }
    storeLocation(latitude, longitude);
}
```

```
var handlePositionError = function(e) {
    log("Position error");
}

var uploadLocations = function(latitude, longitude) {
    var request = new XMLHttpRequest();
    request.open("POST", "http://geodata.example.net:8000/geoupload", true);
    request.send(localStorage.locations);
}

var geolocationConfig = {"maximumAge":20000};

navigator.geolocation.watchPosition(handlePositionUpdate,
                                    handlePositionError,
                                    geolocationConfig);
```

Adding Storage Code

Next, add the code that writes updates to localStorage when the application is offline.

```
var storeLocation = function(latitude, longitude) {
    // load stored location list
    var locations = JSON.parse(localStorage.locations || "[]");
    // add location
    locations.push({"latitude" : latitude, "longitude" : longitude});
    // save new location list
    localStorage.locations = JSON.stringify(locations);
}
```

This application stores coordinates using HTML5 local storage as described in Chapter 9. Local storage is a natural fit for offline-capable applications, because it provides a way to persist data locally in the browser. The data will be available in future sessions. When network connectivity is restored, the application can synchronize with a remote server.

Using storage here has the added benefit of allowing recovery from failed upload requests. If the application experiences a network error for any reason, or if the application is closed (by user action, browser or operating system crash, or page navigation) the data is stored for future transmission.

Adding Offline Event Handling

Every time the location update handler runs, it checks the connectivity status. If the application is online, it will store and upload the coordinates. If the application is offline, it will merely store the coordinates. When the application comes back online, it can update the UI to show the online status and upload any data is stored while online.

```
window.addEventListener("online", function(e) {
    log("Online");
}, true);

window.addEventListener("offline", function(e) {
    log("Offline");
}, true);
```

The connectivity status may change while the application is not actively running. For instance, the user may have closed the browser, refreshed, or navigated to a different site. To handle these cases, our offline application checks to see if it has come back online on each page load. If it has, it will attempt to synchronize with the remote server.

```
// Synchronize with the server if the browser is now online
if(navigator.onLine) {
    uploadLocations();
}
```

Summary

In this chapter, you have seen how HTML5 Offline Web Applications can be used to create compelling applications that can be used even when there is no Internet connection. You can ensure that all your files are cached by specifying the files that are part of the web application in the cache manifest file and then referencing the files from the main HTML page of the application. Then, by adding event listeners for online and offline status changes, you can make your site behave differently based on whether an Internet connection is available or not.

In the final chapter, we will discuss the future of HTML5 programming.

■ ■ ■

## CHAPTER 11

The Future of HTML5

As you have already seen in this book, HTML5 provides powerful programming features. We also discussed the history behind HTML5's development and HTML5's new plugin-free paradigm. In this chapter, we will look at where things are going. We will discuss some of the features that are not fully baked yet but hold tremendous promise.

Browser Support for HTML5

Adoption of HTML5 features is accelerating with each new browser update. Several of the features we covered have actually shipped in browsers while we wrote this book. HTML5 development in browsers is undeniably gaining tremendous momentum.

In an uncharacteristic move, Microsoft has already released several developer previews of its next browser. Internet Explorer 9 will support some important HTML5 features and major speed improvements. Once it ships, the baseline features for modern browsers will include a large portion of the advanced multimedia, storage, and communication features of HTML5.

Today, many developers still struggle to develop consistent web applications that work with older browsers. Internet Explorer 6 represents the harshest of the legacy browsers in common use on the Internet in 2010. But even IE6 has a limited lifetime, as it becomes harder and harder to procure any operating system that supports it. In time, there will be close to zero users browsing the Web with IE6. More and more users of Internet Explorer are being upgraded to the latest versions, and Internet Explorer 9 will be a watershed in web evolution. There will always be an oldest browser to contend with, but that bar rises as time passes; at the time of this writing, the market share of Internet Explorer 6 is under 20% and falling. Most users who upgrade go straight to a modern replacement. In time, the lowest common denominator will include HTML5 Video, Canvas, WebSockets, and whatever other features you may have to emulate today to reach a wider audience.

In this book, we covered features that are largely stable and shipping in multiple browsers. There are additional extensions to HTML and APIs currently in earlier stages of development. In this chapter, we will look at some of the upcoming features. Some are in early experimental stages, while others may see eventual standardization and wide availability with only minor changes from their current state.

HTML Evolves

In this section, we'll explore several exciting features that may appear in browsers in the near future. You probably won't need to wait until 2022 for these, either. There will probably not be a formalized HTML6; the WHATWG has hinted that future development will simply be referred to as "HTML." Development will be incremental, with specific features and their specifications evolving individually, rather than as a consolidated effort. Browsers will take up features as they gain consensus, and the upcoming features might even be widely available in browsers well before HTML5 is set in stone. The community responsible for driving the Web forward is committed to evolving the platform to meet the needs of users and developers.

WebGL

WebGL is an API for 3D graphics on the Web. Historically, several browser vendors including Mozilla, Opera, and Google have worked on separate experimental 3D APIs for JavaScript. Today, WebGL is progressing along a path toward standardization and wide availability across HTML5 browsers. The standardization process is taking place with browser vendors and The Khronos Group, the body responsible for OpenGL, a cross-platform 3D drawing standard created in 1992. OpenGL, currently at specification version 4.0, is widely used in gaming and computer-aided design applications as a counterpart and competitor to Microsoft's Direct3D

As you saw in Chapter 2, you get a 2D drawing context from a `canvas` element by calling `getContext("2d")` on the element. Unsurprisingly, this leaves the door open for additional types of drawing contexts. WebGL also uses the `canvas` element, but through a 3D context. Current implementations use experimental vendor prefixes (`moz-webgl`, `webkit-3d`, etc.) as the arguments to the `getContext()` call. In a WebGL-enabled build of Firefox, for example, you can get a 3D context by calling `getContext("moz-webgl")` on a `canvas` element. The API of the object returned by such a call to `getContext()` is different from the 2D canvas equivalent, as this one provides OpenGL bindings instead of drawing operations. Rather than making calls to draw lines and fill shapes, the WebGL version of the canvas context manages textures and vertex buffers.

HTML in Three Dimensions

WebGL, like the rest of HTML5, will be an integral part of the web platform. Because WebGL renders to a `canvas` element, it is part of the document. You can position and transform 3D `canvas` elements, just as you can place images or 2D canvases on a page. In fact, you can do anything you can do with any other `canvas` element, including overlaying text and video and performing animations. Combining other document elements and a 3D canvas will make heads-up displays (HUDs) and mixed 2D and 3D interfaces much simpler to develop when compared to pure 3D display technologies. Imagine taking a 3D scene and using HTML markup to overlay a simple web user interface on it. Quite unlike the nonnative menus and controls found in many OpenGL applications, WebGL software will incorporate nicely styled HTML5 form elements with ease.

The existing network architecture of the Web will also complement WebGL. WebGL applications will be able to fetch resources such as textures and models from URLs. Multiplayer games can communicate with WebSockets. For example, Figure 11-1 shows an example of this in action. Google recently ported the classic 3D game Quake II to the Web using HTML5 WebSocket, Audio, and WebGL, complete with multiplayer competition. Game logic and graphics were implemented in JavaScript, making calls to a WebGL canvas for rendering. Communication to the server to coordinate player movement was achieved using a persistent WebSocket connection.

Figure 11-1. Quake II

3D Shaders

WebGL is a binding for OpenGL ES 2 in JavaScript, so it uses the programmable graphics pipeline that is standardized in OpenGL, including shaders. Shaders allow highly flexible rendering effects to be applied to a 3D scene, increasing the realism of the display. WebGL shaders are written in GL Shading Language (GLSL). This adds yet another single-purpose language to the web stack. An HTML5 application with WebGL consists of HTML for structure, CSS for style, JavaScript for logic, and GLSL for shaders. Developers can transfer their knowledge of OpenGL shaders to a similar API in a web environment.

WebGL is likely to be a foundational layer for 3D graphics on the Web. Just as JavaScript libraries have abstracted over DOM and provided powerful high-level constructs, there are libraries providing additional functionality on top of WebGL. Libraries are currently under development for scene graphs, 3D file formats such as COLLADA, and complete engines for game development. Figure 11-2 shows Shader Toy—a WebGL shader workbench built by Inigo Quilez that comes with shaders by nine other demoscene artists. This particular screenshot shows Leizex by Rgba. We can expect an explosion of high-level rendering libraries that bring 3D scene creation power to novice Web programmers in the near future.

Figure 11-2. Shader Toy is a WebGL shader workbench

■ **Note** Not only is the WebGL effort bringing OpenGL to JavaScript, it is spinning off a general-purpose binary data API as well. A fast 3D API needs binary buffers. To that end, there is a new proposal for an API for manipulating binary data called `TypedArray`. If the proposal takes off, `TypedArray` will likely be useful throughout HTML5.

Devices

Web applications will need access to multimedia hardware such as webcams, microphones, or attached storage devices. For this, there is already a proposed **device** element to give web applications access to data streams from attached hardware. Of course, there are serious privacy implications, so not every script will be able to use your webcam at will. We will probably see a UI pattern of prompting for user permission as seen in the Geolocation and Storage APIs when an application requests elevated privileges. The obvious application for webcams is video conferencing, but there are many other amazing possibilities for computer vision in web applications including augmented reality and head tracking.

Audio Data API

Programmable audio APIs will do for `<audio>` what `<canvas>` did for `<img>`. Prior to the `canvas` tag, images on the Web were largely opaque to scripts. Image creation and manipulation had to occur on the sidelines—namely, on the server. Now, there are tools for creating and manipulating visual media based on the `canvas` element. Similarly, audio data APIs will enable music creation in HTML5 applications. This will help round out the content-creation capabilities available to web applications and move us closer to a self-hosting world of tools to create media on and for the Web. Imagine editing audio on the Web without having to leave the browser.

Simple playback of sounds can be done with the `<audio>` element. However, any application that manipulates, analyzes, or generates sound on the fly needs a lower-level API. Text-to-speech, speech-to-speech, synthesizers, and music visualization aren't possible without access to audio data.

We can expect the standard audio API to work well with microphone input from the data element as well as files included with audio tags. With `<device>` and an audio data API, you may be able to make an HTML5 application that allows users to record and edit sound from within a page. Audio clips will be able to be stored in local browser storage and reused and combined with `canvas`-based editing tools.

Presently, Mozilla has an experimental implementation available in nightly builds. The Mozilla audio data API could act as a starting point for standard cross-browser audio programming capabilities.

Video Improvements

Earlier in this book, we described in detail the current capabilities of the `<video>` element. While there is still no required video codec specified in HTML5, Google recently released WebM, a high-quality, royalty-free video codec for the Web. Although not all vendors have agreed to support WebM yet, there is significant momentum behind the format.

Additionally, there is increased demand for improvements in the current controls for HTML5 video. In order to fully replace plugin-based rendering of video, HTML's own control will need to introduce better APIs for streaming. Expect this capability to evolve in the next iterations of the media tags; with increased adoption of devices without Flash playback, such as the Apple iPad and iPhone, there is a significant incentive to bring Web video to a large audience with only HTML5.

Touchscreen Device Events

As Web access shifts ever more from desktops and laptops to mobile phones and tablets, HTML5 is also continuing to adapt with changes in interaction handling. When Apple introduced the iPhone, it also introduced into its browser a set of special events that could be used to handle multitouch inputs and device rotation. Although these events have not yet been standardized, they are being picked up by other vendors of mobile devices. Learning them today will allow you to optimize your web applications for the most popular devices now.

Orientation

The simplest event to handle on a mobile device is the orientation event. The orientation event can be added to the document body:

```
<body onorientationchange="rotateDisplay();">
```

In the event handler for the orientation change, your code can reference the `window.orientation` property. This property will give one of the rotation values shown in Table 11-1, which is relative to the orientation the device was in when the page was initially loaded.

Table 11-1. Orientation Values and Their Meanings

Orientation Value	Meaning
0	The page is being held in the same orientation as its original load.
-90	The device has been rotated 90 degrees clockwise (right) since the original load.
180	The device has been rotated upside-down since the original page load.
90	The device has been rotated 90 degrees counter-clockwise (left) since the page was originally loaded.

Once the orientation is known, you can choose to adjust the content accordingly.

Gestures

The next type of event supported by mobile devices is a high-level event known as the *gesture*. Consider gesture events as representing a multitouch change in size or rotation. This is usually performed when the user places two or more fingers on the screen simultaneously and pinches or twists. A twist represents a rotation, while a pinch in or out represents a zoom out or in, respectively. To receive gesture events, your code needs to register one of the handlers shown in Table 11-2.

Table 11-2. Event Handlers for Gestures

Event Handler	Description
ongesturestart	A user has placed multiple fingers on the screen and has begun a movement.
ongesturechange	The user is in the process of moving multiple fingers in a scale or rotation.
ongestureend	The user has completed the scale or rotation by removing fingers.

During the gesture, the event handler is free to check the rotation and scale properties of the corresponding event and update the display accordingly. Listing 11-1 shows an example usage of the gesture handlers.

Listing 11-1. Example Gesture Handler

```
function gestureChange(event) {
  // Retrieve the amount of change in scale caused by the user gesture
  // Consider a value of 1.0 to represent the original size, while smaller
  //  numbers represent a zoom in and larger numbers represent a zoom
  //  out, based on the ratio of the scale value
var scale = event.scale;

  // Retrieve the amount of change in rotation caused by the user gesture
  // The rotation value is in degrees from 0 to 360, where positive values
  //   indicate a rotation clockwise and negative values indicate a counter-
  //   clockwise rotation
var rotation = event.rotation;

  // Update the display based on the rotation.
}

// register our gesture change listener on a document node
node.addEventListener("gesturechange", gestureChange, false);
```

Gesture events are particularly appropriate in applications that need to manipulate objects or displays, such as in diagramming tools or navigation tools.

Touches

For those cases where you need low-level control over device events, the touch events provide as much information as you will likely need. Table 11-3 shows the different touch events.

Table 11-3. Touch Events

Event Handler	Description
ontouchstart	A finger has been placed on the surface of the touch device. Multitouch events will occur as more fingers are placed on the device.
ontouchmove	One or more of the fingers on the device has moved its location in a drag operation.
ontouchend	One or more fingers have been lifted away from the device screen.
ontouchcancel	An unexpected interruption has stopped the touch operations.

Unlike the other mobile device events, the touch events need to represent that there are multiple points of data—the many potential fingers—present at the same time. As such, the API for touch handling is a little bit more complex as shown in Listing 11-2.

Listing 11-2. Touch API

```
function touchMove(event) {
// the touches list contains an entry for every finger currently touching the screen
var touches = event.touches;

  // the changedTouches list contains only those finger touches modified at this
  // moment in time, either by being added, removed, or repositioned
varchangedTouches = event.changedTouches;

  // targetTouches contains only those touches which are placed in the node
  // where this listener is registered
vartargetTouches = event.targetTouches;

  // once you have the touches you'd like to track, you can reference
  // most attributes you would normally get from other event objects
varfirstTouch = touches[0];
varfirstTouchX = firstTouch.pageX;
varfirstTouchY = firstTouch.pageY;
}

// register one of the touch listeners for our example
node.addEventListener("touchmove", touchMove, false);
```

You may find that the device's native event handling interferes with your handling of the touch and gesture events. In those cases, you should make the following call:

```
event.preventDefault();
```

This overrides the behavior of the default browser interface and handles the event yourself. Until the mobile events are standardized, it is recommended that you consult the documentation of the devices you are targeting with your application.

Peer-to-Peer Networking

We haven't seen the end of advanced networking in web applications either. With both HTTP and WebSocket, there is a client (the browser or other user agent) and a server (the host of the URL). Peer-to-peer (P2P) networking allows clients to communicate directly. This is often more efficient than sending all data through a server. Efficiency, of course, reduces hosting costs and improves application performance. P2P should make for faster multiplayer games and collaboration software.

Another immediate application for P2P combined with the `device` element is efficient video chat in HTML5. In peer-to-peer video chat, conversation partners would be able to send data directly to each other without routing through a central server. Outside of HTML5, P2P video chat has been wildly popular in applications like Skype. Because of the high bandwidth required by streaming video, it is likely that neither of those applications would have been possible without peer-to-peer communication.

Browser vendors are already experimenting with P2P networking, such as Opera's Unite technology, which hosts a simplified web server directly in the browser. Opera Unite lets users create and expose services to their peers for chatting, file sharing, and document collaboration.

Of course, P2P networking for the web will require a protocol that takes security and network intermediaries into consideration as well as an API for developers to program against.

Ultimate Direction

So far, we have focused on empowering developers to build powerful HTML5 applications. A different perspective is to consider how HTML5 empowers users of web applications. Many HTML5 features allow you to remove or reduce the complexity of scripts and perform feats that previously required plugins. HTML5 video, for example, lets you specify controls, autoplay, buffering behavior, and a placeholder image without any JavaScript. With CSS3, you can move animation and effects from scripts to styles. This declarative code makes applications more amenable to user styles and ultimately returns power to the people who use your creations every day.

You've seen how the development tools in Firefox and WebKit are exposing information about HTML5 features like storage, as well as critically important JavaScript debugging, profiling, and command-line evaluation. HTML5 development will trend toward simplicity, declarative code, and lightweight tools within the browsers or web applications themselves.

Google feels confident enough about the continuing evolution of HTML that it has announced the imminent release of the Google Chrome operating system, a streamlined operating system built around a browser and media player. Expected in late 2010, Google's operating system aims to include enough functionality using HTML APIs to provide a compelling user experience where applications are delivered using the standardized web infrastructure.

Summary

In this book, you have learned how to use powerful HTML5 APIs. Use them wisely!

In this final chapter, we have given you a glimpse of some of the things that are coming, such as 3D graphics, the new device element, touch events, and P2P networking. Development of HTML5 shows no sign of slowing down and will be very exciting to watch.

Think back for a minute. For those of you who have been surfing the Web, or perhaps even developing for it for ten years or more, consider how far HTML technology has come in just the last few years. Ten years ago, "professional HTML programming" meant learning to use the new features of HTML 4. Cutting edge developers at the time were just discovering dynamic page updates and `XMLHttpRequest`s. The term "Ajax" was still years from introduction, even if the techniques Ajax described were starting to gain traction. Much of the professional programming in browsers was written to wrangle frames and manipulate image maps.

Today, functions that took pages of script can be performed with just markup. Multiple new methods for communication and interaction are now available to all those willing to download one of the many free HTML5 browsers, crack open their favorite text editors, and try their hands at professional HTML5 programming.

We hope you have enjoyed this exploration of web development, and we hope it has inspired your creativity. We look forward to writing about the innovations you create using HTML5 a decade from now.

Index

You Need the Companion eBook

Your purchase of this book entitles you to buy the companion PDF-version eBook for only $10. Take the weightless companion with you anywhere.

We believe this Apress title will prove so indispensable that you'll want to carry it with you everywhere, which is why we are offering the companion eBook (in PDF format) for $10 to customers who purchase this book now. Convenient and fully searchable, the PDF version of any content-rich, page-heavy Apress book makes a valuable addition to your programming library. You can easily find and copy code—or perform examples by quickly toggling between instructions and the application. Even simultaneously tackling a donut, diet soda; and complex code becomes simplified with hands-free eBooks!

Once you purchase your book, getting the $10 companion eBook is simple:

❶ Visit **www.apress.com/promo/tendollars/**.

❷ Complete a basic registration form to receive a randomly generated question about this title.

❸ Answer the question correctly in 60 seconds, and you will receive a promotional code to redeem for the $10.00 eBook.

233 Spring Street, New York, NY 10013

Offer valid through 2/11.